FAMILY MA

WOMEN AND MEN IN HISTORY

This series, published for students, scholars and interested general readers, will tackle themes in gender history from the early medieval period through to the present day. Gender issues are now an integral part of all history courses and yet many traditional texts do not reflect this change. Much exciting work is now being done to redress the gender imbalances of the past, and we hope that these books will make their own substantial contribution to that process. We hope that these will both synthesise and shape future developments in gender studies.

The General Editors of the series are *Patricia Skinner* (University of Southampton) for the medieval period; *Pamela Sharpe* (University of Bristol) for the early modern period; and *Penny Summerfield* (University of Lancaster) for the modern period. *Margaret Walsh* (University of Nottingham) was the Founding Editor of the series.

Published books:

Imperial Women in Byzantium, 1025–1204: Power, Patronage and Ideology   *Barbara Hill*

Masculinity in Medieval Europe   *D. M. Hadley (ed.)*

Gender and Society in Renaissance Italy   *Judith C. Brown and Robert C. Davis (eds)*

Widowhood in Medieval and Early Modern Europe   *Sandra Cavallo and Lyndan Warner (eds)*

Gender, Church and State in Early Modern Germany: Essays by Merry E. Wiesner
Merry E. Wiesner

Manhood in Early Modern England: Honour, Sex and Marriage   *Elizabeth W. Foyster*

English Masculinities, 1600–1800   *Tim Hitchcock and Michele Cohen (eds)*

Disorderly Women in Eighteenth-Century London: Prostitution in the Metropolis, 1730–1830
Tony Henderson

Gender, Power and the Unitarians in England, 1760–1860   *Ruth Watts*

Practical Visionaries: Women, Education and Social Progress, 1790–1930
Mary Hilton and Pam Hirsch (eds)

Women and Work in Russia, 1880–1930: A Study in Continuity through Change
Jane McDermid and Anna Hillyar

More than Munitions: Women, Work and the Engineering Industries, 1900–1950
Clare Wightman

Women in British Public Life, 1914–1950: Gender, Power and Social Policy   *Helen Jones*

The Family Story: Blood, Contract and Intimacy, 1830–1960
Leonore Davidoff, Megan Doolittle, Janet Fink and Katherine Holden

Women and the Second World War in France, 1939–1948: Choices and Constraints
Hanna Diamond

Men and the Emergence of Polite Society, Britain 1660–1800   *Philip Carter*

Everyday Violence in Britain, 1850–1950: Gender and Class   *Shani D'Cruze (ed.)*

Women and Ageing in British Society Since 1500   *Lynn Botelho and Pat Thane (eds)*

Women in Medieval Italian Society, 500–1200   *Patricia Skinner*

Medieval Memories: Men, Women and the Past, 700–1300   *Elisabeth van Houts (ed.)*

FAMILY MATTERS

A history of ideas about family since 1945

MICHAEL PEPLAR

An imprint of **Pearson Education**

London · New York · Toronto · Sydney · Tokyo · Singapore · Hong Kong · Cape Town
New Delhi · Madrid · Paris · Amsterdam · Munich · Milan · Stockholm

Pearson Education Limited

Head Office:
Edinburgh Gate
Harlow CM20 2JE
Tel: +44 (0)1279 623623
Fax: +44 (0)1279 431059

London Office:
128 Long Acre
London WC2E 9AN
Tel: +44 (0)20 7447 2000
Fax: +44 (0)20 7240 5771
Website: www.history-minds.com

First published in Great Britain in 2002

© Pearson Education Limited 2002

The right of Michael Peplar to be identified as Author
of this Work has been asserted by him in accordance
with the Copyright, Designs and Patents Act 1988.

ISBN 0 582 41870 4

British Library Cataloguing in Publication Data
A CIP catalogue record for this book can be obtained from the British Library

Library of Congress Cataloging in Publication Data
A CIP catalog record for this book can be obtained from the Library of Congress

10   9   8   7   6   5   4   3   2
06   05   04   03   02

Typeset in 11/13pt Baskerville MT by 35
Printed in Malaysia, KVP

The Publishers' policy is to use paper manufactured from sustainable forests.

CONTENTS

LIST OF FIGURES AND TABLES

FIGURES

TABLES

ACKNOWLEDGEMENTS

The help of staff at the following libraries: Greenwich Local History Library, the University of Greenwich Main Library in Woolwich (especially Imogen Forster), the Barking Learning Resource Centre at the University of East London, the London Metropolitan Archive, the British Library, The British Library of Economic and Political Science, the University of London Library at Senate House, The Institute of Historical Research (especially Heather Creaton), the Imperial War Museum's Film and Video Department and the British Film Institute.

The people who gave their time to share their memories with me.

Students at the Open University and the Universities of Greenwich and East London where I taught while working on this book, especially students on the University of Greenwich's 'Popular Memory' course.

The general editor of this series, Penny Summerfield, for clear and insightful criticisms which helped to turn the doctoral research into book form. Also the commissioning editor, Hilary Shaw, for encouragement and confidence in the project and Longman's editors Heather McCallum and Jill Birch.

My PhD supervisors Fred Lindop and Joan Ryan, who not only gave excellent supervision but at times offered the opportunity of paid work and a place to live. Also Angela John, Mick Ryan and David Lusted at the University of Greenwich who gave valuable advice and support.

My PhD examiners Mike Kelly and Jeffrey Weeks who offered detailed and helpful suggestions for improving an earlier draft.

Colleagues from the University of East London's Cultural Studies Department, especially Judy Greenway who read drafts of papers and chapters, and Bill Schwartz (now at Goldsmiths' College, University of London) and all who attended seminar papers on the research.

The Nuffield Foundation for funding the transcription of tapes for the University of Greenwich Oral History Archive, and Mary Worley at the University of Greenwich for transcribing the tapes.

The American Oral History Association for the invitation to and funding for my visit to give a paper on work in progress for this book at their annual conference in Philadelphia in 1996.

Nick Copcutt and Stephanie McKeon for proofreading.

Edward Peppitt for help with the book proposal.

Friends and family who have supported my work in many ways, especially my parents and Nick Copcutt, Rachel Rees, Stephanie McKeon, Sophie Verhagen and Jean French. I would like to thank Philippa Thomas and Celia Leach for the loan of computers when my own broke down. I must again acknowledge the financial support of my grandmother, Lily Passmore, without whom this work would probably never have been started.

For Benjamin McKeon

What many books have failed to do is to differentiate adequately between what politicians, preachers and philanthropists say a family should be and how people actually interact in social groups perceived in terms of family.

Diana Gittins
The Family in Question

It may be argued that questions of ideology deal, in some measure, with the point of intersection between everyday talk about marriage and the family and public speech or discourse.

David Morgan
Marriage, Domestic Life and Social Change

CHAPTER ONE

Introduction: The idea of the family

This chapter has several purposes. It aims firstly to introduce 'the family' as a subject of debate in the period 1945 to 1970 and to set this in some historical context by tracing debate back into the nineteenth century and forward to the end of the twentieth. Secondly, as the book is concerned with *ideas* about the family, the chapter will seek to problematise the family and ideology conceptually through a consideration of the etymology of the word 'family' and a critical account of debates concerning ideology. A short survey of the various ways in which historians and sociologists have approached studying the family will follow this, along with a brief introduction to the methodological framework of this study. The book draws upon distinct research strands, namely, official discourse and policy; representation in popular culture; and remembered experience. A fuller account of methodology will appear in chapters dealing with each of these.

The family as subject of debate

'All good things must come to an end'

In the last few months of 1999, as the century drew to a close, two stories connected to ideas about family made the news headlines in Britain. The first was concerned with one of the country's most well known (albeit fictitious) families, the 'Oxo family' of the long-running television advertisement campaign for Oxo stock cubes. The story was that the campaign, which had run since 1983, was to come to an end. In explanation, a spokesman for Oxo was quoted in the *Guardian* as saying: 'The Oxo family has been a great success and extremely popular with viewers over the years, but all

1

good things must come to an end. Family life is changing and we feel it is time for a change of direction.' Lynda Bellingham, the actress who played the part of the mother in the Oxo family, added: 'The whole family set-up has changed socially in the last ten years. I think that people buy pre-cooked meals and I don't actually think that it is realistic, people cooking gravy.'[1]

This series of advertisements and the news story about their demise are connected to a number of contemporary discourses. The Oxo family is a good example of what is often called 'the traditional family'. The advertisements feature a co-resident heterosexual (and presumably married) couple and their three dependent children who together represent the family. The standard narrative of the advertisement involves Lynda Bellingham's character in the kitchen cooking the family meal which all five family members will sit down to later in the day. While the story of the demise of this family may be largely about changes in advertising styles and eating habits in late-twentieth-century Britain, it is also firmly rooted in the long-standing idea of 'the decline of the family' in which the move away from 'the family meal' is one recurring motif. Indeed, it is this that makes the story newsworthy.[2]

'Redefining the family'

The second news story concerned Martin Fitzpatrick's attempt to succeed to his deceased male partner's tenancy of a housing association flat. This seemingly minor story became front page news, and was heralded as 'redefin[ing] the family'.[3] The couple had lived together in the flat for nearly twenty years, with Mr Fitzpatrick providing constant care for his disabled partner for the last eight of those years. After his partner's death, Mr Fitzpatrick had been served an eviction notice and refused the right to take over the tenancy, a right regularly extended to resident members of the deceased's family. Mr Fitzpatrick took his case to the House of Lords, claiming that he was indeed a member of his deceased partner's family. In a historic ruling, the law lords voted by a majority of three to two that he could be classed as a member of his late partner's family. Lord Nicholls, one of the five law lords involved, is reported to have said:

> A man and woman living together in a stable and permanent relationship are capable of being members of a family. Once this is accepted, there can be no rational or other basis on which the like conclusion can be withheld from a similarly stable and permanent sexual relationship between two men or between two women.[4]

The significance of this ruling was that this was the first time that domestic partners of the same sex were judged to be family in law. Since much of the law surrounding inheritance, social security, immigration and taxation uses the term 'family', and since this is not narrowly defined, being a member of a family confers significant rights.

Did this ruling 'redefine the family'? And are definitions or understandings of 'family' determined by law alone? That Martin Fitzgerald considered himself to have been part of his late partner's family before this ruling suggests that private senses of family are not always in line with legal ideas of family. Similarly, the right-wing campaigners who inevitably deplored this law lords ruling have quite different ideas about what constitutes a family. To return to the story about the Oxo family with which we started, it could further be argued that popular cultural representations, and changes within these, also contribute to our sense of what family is. Both of these stories have something important to tell us about ideas concerning the family in Britain at the end of the twentieth century.

'The decline of the family'

Let us turn to another pair of examples from a few years earlier, both of which are concerned with a similar set of anxieties about families. In late October 1995 the writer and broadcaster Melanie Phillips began a week of interviews and discussion about her documentary *Who Killed the Family?* which was broadcast on prime-time terrestrial television. The core of Phillips' argument was that the disintegration of the nuclear family is the most serious problem facing British society, and that this disintegration had produced a generation of dysfunctional and underachieving children.

The programme and concurrent debate saw the involvement of a wide range of broadcasters and other public figures – the Chief Rabbi Jonathan Sacks, columnists Mary Kenny and Suzanne Moore, the philosopher Roger Scruton, and members of both Labour and Conservative front-bench teams – with articles all that week on radio, television and in the print media. There was discussion on BBC Radio Four's *Start the Week*, a double-page spread in the *Guardian*, and an long item on *Newsnight*, the BBC's flagship news programme.

At the same time, a piece of government-proposed legislation, the Family Law Bill, was the subject of especially heated debate in both Parliament and the media. It was subject to an unusual number of amendments and defeats and almost daily reporting in the media. Such discussion focused particularly on the merits or otherwise of the idea of the 'marital offence' in divorce cases; the best environment in which to raise children; and the standing of marriage as an institution in the public eye.

The level of debate prompted by the broadcasting of *Who Killed the Family?* and the publication of the Family Law Bill is indicative of the centrality of debates about the family to British politics in the mid-1990s. This centrality has been in evidence both where the family is the main subject of discussion – as in *Who Killed the Family?* and in the Family Law Bill – or more generally when the family has been brought into discussion on matters ranging from welfare reform to juvenile crime, and from education to genetics. One of the things that is striking about this is that similar kinds of issues were being discussed in relation to the family at many points in the period 1945 to 1970. Another striking feature is that, too often, our contemporary debates about problems with 'the family' are ill-informed of the long history of such debate, perceiving current problems as recent and particular to our own set of social, political, economic and cultural circumstances.

Putting the debate into historical context

Concern about 'the family' was certainly marked in the years after the Second World War, forming a key theme for politicians, journalists, the Church and educationalists. This concern often centred on quite explicit fears about 'the decline of the family', what was causing such decline and how, ideally, the family should be promoted. Specific fears were raised over juvenile delinquency, a decline in personal responsibility (due to the state's new role in welfare), the quality of parenting, 'broken homes', 'latchkey kids', the moral climate of the nation, and what was still sometimes called 'the emancipation of women'. The following extracts give something of the flavour of these concerns.

The 1947 Denning Report into Procedure in Matrimonial Causes noted that

> every thinking person is profoundly disturbed by the prevalence of divorce and its effects on the family life and the national character . . .[5]

while the 1949 Report of Departmental Committee on Grants for the Development of Marriage Guidance thought

> it unnecessary for us to draw attention to the deterioration in marriage standards which has shown itself in recent years because this is common knowledge.[6]

In the same year, Donald Coggan, then Archbishop of York, told a National Union of Teachers Conference,

> it is part of the sickness of modern society that many parents have abdicated their responsibilities in the upbringing of children, and, consequently, the

school teacher of today finds himself necessarily concerned with the total health and character-formation of the child in his care.[7]

The *Times Education Supplement* noted that

many parents are now happy to let the state and the schools do things for their children that they would not have dreamt of allowing before the war . . . Many people feel that the Welfare State merely gives equality of opportunity for parents to be irresponsible. They fear that we shall soon begin to wonder what parents are for.

And an editorial made a connection between criminal violence and the family:

If adolescents are half as criminal and as vicious as the publicity given to them suggests, the root cause, as is generally agreed, must lie in the breakdown of family life and social standards generally.[8]

Although we can see here some very time-specific responses to, for example, the development of the welfare state and changes in social relations, this *kind* of concern about 'the family' resonates with late-twentieth-century concerns. It is, however, certainly not unique to either of these periods. There was a perceived state of crisis in the (usually working-class) family for many social reformers of the nineteenth century. Towards the end of that century, and particularly after the Boer War, these concerns were centred around the size of poor and working-class families, the quality of mothering and the resultant health and fitness of the nation. Moving forward to the period beyond 1970, we can note a return to a sense of crisis and calls for the promotion of family values, which culminated in that 'flashpoint of the social',[9] the debate around the passing into law of section 28 of the Local Government Act 1988.

Problematising the family

The etymology of 'the family'

One thing which becomes clear when discussing the family is that the idea of 'the family' is not a simple one. Different definitions and assumptions lead to different concerns and conclusions. There is, then, a need, to understand more precisely what is meant by 'the family'.

Often when concern about the family is expressed, it is the 'traditional family' (such as the Oxo family discussed above) which is seen to be at risk. In the period under discussion, it is this kind of family which is often seen as the generic type, as evidenced in this description by a sociologist in 1947:

> Typically, a family comes into being when a couple is married. The family gains in size with the birth of each child. From the time when the last child is born until the first child leaves home, the family remains stable in size. As the children leave home, for employment or marriage, the size of the family shrinks gradually back to the original two persons. Eventually one and then the other of the parents die and the family cycle has come to an end.[10]

Yet the word 'family' is currently used to describe a wide variety of different things: the nuclear family; a kinship group; 'great' families; a family of languages, plants etc.; and a feeling of community or closeness (as in 'family-like'). Raymond Williams in his *Keywords* provides a basis for understanding the modern development of some of these uses. He traces the use of 'family' to mean a 'house' (for example House of Windsor), a household (both with and without servants) and reflects on the modern distinction between the nuclear and the extended family, which he has related to the rise of the bourgeois family. These distinctions, and the processes by which they came about, are both important, for, as Williams argues,

> it is a history worth remembering when we hear that 'the family as an institution is breaking up' or that in times gone by and hopefully still today, 'the family is the necessary foundation of all order and morality'. In these and similar contemporary uses it can be useful to remember the major historical variations, with some of their surviving complexities and the sense, through these of radically changing definitions of primary relationships.[11]

Diana Gittins has taken up the challenge of analysing definitions of the family, calling into question the assumption that there is anything which can be usefully called *the* family. Importantly, she argues that as such a term covers such complexity and range of human experience, it is 'essential to start thinking of *families* rather than the family'.[12] It has been further argued that there is a need to locate families within a culture and understand them within that context. As Michele Barrett and Mary McIntosh commented in the 1980s, the family is specific to time and place – it is not culture-free.[13] Also, as Michele Barrett has argued elsewhere, 'even to conceptualize "*the* family" is to concede the existence of an institution that, in whatever historical context it is found, is essentially and naturally there'.[14] Thus it has been argued, a vital part of what constitutes 'the family' must be that which is ideologised.

Demographic change

Developments in the social organisation and practice of family life which are shown up by demographic research are particularly interesting in the light of the concern being expressed about the family's decline in the years after the Second World War. From the end of the war until the early 1970s there was a move towards earlier marriage for both men and women. While marriage rates for those aged 25 and over marrying for the first time remained stable throughout the period, the proportion of people marrying under the age of 25 rose consistently. Furthermore, although the number of divorces surged in the mid-1940s, this was short-lived and from the late 1940s up to 1960 the divorce rate fell to less than half its 1947 figure and did not rise again significantly until the implementation of the divorce reform of 1969. Fears of further decline in birth rates proved unfounded in the wake of the postwar 'baby boom'. The birth rate peaked in 1947, remained lower but stable in the early 1950s, and moved towards a general increase until the late 1960s.[15]

It is no simple task to interpret these demographic trends. It may seem that the traditional family was proving itself to be highly resilient, coming out of the war years with new vigour. Yet these statistical changes do not show the whole picture and in particular do not give us much indication (except in the brief increase in divorce) of the challenges that there had been to the stability of this model of the family. Nor do they provide us with many clues as to why there was such widespread and recurrent concern about 'the family'.

Ideology, theory, method

This section considers some of the major debates that have taken place on the notion of 'ideology'. Definitions and understandings of ideology have been fiercely contested and the concept both championed and derided in recent cultural theory.[16] To locate the present text within these debates, I will explain what I mean by the word 'ideology' and how I will use this concept in this book. To do this, I will take the reader through the processes by which I arrived at this understanding. I will show examples of the work and positions I will be drawing on, acknowledging problems and criticisms to which these positions have been vulnerable. I will also consider why it is (still) important to study ideology.

As a starting point, let us consider a set of observations made by Terry Eagleton in his *Ideology*.[17] Here Eagleton lists some definitions of ideology currently in circulation. Reading through these, I began mentally to construct a matrix in which some of these definitions could be shaped towards my own understanding of ideology. Equally, I discarded other definitions which had no use for my project.

The definitions I found useful were these:

1. The process of production of meaning, signs and values in social life.
2. A body of ideas characteristic of a particular social group or class.
3. Ideas which help to legitimate a dominant power.
4. Forms of thought motivated by social interests.
5. The conjunction of discourse and power.
6. The medium in which conscious social actors make sense of their world.
7. The process whereby social life is converted to a natural reality.

Evidently, within these various definitions, there are very different ideas about what ideology 'is'. A number of questions arose immediately from considering these. If ideology is the process of production of meanings, signs and values in social life, how does this process work, and to what ends? If ideology can be usefully understood to be a body of ideas characteristic of a particular social group or class, when and how does it become 'ideas which help to legitimate a dominant political power'? It became clear that a single definition of ideology would not do. I came to agree with Eagleton's argument that

> the word 'ideology . . . is a *text*, woven of a whole tissue of different conceptual strands; it is traced through by divergent histories, and it is probably more important to assess what is valuable or can be discarded in each of these lineages than to merge them forcibly into some Grand Global Theory.[18]

Therefore, to locate myself within these ongoing debates, I will consider those conceptual strands which I find most useful and which I will be drawing upon in my understanding of ideology. Before doing this, it will be equally useful to outline those conceptual strands which I have *not* found useful, that is the strands which relate to those of Eagleton's definitions which I am discarding.

Firstly, I am less concerned with seeing ideology as 'false consciousness'. This conceptual strand comes directly from the work of Marx and Engels, though as Stuart Hall has shown, no comprehensive, fully prepackaged theory exists in their work[19] – no general explanation of how social ideas work was developed comparable to the work on economic forms. Where Marx did consider ideology, it was most often to refer to specific manifestations of bourgeois thought, and in particular the features of such thought which were deemed negative or distorted. In *The German Ideology* and *The Poverty of Philosophy*, Marx and Engels were combating the anti-materialist bourgeois philosophies with which 'ideology' was to become associated: Hegelianism, religion, idealist philosophy and political economy. Hall argues that it is possible to read Marx's writing on ideology differently, especially outside of these two texts, in ways which reduce the apparent antagonism between the use of ideology in Marx's and Gramsci's work. However, it is with the notion of 'false consciousness' that early Marxist formulations on ideology are most closely associated.

Classically, in analyses of capitalism within this conceptual strand, the working class is seen to have false consciousness foisted upon it by the ideology of the ruling class, or, less pejoratively, that ideology forms a veil over the eyes of the working class which screens their 'real' relations to the world around them.[20] Importantly in this model, ruling ideas are seen to be those of the ruling class. The purpose of studying ideology is therefore to raise the consciousness of the working class, to demystify the distortion and reveal the true nature of capitalism, and in the process to reveal the truth about people's existence.

This conception of ideology has been challenged from a number of perspectives. One problem that has been identified is that by designating some thought 'ideological' there is an implication that there is other thought which is *not* ideological. A further implication, that the concept of non-ideological thought is akin to the concept of absolute truth, is one which has not been overlooked by post-structural and postmodern writers, and a number of positions have followed on from this observation. These positions will not feature in my own use of the concept of ideology, but need to be addressed briefly. In particular, there is the position which has become known as 'the end of ideology'. Although debates about the end of ideology first emerged in the United States after the Second World War, it is the much later debates of a number of post-structuralists and others that I am concerned with in this context. The earlier debates about the end of ideology have more in common with what Fukuyama later called 'the end of history'. The later post-structuralist/postmodern debates about the end of ideology relied initially on the critique of 'false consciousness' and mystification, and put forward a suggestion that if there was no absolute truth, and that nothing un-ideological existed, then everything was ideology and as such the concept has no useful meaning. This relates to other arguments about representation and the organisation of perception in which it has been suggested that there is no reality except representation itself. In this way, ideology has been seen as the confusion of linguistic and phenomenal reality.[21]

While these debates certainly force a sharpening of the epistemology of ideology, they are not my real concern here. I do not accept that ideology is a redundant concept. It may be that there is no thought which is un-ideological, but it is possible to argue that some ways of thinking are more ideologically significant than others. It is also possible to make efforts to see where and how ideas emerge within a culture. It is these two crucial ways of thinking about ideology which link the various conceptual strands I will draw upon in my understanding of ideology, and to which I turn next.

If the concern with mystification and false consciousness forms one major strand of Marxist thought on ideology, an interest in the function of ideas within a culture forms another. A different set of problems relating to early Marxist conceptions of ideology and false consciousness has been identified within this particular materialist tradition of ideology. In particular there has been a concern that within the 'false consciousness' conception of ideology there is a tendency towards economic determinism. This tendency was countered within the culturalist tradition by placing particular emphasis on re-sisting simple notions of economic determinism and the base-superstructure model in order to recover the importance of culture.

Raymond Williams is usually placed within this tradition, because his work in the late 1950s and 1960s struck a chord with E.P. Thompson's work in *The Making of the English Working Class*.[22] Although at that time Williams was not working within an obviously Marxist framework, his think-ing on culture and society had much in common with Thompson's post-1956 rethinking of ideology in which the determination of class domination (where ruling ideas are necessarily those of the ruling class) was resisted in favour of a recovered sense of human agency and an insistence on the importance of subjective experience. Importantly within this culturalist tra-dition, there is also an emphasis on 'bottom-up' analyses and an insistence on the importance of ethnographic studies. Williams's emphasis at this stage was on culture as 'a whole way of life', similar to anthropological understandings of culture, though it was this rather consensualising view of culture which exposed differences with Thompson, who favoured an under-standing of culture as a struggle between whole *ways* of life.

In a different vein, though at a similar time, the theoretical insights of structuralism emerged into this debate, offering different ways of addressing the issue of economic determinism. In particular, Althusser's work in the 1960s and 1970s marked a break with the early Marxist formulation of ideology and false consciousness. Instead of false consciousness, Althusser argued for ideology as a conceptual framework through which people make sense of and live out the material conditions within which they find them-selves. He suggested that ideology shapes and forms people's consciousness of reality, and as such, the world it constructs is the one which people will always inhabit.[23] This move enabled a more discursive conception of ideology to emerge and also enabled a move away from the simpler base and super-structure model of society. It did, however, also produce conflict with the culturalist tradition, particularly over the issue of agency and over structur-alism's tendency towards 'top-down' analyses in contrast to culturalism's 'bottom-up' analyses.[24]

It is the turn towards Gramsci, and particularly the concept of hegemony, which offers a bridge between these two traditions. The concept of hegemony, developed initially by Gramsci in the 1930s, is the means by which a ruling group maintains its dominance not by repressive force but through winning consent. Of particular concern to Gramsci is how this consent is obtained and maintained through a number of stages in the development of hegemonic rule. Central to this is his understanding of the workings of 'common sense' and the ways in which dominant ideas are formed and accepted as natural. The concept of hegemony is useful in uniting two of the key definitions of ideology listed above, that is 'ideas which help to legitimate a dominant political power' and 'the process whereby social life is converted to a nat-ural reality'. It is also useful in bringing together concerns about economics, culture and individual agency. As Graeme Turner has argued,

> Gramsci's theory of hegemony does seem well designed for its ultimate deployment as the consensual principle within cultural studies conceptions of ideology. It does allow for power to flow 'bottom-up', and severely qualifies assumptions about the effectiveness of power imposed from the 'top-down'.[25]

Significantly, Gramsci saw ideology as a site of perpetual contestation and, within this, popular culture as a source of particular resistance.

Within this turn to Gramsci there has been a concern for work on semiotics and ideology, and this forms another conceptual strand which I will be drawing upon. An important theme within semiotics is the analysis of the naturalisation of social reality (not unlike the Gramscian notion of common sense), and in particular the uncovering of the latent meanings of everyday life. Part of my work will be concerned with uncovering the latent meanings in discourse on the family in which I will be particularly interested in the play of social and political power within language itself, especially within official discourse, but also elsewhere. I will be drawing upon ideas about language and 'the real' which are expressed here by John B. Thompson: 'Once we recognise that ideology operates through language and that language is the medium of social action, we must also acknowledge that ideology is partially constitutive of what in our societies is "real".'[26]

Gramscian conceptions of ideology have not been accepted wholesale, and within the turn to Gramsci a number of criticisms have emerged. As

Gramsci's conception of hegemony centres mainly around consent rather than coercion, he sees hegemony as being located primarily in civil society – those institutions intermediate between the state and the economy. Perry Anderson has criticised Gramsci for not locating hegemony also within the state.[27] For me this is a crucial step to take, as part of my concern with ideology will be about examining the ways in which the state is influential in distilling ideas central to hegemony.

Other critics have turned their focus on resistance and difference, that is the ways in which ideology fails to determine and fails to interpolate the subject, and where hegemonic ideas are resisted. Michel de Certeau's work has been influential here, emphasising the winning of small victories, the 'making over' of popular culture to people's own ends and focusing on the subversive possibilities of consumption.[28] It is possible to see these developments as building upon work on agency, though the need to retain a clear perspective on the conflict between determination and agency can equally be asserted. Though the attention to difference can be valuable, it can lead to a kind of relativism which is absent in other analyses of culture.

Debates about agency and structure were refreshed in the 1990s by the publication of Ulrich Beck's *Risk Society: Towards a New Modernity* (Sage, 1992). With his notion of reflexive modernisation, Beck has suggested that there is a changing relationship between social structures and social agents in which, when modernisation reaches a certain level, social agents tend to become less constrained by social structures and more individualised. Moreover, he argues that structural change *forces* social actors to become more and more free from structure, and that, for modernisation to be furthered, such agents need to release themselves from structural constraint, thereby actively shaping the modernisation process.

Beck argues that reflexive modernisation is taking place in a number of spheres, including the personal and private. Here his work begins to converge with Anthony Giddens' on modernity and the transformation of intimacy. Both suggest that structural change in the private sphere results in the individualisation of social agents who then need to make decisions about the form and shape of interpersonal relationships and family and domestic arrangements, with Giddens arguing that this becomes a crucial site for the formation of identity.

The conceptual strands in debates on ideology discussed here will inform the analysis that follows; and where clear preferences for particular theoretical traditions has been expressed, these will shape the selection and questioning of sources and the subsequent analysis produced. In the concluding chapter (Chapter Six), I will return to these various conceptual strands and ask what the evidence and argument from the different chapters can contribute to these debates.

Studying families

In the sections above I have sought to problematise the family conceptually and to explore the different meanings which have been attached to the idea of family in Britain in the recent past. These different meanings are necessarily tied up with the ways in which 'family' has been researched and studied, both in the past and in the present. This section surveys these studies in order to expand upon discussion of the idea of the family and also to locate this book more firmly within the tradition of writing on family matters.

The study of the family in its historical setting has been an expanding field since the 1960s, though historical studies of the family in the period after 1945 are still scarce. Much historical research has, however, been carried out on earlier periods, and this has been conducted in a number of ways. Much of this work, especially in the earlier years, was concerned with how 'the family' was constituted in pre-industrial society and the ways in which it changed and developed into a modern form. Controversy has characterised the development of this work. From one point of view, Michael Anderson and others have argued for the complexity of and difference in family forms over time, aiming to show that

> the one unambiguous fact which has emerged in the last twenty years [since 1960] is that there can be no simple history of *the* western family since the sixteenth century because there is not, nor has there ever been, a single family system. The west has been characterised by a diversity of family forms, by diversity of family functions and by diversity in attitudes to family relationships not only over time but at any one point in time. There is, except at the most trivial level, no western family type.[29]

Though there is much support for this point of view, it is by no means universally accepted and others have argued directly against it. Peter Laslett, in his work from the mid-1960s onwards, suggests that the mean average household size has remained constant (at 4.85) from the late sixteenth century to the end of the nineteenth, and from this he forms the theory that the family has invariably been nuclear.[30]

Such demographic analysis of past communities has been a popular way of looking at family history since the 1960s, with the work of Laslett and the Cambridge Group for the History of Population and Social Structure being prominent. During the 1960s and 1970s an alternative approach was developed by a series of studies known collectively as 'the sentiments school', that is work which had a qualitative rather than a quantitative focus on family life and which often sought to trace the development of emotions and sentiments in families as a key feature in a perceived change from 'traditional' to 'modern' families.[31] Work on changes in meaning has also been evident in the development of cultural histories of family, such as Leonore Davidoff and Catherine Hall's *Family Fortunes*, and Davidoff *et al.*'s *The Family Story*.[32] Oral historians have also developed a body of work on family life, a recent example being Elizabeth Roberts' *Women and Families*.[33]

Historians have only recently begun to concern themselves with studies of family in the period after 1945. Most of the work on families since the Second World War has been done by sociologists, with functionalism dominating the earlier part of the period. At that time a consensus grew in which a functional fit was seen to exist between the 'modern nuclear family' and industrial society. As the appeal of functionalism waned, sociological work on families diversified and has been further carried out in various fields of contemporary sociology. Recent work has included studies of the formation, composition and workings of new households; youth transitions; divorce, remarriage and the dynamics of step-families; parenting and child care; and of family obligation and responsibility.[34]

More broadly, sociological work has been done on developments in the organisation of everyday life as a whole, including new critiques of the interpersonal domain. The essence of this critique is captured in Anthony Giddens's *The Transformation of Intimacy* in which he argues that, though filtered through existing inequalities and traditions, modern cultures have witnessed a radical democratisation of the interpersonal domain in which equal partners have emerged with the freedom to choose lifestyles and forms of partnership.[35] Thus, it is argued, late modernity has seen the emergence of 'pure relationships', entered into solely for what they can bring to each partner and existing only so long as those (usually emotional) benefits remain. Connected to this, others have commented on the convergence of patterns in both heterosexual and homosexual ways of life centred around the search for and maintenance of a satisfactory primary emotional relationship as a key part of personal identity.[36] The implications that this has for homosexuality as heterosexuality's 'dark shadow' have not gone unnoticed.[37]

*

Some of these ways of thinking and writing about family will necessarily be drawn upon in this book. As the book is concerned primarily with ideas about the family, it will have more in common with the tradition of the 'sentiments school' of historical writing – especially as developed through cultural history – than with demographic analysis. It will, however, be very much aware of the criticisms to which this tradition has been vulnerable and will moreover be filtered through the critiques of the culture of familiarism, as well as the questioning of epistemology implicit in the previous discussion of ideology, theory and method. It will also draw upon contemporary sociological debates about 'the family' and the organisation of everyday life, though it will not attempt the kind of empirical study characteristic of that discipline.

So, to summarise what this will all mean in terms of the work that will follow: I have chosen to utilise three distinct research strands – official discourse/public policy, popular cultural representation, and remembered experience – which are not usually studied together. This choice of research material has been influenced by the discussion of theoretical perspectives above. Particularly important here are the challenge to economic determinism suggested by the idea that popular culture is a site of particular contestation of hegemony, and the idea that the consideration of human agency – as evidenced here in oral source – is crucial for understanding ideology.

In this book, I will first concentrate (in Chapters Two and Three) on official discourse and public policy. This will involve an assessment of the production of ideas about the family in these texts, and part of this analysis will be concerned with the ideas at work within the use of language itself. I will also consider the role of organisations at the periphery of and formally outside of the state – charities, social services etc. – in the formation of prevalent ideas about the family to acknowledge that, although the state may represent the official 'distilled' public voice, this voice has many constituent parts and the state's position at any given moment involves many different components.

Next, in Chapter Four, I will turn my attention to the issue of popular cultural representation. By representation I do not mean the kind of empiricist representation where the signified is seen to exist prior to its signifier and is then merely reflected by it. Instead I mean what Richard Dyer has called 'images of' analysis of the representation of cultural groupings and the issue of who is being represented where and by whom. This kind of work relies on a rejection of the 'end of ideology' and 'there is no reality except representation itself' theories mentioned above. In this I will agree with Dyer when he argues that he

> accept[s] that one apprehends reality only through representations of reality, through texts, discourse, images; there is no such thing as unmediated access to reality. But because one can see reality only through representation, it does not follow that one does not see reality at all. Partial – selective, incomplete, from a point of view – vision of something is not no vision of it whatsoever.[38]

For reasons explained in Chapter Four, this work on the representation of the family will focus in particular on film. In considering cinematic representation I will draw upon John Hill's suggestion that films do more than just reflect society: they also actively explain and interpret the way in which the world is to be perceived and understood.[39]

The third strand, developed in Chapter Five, will be concerned with examining remembered experience of the period 1945 to 1970 in a study of people who were living in what was to become the London Borough of Greenwich. By using oral history I am seeking to uncover people's memories of the family as it was experienced by them, and what ideas about family they lived with. This will involve looking at some issues around the theory of oral history. I will explore these through focusing on two interrelated themes: memory as a cultural product, and the ways in which the past and the present are related.

Chapter Six will consider the juxtaposition of evidence from the various strands, making links and drawing conclusions. It will address the issue of how to evaluate evidence from such disparate sources, reflecting on methodological issues, and will be informed by the theoretical positions drawn upon in the book and outlined in Chapter One.

A final postscript chapter will bring elements of the history up to date with a survey of major trends and developments in the practice of family life since the end of the 1960s. There will be consideration here of both demographic changes and developments within the social organisation of domestic life as well as a survey of how public policy on families has developed over the period. The chapter will also attempt to put such trends and developments into a wider cultural context.

Although some issues may recur in each of these chapters, the 'family matters' discussed in the various strands will necessarily differ as the concerns expressed in the various elements of the culture (or at least in those sources available to the researcher) also differed. Rather than try to discuss a uniform set of issues in the various strands, I have taken the issues which were most striking or which recurred most frequently in the various sources consulted.

CHAPTER TWO

'Family planning'

Families, policy and the law

This chapter is organised both chronologically and thematically. Chronologically because it addresses the popular idea that there is a sharp division
between, on the one hand, the immediate postwar years and 1950s, and,
on the other, the 1960s. This perceived division is not confined merely to
conservative thinking, although it is especially strong there, often manifesting
as ideas of a 'golden age' of 1950s order and cohesion contrasted with a
chaotic, demoralised post-1960s Britain. In much radical thought, too, the
1960s are a watershed, this time of liberation and new expression. On closer
examination this division is not so clear-cut, and so one of the organising
themes of the chapter will be the changes and continuities in official discourse
between these two notional periods. A second theme will be concerned with
the new (and sometimes old) ways in which the state intervened in families.
The chapter starts, however, with ideas about the nation and nationhood,
race and ethnicity, and how in official discourse these are integral to thinking
about the family in the 1940s and 1950s.

Note on sources

The chapter is concerned with government-sponsored enquiries, policy decisions and legislative changes. The selection of official texts for discussion
was made by careful analysis of lists of official publications for the period
1945 to 1970 and close analysis of those publications most tied up with
ideas about family. Royal Commissions are given particular attention because
of their status as bodies reflective of diverse opinion, entrusted to garner the
widest possible ideas and voices. They are therefore taken to be especially
useful in looking at prevalent ideas and consensuses. The policies of welfarism,

where they are concerned with or have an especial impact upon families, have also been included for analysis and are discussed in connection with Royal Commission and other committee recommendations. Particular attention is paid to the report of the Wolfenden Committee as this is often argued to be the defining voice of what some call permissiveness and which others have called the legislation of consent.[1] The legislation from this period which has an impact upon and helps shape the organisation of sexuality and family life is given similar attention. The chapter assumes that together these various official texts – reports, policies and legislation – add up to the prevalent official discourse on ideas about family.

Families and the national interest

Once the Second World War was over, two themes of concern prevalent in national debate were: (1) fears over population decline, and (2) an outcry over failure rates in marriage. These concerns were both related to the stability of the family – the bedrock of society and yet, in Christopher Lasch's useful phrase, an oddly fragile one – and the well-being of the nation. The two concerns were inextricably linked.

Concern about population was not new in 1945. The concern which emerged at that time can be related to the new thinking about population which, with the beginnings of the census and the compulsory registration of births, deaths and marriages, became possible in the nineteenth century when population became reified, quantified and measured. In particular, the concern about birth rates (and more specifically the issue of population replacement levels) was one which originated in the 1930s, when the idea that the number of births was below the level of replacement formed the basis of demographic discussion in Britain and elsewhere in Europe. When a Royal Commission was set up to look at the issue of population, its members saw this as their primary concern. This Royal Commission was further instructed 'to consider what measures, if any, should be taken in the national interest to influence the future trend of population'.[2]

When the Royal Commission on Population (RCP) reported in 1949, its most significant message was a belief that the average family size was still insufficient for the continued replacement of the population. This was 'not due to any change in the proportion of people marrying . . . but to a decline in the number of children born per married couple'.[3] This trend of family limitation was seen to be deliberate and a cause for serious concern both in the way in which it was occurring and in what its consequences might be.

Ironically, by the time the report was published in 1949, public concern over this issue was declining on a wave of optimism following the postwar baby boom. The voice of the Commission was influential though, and it was central in directing and filtering ideas about the family in these years. As a Royal Commission it comprised the widest and most powerful opinion about matters to do with fertility, marriage and the family. Its message is therefore worth considering in some detail.

It is illuminating to look further into the concern expressed over replacement levels. In one sense the Commission sees sub-replacement levels as evidence of a cultural malaise:

> There is much to be said for the view that a failure of a society to reproduce itself indicates something wrong in its attitude to life which is likely to involve other forms of decadence. The cult of childlessness and the vogue of the one-child family were symptoms of something profoundly unsatisfactory in the *zeitgeist* of the inter-war period, which it may not be fanciful to connect with the sophistications and complacencies which contributed to the catastrophe of the second world war.[4]

The Commission does not specify what 'other forms of decadence' it has in mind, and so we are left to speculate. What is clearer is the call for a kind of 'back to basics', a move away from sophistication, complacency and decadence which the Commission saw as fundamentally threatening to Britain, the Empire and perhaps Britishness itself.

The report continues with an airing of its fears concerning the 'fundamental issues of the maintenance and extension of Western values and culture',[5] urging the need for the number of births to exceed the replacement levels in 'Western peoples' to ensure the continued influence of western ideas. This relates further to a desire to maintain white emigration to the Commonwealth, the Dominions and the United States. The Commission expressed a belief that migration was essential if Britain was to continue its economic links with those parts of the world and maintain its international standing in more general terms. From this we can see the beginnings of an equation where the health of the family relates directly to the health of the nation and, by implication, the race.

This is underlined by concern that sub-replacement birth rates may result in a need for immigrant workers in certain areas, an outcome which the Commission sees as 'undesirable':

> Immigration on a large scale into a fully established society like ours could only be welcomed without reserve if the immigrants were of good human stock and were not prevented by their religion or their race from intermarrying with the host population and becoming merged in it.[6]

Past examples we are given of immigrants of 'good human stock' are French Protestant and Flemish Protestant refugees, in other words white, non-Catholic Christians. This would seem to suggest that immigrants would need to be invisible to be acceptable, and might explain why the Irish seem to be pointedly excluded from this list. Perhaps the Commission could not see Asian or Afro-Caribbean people as being 'of good human stock', certainly it could neither envisage autonomous cultural groups establishing themselves in Britain nor black integration into British culture.

We can also see here further evidence of the way in which the idea of marriage, and a particular view of marriage, is so deeply embedded into public policy. Racial intermarriage is unthinkable in the Commission's eyes. It concludes,

> all these considerations point to the conclusion that continuous large scale immigration would probably be impracticable and would certainly be undesirable, and the possibility – it can be regarded as no more than a possibility – that circumstances might compel us to consider or attempt it is among the undesirable consequences of the maintenance of family size below replacement level.[7]

This concern over the state of the nation extends to what amount to eugenicist fears over the birth rates of different classes. The Commission took expert evidence which showed that, on average, 'the more intelligent have smaller families than the less intelligent'. This was a cause for concern 'since a large part of intelligence is inherited, there is in process with each generation a progressive lowering of the average level of innate intelligence of the nation'.[8] The Commission urges that there is a need for further research into this differential fertility, concluding

> it is clearly undesirable for the welfare and cultural standards of the nation that our social arrangements should be such as to induce those in the higher income groups to keep their families not only below replacement level but below the level of others.[9]

This resonates with the eugenicist ideas which were evident in Beveridge's thinking at the time of the drafting of his famous *Report on Social Insurance and Allied Services* (Cmnd 6404), published in 1942. Beveridge was keen to maintain tax allowances for men with children, alongside family allowances, as tax allowances were more beneficial to the middle and professional classes – 'the more successful in society' – and would encourage them to have more children.[10]

The eugenics/imperialism/racism tie up, which is evident in the RCP report, has a long history and one which has been linked to periods of concern about the state of the nation, such as at the turn of the century with the state's investigations into 'physical deterioration'. It is interesting to note that such ideas were alive and kicking in early postwar Britain. It is also interesting to note that concern for the family seems here to cloak other concerns, particularly about Britain's position in the world and the organisation of ideas about gender, sexuality and race in the postwar world. It would seem that responses to a whole range of issues are being framed in terms of problems with 'the family'.

These ideas emerging from the five years of deliberation by the RCP are relevant to the outcry over divorce rates which became strong in the late 1940s. This second major theme of concern over the family spawned several enquiries into marriage and divorce. The first of these enquiries was the *Report into Procedure in Matrimonial Causes* (Denning Report). This Home Office committee was established in 1946 to look into the ways in which the law dealt with divorce and the nullity of marriage and to see how a reconciliation could be effected in a marriage which had broken down. This latter concern was in direct response to the rising divorce rate and the fears which it raised: 'Every thinking person is profoundly disturbed by the prevalence of divorce and its effects on the family life and the national character'.[11] The Royal Commission on Marriage and Divorce (RCMD), established five years later, went so far as to call divorce a 'deep-rooted evil' and chose to pay particular attention to that part of its briefing which referred to 'the need to promote and maintain healthy and happy married life'. Indeed, it saw this phrase as underlining the 'grave responsibility' of its task.[12]

Precisely why the rise in divorce was seen to be so disturbing has to do with the vital role that marriage was seen to play in society. This may be an obvious point but it is one worth exploring. The Denning Committee pointed to the importance of marriage in its summing-up:

> We have throughout our enquiry had in mind the principle that the pre-servation of the marriage tie is of the highest importance in the interests of society.[13]

This idea appears again in a Home Office report of 1949 which called the 'deterioration in marriage standards' a 'social problem of considerable magnitude going to the roots of national life'.[14] This is echoed by the RCMD with its clear view about the role that marriage plays in society:

> The Western world has recognised that it is in the best interests of all concerned – the community, the parties to a marriage and their children – that marriage should be monogamous and that it should last for life . . . it is obvious that

life-long marriage is the basis of a secure and stable family life, and that to ensure their well-being children must have that background.'[15]

The idea expressed here, that the preservation of marriage is in the best interests of all concerned, extends to an acknowledgement that it is in the interests of the nation as well: 'The nation's well being depends largely upon the quality of married life amongst its members.'[16]

While this message about the importance of marriage comes across quite clearly, none of these enquiries is explicit about why this is so. It may be that this is because it was taken for granted, that this was obvious, in the same way that the deterioration of marriage standards was seen to need no explanation here:

> It is unnecessary for us to draw attention to the deterioration in marriage standards which has shown itself in recent years because this is common knowledge.[17]

Some evidence given to the RCMD from the Church does suggest that divorce opens up the possibility of the expression of sexuality which would ordinarily be suppressed. This is given as the reason for opposing moves to relax the law so as to allow a divorced person to marry their former brother-in-law or sister-in-law:

> It is supremely important for the stability of the family unit and for the protection of its members from indulging in unlicensed thoughts or desires that there should be the strongest barrier against any thoughts or possibility of marriage with the brothers or sisters of a partner.[18]

However, the clearest indications of why divorce is found to be quite so disturbing come in the thoughts emerging from enquiries into the causes of the increase in divorce rates. These were talked of as a short-term and a long-term set of problems. There was much agreement that a prolonged and involved war had resulted in a rise in the divorce rate after lengthy separations and hasty wartime marriages. This coincided with extension of the grounds for divorce in 1937 and the introduction of legal aid for divorce after the war, producing what Denning referred to as a 'temporary blip'. A Home Office report which appeared soon after the Denning Report pointed also to the employment of married women in industrial occupations during the war as a reason for the increase in divorce.

In the longer term, a loss of community life and the isolation of families and individuals as a result of industrialisation were cited.[19] The RCMD took up this analysis of the longer-term roots of the increase in divorce, suggesting there was now a 'tendency to take the duties and responsibilities of marriage less seriously than formerly'. It further suggested that more widespread education and improved standards of living had meant that greater demands were being made of marriage. It singled out women's emancipation as a particularly strong element in this greater expectation of what marriage should have to offer. It is noticeable that these last reasons which were given for the rise in the divorce rate are similar to those which the RCP saw as significant in the decline in family size. The idea that women were expecting or demanding more from marriage (and were thus less prepared to put up with an unsatisfactory marriage) relates directly to the idea, set out by the RCP, that women wanted fewer children because the burden of responsibility fell so heavily on them.

There are other ways, too, in which the concerns of both falling family size and rising divorce rate overlap. It is significant, for example, that within the RCP report 'family' means most definitely 'within marriage'. Throughout the report, population is seen to be dependent on family size and there is an assumption that this in turn is dependent on the state of marriage and constituent factors like the average age of people marrying. Illegitimate births, which were at around 10 per cent of all births in 1945 and at 5.5 per cent in 1948 were dismissed as unimportant. (Indeed, women who had children outside of marriage were being depicted in psycho-sociological literature of the time as pathologically disturbed.[20]) Predictions for future trends in birth rates were seen to depend firmly on 'the level of marital fertility rates and therefore on the size of the family.'[21] A potential future gender imbalance in the population is predicted, with a small 'excess' of men at reproductive ages, presupposing both heterosexuality and a desire to reproduce.

In other reports of the period there is evidence that 'the family' is being held in higher regard than ever before. The *Report of the Scottish Home Department Committee on Homeless Children*, for example, saw that

> the lesson which above all else the war years have taught us is the value of the home. It is upon the family that our position as a nation is built.

and

> the war has sharpened the nation's consciousness of the need and value of service and has bxrought into prominence the vital place in our lives of the family and the home.[22]

The report goes on to talk specifically of 'the growing awareness of the importance of the family', while the *Report of the Royal Commission on Population* stressed that the family has tended to be overlooked or given only a minor place in social policy and urged that the family should in future be given a central place in policy planning. Concerns about family which were in evidence in the many related enquiries of the early postwar years were, then, appearing against a backdrop of renewed regard for 'the family'.

Reforms in the provision of the state care of children were also to be organised with the model of the two-parent, gender-differentiated family in mind. In 1946 the Home Office published a report from its Care of Children Committee which established the following for female workers:

> The House Mother or Assistant Matron should be a woman suitable to take charge of a 'family' group of up to twelve children from (say) two years of age to fourteen or fifteen. She must play the part of a mother to the children and be able to create for them the atmosphere of affection and security necessary to their happiness . . . and give them the kind of training in character and social habits which is normally given in the home.

There was also a need for a particular kind of male role model:

> The corresponding male worker must play the father's part. His duties call for equal understanding of and interest in the children but his domestic work will lie on the side of out-of-door recreational activities rather than the physical care of the child.[23]

The sanctity of the family home is reiterated in this report by the Committee's concern not to intervene in the care of children while still in the parental home, even where the child is suffering from neglect, malnutrition or 'other evils'. The Committee argued that, 'during the period leading up to a child's removal from his home he may indeed be said to be deprived of a "normal" home life . . . but the difficulty of drawing the line among children in their homes is obvious.'[24]

From the evidence of these various enquiries into subjects relevant to families and family life, we can begin to build up a picture of what was being suggested in official discourse to be in the national interest in the ten years or so after the war. This could be summed up as the healthy flourishing of the family as an institution and as the basis of everyone's domestic life, involving life-long marriage and the production of three or four healthy children, cared for primarily by their mothers in the home. In order for this to be achieved it would be necessary for women to be content with being primarily in the home and for children to be less of an economic burden to their families.

That all this was seen to be necessary has to do with the broader theme of reconstruction and reconciliation which was at the heart of government policy after the war. The disarray which was noted in family life was reflected in the economic and physical damage evident in the country at large. In the process of reconstruction it became clear that repairing the damage done to the family was essential to the rebuilding in other areas. As such, reconstruction came to imply more than a physical rebuilding of a damaged infrastructure and economic base. In a sense there was also to be a reconstruction of society. A nation which had been torn apart by war and yet drawn together (so we are led to believe) by 'wartime spirit' faced the possibility of further social disintegration once that spirit had evaporated. It can be argued that reconstruction, as part of an effort of national reconciliation, imbued with family values, was at least in part an attempt to blur class differences and gender antagonism thrown up by the war. As Liz Heron argues,

> it is the family, in the comforting sameness of its image, replicated a million times across the barriers of wealth and class that can transcend and overwhelm the significance of the other structures and institutions in which ordinary lives are caught.[25]

In order to bring about this kind of reconstruction, greater state intervention in family life in the area of social policy was advocated along with a call for the needs of the family, as well as the need to promote healthy family life, to be at the centre of other policy areas. This, in essence, is what was recommended by the various commissions and committees. The next section will look at these recommendations and actual policy changes.

Family, social policy and state intervention

Roy Parker has argued that there has never been any explicit 'family policy' in Britain. There have been policies which have *affected* families and which have contained powerful assumptions *about* families, but 'the family' as an overt subject of social legislation is, he argues, significantly absent. Thus 'it is politically much less hazardous for a government to adopt family policies which are implicit, fragmented or disguised as the incidental effects of other initiatives'.[26] The early postwar years may well be the period in recent British history (at least until the advent of 'New' Labour in 1997) in which this is *least* the case. Perhaps the spirit of reconstruction enabled a more explicit approach to the formation of policy on families. Certainly, both the reports of the various enquiries discussed above and many of the policies enacted from them suggest more coherence on the subject of family and policy than Parker sees.

Furthermore, while the development of the welfare state has most often been characterised as a response to the rise of class politics, it can be seen equally to be concerned with the promotion of particular ideas about gender and families. Susan Pedersen has recognised this argument in her recent study of the origins of welfarism in western European states. In *Family, Dependence and the Origins of the Welfare State* she argues that

> the social reformers and activists who shaped early welfare policies in Britain and France were often quite as concerned with gender relations and family maintenance as they were with social class . . . [they] sought to redistribute income and resources not simply across class lines but towards families with dependent children and the mothers occupied in caring for them.[27]

In Britain after the Second World War this is clearly in evidence in the introduction of family allowances – suggested by Beveridge as one of the three measures needed to make social insurance work – and the related system of child tax allowance. The latter provided tax breaks for married men with children, while the former (after a successful campaign headed by Eleanor Rathbone) provided mothers with a flat payment – initially 5 shillings each at a time when the average male manual wage was £6[28] – for the second and any subsequent child.[29] It is possible to see a connection here with the concern over population levels which led to the Royal Commission on Population, as it was sometimes argued that making payments for second and subsequent children would make the three- or four-child family more financially viable for the majority of people, increasing the birth rates.[30]

The RCP report had also paid close attention to the social and economic position of the family, focusing firstly on the effects that having children had on the standard of living of the family unit and secondly on the position of women in the family. It concluded that the development of social policy throughout the century had tended to accentuate the relative difficulties of parenthood. It suggested that in the process of social advance the family had been overlooked or given only a minor place in social policy and consequently the state had done little to alleviate the difficulties of raising a family. It singled out two particular effects that this had had. In economic terms it had meant that the addition of children had involved a substantial fall in the average family's standard of living. In social terms it saw the worst effect being felt by mothers who had not gained access to the growth in leisure time which had been a feature of the period. In the eyes of the Commission, the overall effect had been 'to lower the status of the family in the national life'.[31] The proposals the RCP made were aimed at changing these particular effects of parenthood and consequently raising the status of the family once again.

To ease the financial burden of parenthood the Commission recommended increases in the scope and scale of family allowances, a lump sum to be given by the state after the birth of a child and income tax allowances for children. This was to be the means by which family income could be maximised, though rates of family allowance were not raised until the later Wilson government of 1966–70.[32]

It might have been expected that, given their experience of war work, women's employment outside of the home might have been made easier, as a way of increasing family incomes. The Commission chose instead to focus on improving the material conditions of motherhood as an occupation. This again resonates with the Beveridge Report. Beveridge, using figures from the 1931 census which showed that more than seven out of eight married women did not do paid work, argued that policy should be framed with reference to the seven and not the one, and so assumed that during marriage women would not be engaged in paid employment.[33] Furthermore, Beveridge worked with a model of marriage where husband and wife were a 'team', the man going out to work to earn a family wage and the woman remaining in the home. The postwar government did not appear to question this reasoning and the model was to become fundamental in the establishing of the welfare state. The system of family allowance payments and child tax allowance relied on such a model. While it can be criticised for reproducing a set of conservative options for men and women, this model was to be made unworkable with the rise in the divorce rate, the rise in the number of one-parent families and the implications these social factors had for a system which relied on the idea that a man would provide for the family and the family would be insured against want through him.

The Beveridge Report had seriously addressed the role of and conditions for women in the new welfare society. Women as 'housewives and mothers have vital work to do in ensuring the adequate continuance of the race'[34] it said, and recommended provision of new benefits and an attitude to motherhood which had much in common with the recommendations of the RCP. To ease the burden of motherhood the RCP report recommended a plethora of 'Family Services'. There were to be home helps, babysitters, day nurseries and nursery schools as part of the normal running of the household. Residential nurseries were to be established for when mothers were ill or for during confinement. Schemes to provide holidays for mothers were to be set up along with rest homes and facilities for mothers and children in trains and at stations. Many of these services were established, and examples of their workings are discussed in Chapter Three.

In a sense, these were radical proposals amounting to the state's recognition of the difficulties inherent in most women's day-to-day lives in the mid-twentieth century in Britain. The general aim of these family services was 'to reduce the work and worry of mothers of young children' in recognition of the idea that women should be given help in order to enjoy some leisure time and 'a tolerable life'.[35] There is a conscious progression from the idea that help should be given to women in times of household emergency – illness, confinement, the need to care for an elderly relative – to the idea that help should be given in the normal running of the home where a mother is responsible for more than one or two small children. A key part of this was to be the provision of part-time day nurseries to afford a few hours' relief for the mother. This is heralded as 'an important contribution to family welfare'.[36]

But this relief for the mother in the home was to come at a cost – the loss of provision of full-time day nurseries for mothers who worked outside of the home. Day nurseries had originally been established by voluntary agencies to care for the children of women who went out to work. During the war the state intervened to provide more nurseries to facilitate women's war work. Now this emergency was over and new (and old) concerns about the family were emerging, women were to return to the home, and motherhood was to be made more attractive. Full-time nurseries for mothers who went out to work 'would become subsidiary'. From the combination of both of these main themes in the proposals of the RCP – financial support for the family from the state and practical support for the mother in the home – a formula for population growth is achieved by a reiteration of the idea of the family wage, with state support, coupled with new ideas about women's need for a more fulfilling life. Both of these were to be brought about by a new role for the state in creating a domestic environment conducive to pronatalist ends.

This role was to extend as far as intervention to uphold such a domestic environment through measures to dissuade people from divorce. In recommending policy on marriage and divorce up to the mid-1950s, the various committees and commissions were unanimous in two areas of major concern: that it was essential for the state to enable and encourage the reconciliation of marriages before divorce became final; and that there was a need to educate the population about marriage and domestic life. The first of these points is clearly stated in both the Denning Report and the RCMD:

> The reconciliation of estranged parties to marriage is of the utmost importance to the State as well as to the parties and their children. It is indeed so important that the State itself should do all it can to assist reconciliation . . . The unity of the family is so important that, when parties are estranged, reconciliation should be attempted in every case where there is a prospect of success.[37]

Successful marriage and the maintenance of the unity of family life are so important that, where husband and wife have become estranged, an attempt should be made wherever possible to bring them together again . . . The State has thus an interest in furthering reconciliation wherever possible.[38]

To this end the Home Office set about giving financial support to voluntary agencies like the National Marriage Guidance Council – which had been established in 1938 precisely to deal with this issue – and also to other organisations which began to offer marriage guidance as part of their service. The Home Office also established the Marriage Guidance Training Board in 1949.

The second area of agreement – that there was a need for education on marriage – linked the philosophy of the enquiries into marriage and divorce with that of the RCP. It also marked out one of the main policy areas in which the interests of the family would be made more central. There was a consensus here that education (in the broadest sense) could be used as a preventative measure against divorce. The work of the agencies involved in marriage guidance was to be one way in which this was to be achieved, but the RCP report suggested that education on marriage should be carried out in a number of other ways, too: through the inclusion of sex education in the curriculum; through improving the status of 'the practical crafts of homemaking' and other subjects related to married life; and through courses for adults in the psychological aspects of marriage. The Commission called for the cooperation of the Churches and voluntary organisations with schools to make this possible. This was to be one of the ways in which the family was to be put in a more prominent position in a broad range of policies.

There were problems associated with the formal introduction of sex education and other matters into schools as government was reluctant to intervene in the curriculum[39] and for a variety of reasons there was a lack of definite leadership from local education authorities.[40] It is also difficult to assess the extent to which churches and voluntary organisations took up this call, though representatives from churches and a variety of voluntary organisations were involved – either directly through sitting on committees or indirectly by giving evidence – in the researches of government-sponsored enquiries. Other changes in education policy had more certain impacts upon families, particularly in the raising of the school-leaving age to 15 and then to 16 and the general expansion of further and higher education. These measures combined to increase the economic and practical dependence of children, arguably making children more of an economic liability within families. (There was therefore something of a tension between these measures and the system of family allowances, aimed to reduce the financial burden of parenthood, which was partly resolved by the continuation of payments for children under the age of 18 while in full-time education.) Lorraine Fox Harding has further suggested that this 'extension of childhood' may have contributed to (or perhaps been a reflection of?) the wider change in general attitudes to children and their place in society.[41]

While seeking to raise the profile of the family across a range of government policy, the RCP had in fact concentrated its recommendations on two specific policy areas: education (as seen above) and housing. 'The family should be given a central place in town and country planning', it said, suggesting that the particular needs of families with young children should be met with the provision of parks, health centres, nursery buildings and facilities for family recreation. This echoed widespread concerns about housing and the need for this aspect of reconstruction to be well thought out.

The problem of a lack of suitable housing was a serious one. There were around 700,000 fewer houses in 1945 than there had been before the war and the large increase in births and marriages compounded the demand for housing.[42] Not only new homes but entire areas of cities needed rebuilding, providing an unusual opportunity for restructuring. The new Labour government was keen on achieving what it believed to be the right type, quality and mix of housing as well building on a massive scale.[43] Various studies have shown that this concern for improved housing developed in the context of the promotion of family life. Indeed, the RCP saw the housing shortage as one of the 'main deterrents of parenthood', while urging for the provision of larger houses.[44] Graham Crow, in his study of housing after the war, argues that the recent history of declining birth rates and perceived worsening of standards of mothering meant that there was a concern that new houses should have sufficient space and be conveniently organised for bringing up children. He suggests that the 1950s was to be the period in which

> the modern domestic ideal of an affluent nuclear family living in a home of their own and enjoying the benefits of leisurely home life took shape, with the emphasis placed on the privacy of the individual household rather than the wider community. Moreover this new privatised life style was presented as a universal opportunity rather than something open only to a privileged part of the population as (for example) the bourgeois domestic ideal of the Victorians had been.[45]

Developments in domestic architecture – which Denise Riley called 'a revolution towards streamlined, rational kitchens and a good number of bedrooms'[46] – have similarly been criticised for their reaffirmation of women's domestic role. Women became cut off from the outside world in kitchens located at the back of the house in design changes which Jennifer Craik argues formed part of the ideological shift in emphasis from the kitchen reflecting the family's public status to its 'making visible and institutionalizing the dominant role of the woman in the family'.[47] It was this kind of housing which the Labour government had promoted in the early postwar years and which had been particularly associated with Hugh Dalton.[48] Although subsequent Conservative governments tended to reduce the unit cost of housing, and therefore arguably its quality, the consensus on the type of housing to be built does not seem to have been questioned until the development of the high-rise in the 1960s. These criticisms of housing design need, however, to be examined in the context of planning ideals, particularly in the public sector, which were very much orientated towards communal facilities and the open-plan model. Some examples of assumptions in housing policy at a local level are examined in the next chapter.

What overall picture, then, emerges of developments in this family–state relationship? Clearly, the period from the end of the Second World War to the mid-1950s saw a considerable shift in the relationship. There was a marked increase in the state's intention to intervene in families, which developed in conjunction with the development of the principle of universality in social policy. It could, though, create a false divide to see this as a specifically postwar development. The radical idea of universality had become accepted during the war and thus forms something of a continuity in 1940s and 1950s government policy. It has also been suggested that during the war there had been a growing sense of approval for greater state intervention in matters of national efficiency.[49] Jane Lewis, for example, points out that during the 1940s there was no opposition among commentators on the family to the idea of state intervention.[50] Indeed it may be that the war initiated an exaggerated belief in (and acceptance of?) the state's power to control. The immediate postwar years can be seen as a time in which the state sought to reinforce the influence it had gained in wartime to work against a longer-running trend for individuals and families to withdraw increasingly into a more private lifestyle. Whatever its roots, the kind of intervention discussed above, taken with the concept of universality, meant the state could be unprecedentedly involved with individual family lives. As Janet Walker has argued, 'here was the turning point which legalised state intervention in the life of every family'.[51]

The two key developments within this can be summed up as an active pronatalism and, later, a desire to 'rebuild' the family. By the end of the 1940s, the baby boom saw specifically pronatalist concerns wane only to be swamped by new desires to 'rebuild' the family. This latter idea relied on notions of the ideal (bourgeois) family with legal definitions of what constituted family and the roles that members should play within it. It is interesting that this concern to rebuild the family should coincide with the emergence of an ideology of companionate marriage which Janet Finch and Penny Summer-field have called 'the most distinctive feature of domestic life' in this period.[52] In many ways, what the RCP had been trying to achieve was the reconciliation of this modern kind of marriage with the three- or four-child family.

In a time of economic reconstruction this kind of ideological manoeuvring necessitated a few twists. Young married women were to be enticed into motherhood by improvements in material conditions. Concern was to be expressed here for the conditions which mothers had had to put up with, yet it was to be emphasised that a woman's place was in the home. At the same time, older married women were to be encouraged to return to work as a matter of national duty. A shortage of labour marked the era of reconstruction and now, once again, women's labour was needed outside the home. Calls were made for married women who no longer had children to care for to return to the workforce, especially if they had skills or training in areas of greatest need, such as teaching. This meant that at some stages of their lives – before marriage and after child care – women were not expected to stay in the home. Women were, in effect, to be a labour resource which could be called upon primarily in case of emergency. As Liz Heron has argued, 'to all ideological intents and purposes women did not work outside the home, while in effect they did and have continued to do so in increasing numbers'.[53]

One final important feature of state intervention in families up to the mid-1950s was the call to tighten up legislation in relation to the family and private morals. The RCMD could not support the idea of making divorce more difficult as it thought public opinion would not support it. It preferred instead to rely on 'fostering in the individual the will to do his duty by the community; in strengthening his resolution to make marriage a union for life; in inculcating a proper sense of his responsibility towards his children'.[54] The Commission recommended against allowing divorce on the grounds of an irretrievable breakdown in the marriage, preferring to retain the idea of divorce based on the matrimonial offence. Its one concession to this was to allow for a limited extension on the grounds of a separation of at least seven years. The Commission may have been persuaded on this by some who saw that marriage had been brought into disrepute by the number of 'dead marriages' which could not be ended by divorce under existing laws. It was suggested that a more reasonable law would increase morality and strengthen marriage rather than undermine them.[55]

The Commission did however refer to a tendency 'to resort too readily and too lightly to divorce' and warned that

> unless this tendency is checked, there is a real danger that the conception of marriage as a life-long union of one man with one woman may be abandoned.

'This would be an irreparable loss to the community. There are some of us who think that if this tendency continues unchecked, *it may become necessary to consider whether the community as a whole would not be happier and more stable if it abolished divorce altogether* and accepted the inevitable individual hardships that this would cause.[56]

The suggestion that it may become necessary to consider abolishing divorce altogether is clearly a minority view here; however, it is difficult not to read a hard line on divorce from the tone of the whole report. Yet scarcely more than a decade later, fundamental divorce reform was to come, shifting the principal basis for divorce from that of matrimonial offence to that of irretrievable breakdown for which matrimonial offences could – but need not – be cited. This fundamental shift has been seen as part of the mood of 'permissiveness' in liberalising legislation in the 1960s. There is, however, much continuity within this change, and the ideological developments can be seen to be much less dramatic than the liberalising of legislation may suggest.

Family and 'the legislation of consent'

What happened in the late 1950s and 1960s was a significant shift in the state's attitude to sexuality, marriage and the family in which immorality was no longer necessarily synonymous with illegality. There was a relaxation of the laws on private morals which involved a distinction between the public good and private morality. Stuart Hall, in his seminal text on the 'permissive' legislation, has characterised this as 'a sharper distinction between "public" and "private"; between the *state* and *civil society*'.[57]

This shift can be clearly seen in the *Report of the Committee on Homosexual Offences and Prostitution* (Wolfenden Report).[58] Even though this appeared only two years after the report of the Royal Commission on Marriage and Divorce, the tone of the Wolfenden Report is representative in many ways of the 'permissive' legislation which was to come in the 1960s. The report states unequivocally its view on how the state should and should not interfere in private morality. The Committee considered itself 'not charged to enter into matters of private moral conduct . . . except in so far as they directly affect the public good'. It added,

It is not, in our view, the function of the law to intervene in the private lives of citizens, or to seek to enforce any particular pattern of behaviour.[59]

This is clearly out of step with the prevailing philosophy of the RCMD in particular and the other reports considered above in general. That the philosophy of the Wolfenden Report should be taken up in legislative changes concerned with private morality and the public good evidently needs to be commented upon. We should note firstly that while Wolfenden's recommendations on prostitution were enacted almost immediately, the recommendations on the changes in the law concerning male homosexuality were delayed by ten years. Similarly, the often linked reforms of the law on abortion, divorce and family planning did not take place until the late 1960s. This can in part be attributed to party politics and personality. The change in government in 1964, which brought the Labour Party back into power, was compounded by the party's outright victory in 1966. These electoral victories saw the appointment of Roy Jenkins to the Home Office where he was to develop a reputation as a reforming Home Secretary.

However, while acknowledging this particular set of circumstances, it is possible to overestimate the part that changes of administration may play in alterations to official policy connected to ideas about the family. It is all too tempting to see the 'legislation of consent' as simply a break from the past occasioned by a new Labour government. It may be noted that, in contrast, in the discussion so far on the ideas about the family in official discourse before Wolfenden, changes in government have barely been noted. I would suggest that, in this earlier period at least, this is because ideas about the family formed one area of consensus. There is currently a move towards questioning the 'myth of consensus' in British postwar politics,[60] but ideas about and attitudes to the family have been exempted from this discussion so far. Changes in administration *may* lead to distinct changes to policy and legislation relating to the family (and the 1964 and 1966 Labour governments would seem to be examples of this), but such change should not be assumed in this period. Furthermore, as will be argued here, the *continuities* evident in different administrations' attitudes towards the family (including the 1964–70 Labour administration) are sometimes lost in superficial analyses of policy and legislative change.

Within the ideology of the family, the philosophy of Wolfenden and the legislation which followed from it amounted to an acknowledgement that sexuality did exist – and more importantly could legally exist – outside of marriage. The partial decriminalisation of adult male homosexuality sanctioned this expression of sexuality (albeit tacitly) for the first time in over a hundred years, while the partial legalisation of abortion involved, in part, an acknowledgement of women's sexuality outside of marriage – it was imagined (erroneously) that it would mainly be unmarried women who would make use of this facility. The inclusion of contraceptive advice within the mainstream of the health service strengthened this new admission of women's sexuality. In a sense, the changes in the divorce law confirmed this, too. Before the Divorce (Reform) Act 1969, the principle of matrimonial offence had involved the creation of both a guilty and an innocent party. The offences committed were against the sanctity of marriage and monogamy within it. In accepting the idea of 'irretrievable breakdown' as a mechanism through which a dead marriage could be dissolved, the state rejected its previous concern for the establishment of moral blame.

These were all significant advances and perhaps it is right to connect them to the change in government. It may also be that this was the reshaping of the consensus. While aspects of the philosophy of Wolfenden and the changes in the law associated with this may seem to suggest a complete break with the past, there was much continuity within this change.

Arguably there was, underlying these legislative reforms, no real change in the position marriage and the family held as a set of ideals for the state. The liberalism of Wolfenden was double-edged and it is important to remember that the report was commissioned in response to public fears about a perceived increase in homosexual behaviour and prostitution. Although prosecutions for male homosexual offences had risen sharply since the 1940s, the Wolfenden Committee could find no conclusive evidence that homosexuality was becoming more popular, but pointed to a number of factors which could mean that this was likely. These included specific references to the war, and the break-up of families and the separation of the sexes which had occurred. The Committee also pointed to less tangible developments, suggesting

it is likely that the emotional insecurity, community instability and weakening of the family, inherent in the social changes of our civilisation, have been factors contributing to an increase in homosexual behaviour.[61]

The Committee agreed that homosexuality has damaging effects on family life as divorces may occur when married men indulge in homosexual behaviour while other men may feel precluded from marrying 'when perhaps they could have had good marriages'.

These concerns for the family, not at all dissimilar in essence to those being expressed ten years earlier, may seem at odds with the more liberal nature of Wolfenden's recommendations for partial decriminalisation. Yet while acknowledging the threat to the family which homosexuality may pose, the underlying philosophy of the report towards greater equality of application in the law and a retreat from policing private morality produces the kind of compromise which is demonstrated here:

We deplore this damage to what we regard as the basic unit of society . . . but marriages also break up or are prevented by lesbian tendencies and are broken up by adultery and fornication. All of these are *not* criminalised in the way male homosexuality is and therefore there is no basis for criminalising male homosexuality on these grounds . . . These practices are all reprehensible from the point of view of harm to the family but male homosexuality should not be singled out.

Neither did divorce reform seek to undermine marriage as an institution. As Stuart Hall has argued, 'the 1969 Act did not shift an inch from the orthodox defence of the institutional basis of marriage and the regulation of sexuality by marriage. Its first and principal aim was "to buttress the stability of marriage".'[62] This aim, directly in line with Denning and the RCMD can be clearly seen in the debate in Parliament in the passage of divorce reform. Alec Jones in proposing the 1968 bill agreed wholeheartedly with the RCMD that it was in the best interests of the individual and the wider community that marriage should be monogamous and should last for life. He also stated his belief that this was a view shared by the majority of the supporters of the bill. To reiterate his own position he announced, 'if it were possible to legislate for this ideal state of affairs, to make all marriages stable and happy marriages, then I would welcome the opportunity of introducing such a bill'.[63] We ought perhaps to allow for the possibility that politicians sometimes may say what needs to be said in order to get legislation through Parliament. But still, this does not detract from the significance which must be given to the fact that it was these kinds of ideas which necessarily framed the debate.

Opponents of the bill, such as Bruce Campbell, argued that the change in the law would give another surge forward to the disintegration of family life. Yet questions were also raised as to whether the existing law could be said to uphold the sanctity of marriage. The number of 'dead' marriages, forced to exist in name only, were seen to cause 'increasing harm to the community and injury to the ideal of marriage itself'.[64] Thus debate centred not around widening the parameters of private morality, but around the best ways in which to promote marriage and the stability of family life.

This was again the key idea which emerged from parliamentary debate on the 1967 NHS (Family Planning) Bill which, when enacted, empowered, though did not require, local authorities to provide family planning services. The proposer of the bill, Edwin Brooks, painted a picture of deteriorating social relationships which could be radically improved through the introduction of contraceptive advice on the NHS.

Marriages are founded not on mutual love but on a momentary and, perhaps, bitterly regretted impulse. Children, the innocent victims, are resented and even rejected. Illegal back-street abortions occur in squalor and misery. These are the tragedies of infatuation gone sour, and we see the legacy in divorce and the desolation of the children affected.[65]

He adds that the bill, 'far from being an incitement to promiscuity is an incentive to loving and responsible parenthood'. This view is echoed here by the Minister of Health, Kenneth Robinson:

> It is generally accepted today that voluntary parenthood is an important factor in strengthening family life. I am convinced it is an essential aspect of family welfare . . . We all know that unhappy homes and strained family relationships can be as destructive to the full life of the individual, and indeed of the community, as the ravages of physical disease.[66]

In practice, provision of family planning services was patchy after the NHS (Family Planning) Act 1967, with the widespread outcry over 'sex on the rates' in many local newspapers perhaps influencing local authorities' decisions over whether or not to provide such services and if they did, whether to provide them free of charge, as the Act allowed.[67]

Given this reaffirmation of the centrality of marriage and the family, it is perhaps not surprising that this new distinction between the state and civil society did not mean that the state was about to abdicate its role in intervening in and regulating the family. There may have been some relaxation on the regulation of private morality but there was a clear move towards tightening up control 'in the public good'.

In the case of homosexuality, this meant more severe penalties for soliciting and importuning and 'acts of gross indecency' – together protecting the public from that which it might find shocking and protecting children from the 'threat' of homosexuality – while consenting, private sexual behaviour was to be accepted within limits. This 'privatising' of sexual behaviour is mirrored in new recommendations for the regulation of prostitution, moving it out of sight of the public while clamping down on any public evidence of it, with stricter penalties for street offences. Recommendations for regulation included a new role for moral welfare workers, particularly in the case of first offenders, and new powers to remand first and second offenders into custody so that a social/medical report could be made.

In the case of abortion, new regulators were to be employed in the form of medical doctors in an effort to bring abortion within state control. In proposing the legislation to make this possible, David Steel states clearly the intention to 'stamp out back-street abortions' and not 'to leave a wide door open for abortion on request'.[68] This desire to bring things within state control is again in evidence in the provision of family planning advice, not just through the mechanism of this advice being provided by the NHS but also through the minister of health being given powers to decide whether and to what extent individual local health authorities could provide such a service.

Finally, the divorce reform enacted in 1969 made divorce easier at the same time as increasing the effort to preserve marriages. One-fifth of the Act is devoted to 'provisions designed to encourage reconciliation'. This was to mean that the solicitor for the petitioner was now required to certify that s/he had discussed reconciliation with the client and had passed on the names and addresses of those statutory and voluntary agencies qualified to help effect a reconciliation. Furthermore, courts were now to have the power to adjourn proceedings if it was believed that there was a reasonable possibility of reconciliation. This emphasis on reconciliation was strengthened by the new role given to the courts in determining whether, in their view, a marriage had irretrievably broken down.

Much of this intervention into families was in practice to take place at the local level through interaction between local health authorities, councils and voluntary agencies. This was to include the development of family social services and children's welfare services. In order to look at this in detail, the next chapter will focus on developments in the provision of social welfare in two London boroughs.

CHAPTER THREE

Families, charities and local authorities

Chapter Two was concerned with families and official discourse at the 'macro' level. This chapter will attempt to assess families and official discourse at a micro level by focusing firstly on a case study of two London metropolitan boroughs – Greenwich and Woolwich – which later came to form the London Borough of Greenwich; secondly on the interaction between statutory authorities and voluntary agencies in the provision of social welfare; and thirdly on the interaction between the local and the national.

There are some problems which become immediately apparent in carrying out such a study. In *The State or the Market*, Martin Loncy argues that 'the history of welfare policy is unintelligible without reference to the family as a central organising principle'.[1] Yet Andrew Land *et al.*, in their introduction to sources on the welfare state at the Public Record Office, point to the difficulties there are in locating sources in which *ideas* are discussed. 'Anyone hoping to locate in the public records regular debates on the purpose, development or impact of welfare policy' will, they tell us, 'be disappointed.'[2] In looking at policy at the local level in this period I am more in sympathy with Roy Parker's argument (discussed in the previous chapter) that there was never anything as explicit as 'family policy' in British politics.[3]

Particular problems arise in the case of the Greenwich and Woolwich areas. Policy on the family is elusive, not least because responsibility for making this policy is shifted around. Certain responsibilities are transferred from the Metropolitan Boroughs of Woolwich and Greenwich to the London County Council (LCC) but are later transferred back again. Parts of local government are disbanded or merged at particular moments in this history. This shifting of responsibilities often leads to a drying up of sources as no systematic referral of documents to local history libraries exists until after this period. To compound the problem of sources, the published minutes of these councils, and even more so those of the LCC, are exceptionally dry, conforming to a very exact idea of minutes as the recording of decisions. Furthermore, some of the most promising sources appear to be no longer in existence. These include the unpublished minutes of both metropolitan boroughs (referred to obliquely in full council minutes), which seem to exist only up until the late 1930s. These silences clearly pose problems for the researcher and beg the question of how to proceed with such a study.

Fortunately, other local government papers do exist, although again holdings in local archives can be patchy. The medical officer of health reports are a useful source of information, and a good run of these is held in local archives. There exist occasional documents, such as tenants' handbooks or promotional material for council 'health weeks', which can be drawn upon. There also exist a number of voluntary agency papers for the area, some of which illuminate the relationship between voluntary and statutory bodies in the provision of social welfare.

Furthermore, we can take Loney's contention that the provision of welfare services is unintelligible without reference to the family, and add that we need also to determine what *senses* of family predominate. To arrive at an answer to this question we can proceed in a number of ways. Certainly, there are specific policy decisions which can be analysed and particular changes in the provision of welfare services over time which can be noted. Textual analysis of local authority and voluntary agency papers can be used to explore ideas implicit in the formation and publication of policy. National concerns can be used to form useful reference points for understanding local concerns and we can observe the relationships that exist between centre and locale. Finally, developments in the relationship between the local authority and the voluntary sector in the provision of welfare or family services can also be charted.

The local authorities: policy, language, debate

With these methods of analysis in mind, I will examine the following specific areas of policy and discussion: the monitoring of the local population, including the identification of problematic people; family planning; housing; and the provision of relief from domestic work, including nursery care and the care of the elderly. Some of these (for example family planning) relate directly to issues discussed in the previous chapter. Rather than try to force the national issues to match up with local issues, I have instead taken what seemed to be the most striking and frequently recurring issues at each level. That there should be different concerns at the local and national levels is a point which is considered later in this chapter and again in Chapter Six.

Monitoring the local population

An important part of local authority work in the field of welfare and social services is concerned with monitoring the local population with a view to making interventions where deemed necessary. This monitoring has both general and particular aspects. From the generalist perspective, statistics are collected relating to the whole borough population on matters such as birth, death and disease. From the particular perspective, various 'problem' groups are distinguished and monitored separately. These include 'problem families', illegitimate babies and unsupported mothers. Interventions can either be made across the borough population as a whole (for instance in the provision of new general services) or target specific groups.

From the generalist perspective, one of the most important monitoring procedures is carried out by the medical officer of health (MOH) and is collated in the MOH's annual report. The MOH's 'vital statistics' for the boroughs are collected and presented at the beginning of the report. The 'vital statistics' include births, deaths, maternal deaths, infant mortality, inquests, accidents, deaths from specific diseases – cancer, polio, tuberculosis, etc. – and marriages. With the exception of marriage, these all have an immediate and obvious impact on crude population figures. Marriage figures may lack this immediate influence on population statistics, but in the first MOH report of the new London borough of Greenwich in 1965, the MOH explained that figures for marriage are included because, 'as over ninety per cent of all births are legitimate it follows that the extent to which people marry exerts a powerful influence on the fertility rate'.[4]

In connection with these 'vital statistics', one area of early policy debate which is noticeable by its absence is that of population decline. Whereas, as we have seen in the previous chapter, this appears as an issue of some concern nationally, in the metropolitan boroughs of Greenwich and Woolwich population statistics are produced without comment or discussion relevant to this national debate. Instead, comment is centred on a sense of gradual improvement in public health and on improvements in figures for infant mortality, death rates etc. (This sense of gradual improvement will be returned to later in this section.) Some decline in the boroughs' population is noted, but this is seen to be to do with natural fluctuations connected to work patterns and is not marked as a cause for alarm.

The concerns about population expressed at a national level do offer a reference point for discussion of local statistics though, and the figures produced in the MOH report are interesting in the light of this national concern. Tables 3.1, 3.2 and 3.3 compare local with national statistics.[5] A number of points emerge from these figures. Firstly, it is interesting to consider these figures in the light of the findings of the Royal Commission

Table 3.1   Comparative birth rates per thousand of the population, 1945–49

Year	Greenwich	Woolwich	London	England and Wales
1945	18.59	17.5	15.7	16.1
1946	22.65	21.6	21.5	19.1
1947	23.61	22.8	22.7	20.5
1948	19.79	17.7	20.1	17.9
1949	17.76	17.4	18.5	16.7
5-year average	20.48	19.4	19.7	18.06

Source: Metropolitan Borough of Greenwich, *Report of the Medical Officer of Health*, 1945–49, and Metropolitan Borough of Woolwich, *Annual Report on the Health of the Metropolitan Borough of Woolwich*, 1945–55.

Table 3.2   Comparative death rates per thousand of the population, 1945–49

Year	Greenwich	Woolwich	London	England and Wales
1945	12.78	12.8	13.8	11.4
1946	11.38	11.4	?	?
1947	11.61	11.6	12.8	12.0
1948	10.21	11.0	11.6	10.8
1949	10.8	10.9	12.2	11.7
5-year average	11.36	11.54	12.6	11.48

Source: Metropolitan Borough of Greenwich, *Report of the Medical Officer of Health*, 1945–49, and Metropolitan Borough of Woolwich, *Annual Report on the Health of the Metropolitan Borough of Woolwich*, 1945–55.

Table 3.3   Comparative infant mortality rates per thousand live births, 1945–49

Year	Greenwich[a]	Woolwich[a]	London	England and Wales
1945	43 (40/78)	41 (38/70)	?	?
1946	34 (35/21)	31 (31/36)	41	43
1947	26	27 (26/42)	?	?
1948	26 (26/38)	29 (27/55)	?	?
1949	24	29	29	32

[a] Figures in brackets refer to legitimate/illegitimate infant mortality rates.
Source: Metropolitan Borough of Greenwich, *Report of the Medical Officer of Health*, 1945–49, and Metropolitan Borough of Woolwich, *Annual Report on the Health of the Metropolitan Borough of Woolwich*, 1945–55.

on Population (RCP). What is most immediately obvious is that birth rates in the two boroughs do *not* fall below replacement levels but in fact indicate a rise in absolute population levels. This is compounded by the falling rate of infant mortality. While these may be national trends, the figures for Greenwich and Woolwich suggest that, in this part of London, these trends are noticeably accentuated. A five-year average of birth and death rates (1945–49) shows births per thousand of the population exceeding deaths by 6.58 in the whole of England and Wales and by 7.86 and 9.12 in Woolwich and Greenwich respectively. Again, favourable infant mortality rates in these two London boroughs strengthen this difference.

If we can accept that in Greenwich and Woolwich the RCP's fears over sub-replacement levels of population are not borne out, does this tell us anything about those fears? We know that those fears were receding in public debate by the time the Commission reported in 1949. However, we must remember that the Commission's fears were not confined to absolute population figures, but were differentiated along class lines. As these two London boroughs formed a predominantly working-class, inner-city area, it is tempting to see the differences in population growth as evidence which could support the RCP's eugenicist fears over class difference in population growth.

While no clear evidence exists to secure this argument, inferences in the MOH reports may lend the argument some support. Although these comments date from the late 1960s, the MOH in question was a long-standing official and had been employed by Greenwich council in the same capacity in the 1950s. His report of 1968 makes this statement:

> Generally, like attracts like and over generations the genetically well-endowed mate with others equally endowed, with the converse also being true. This 'natural' selection inevitably leads to a stratification of society where the tendency is for tallness to beget tallness, smallness to beget smallness and intelligence to beget intelligence etc.[6]

He elaborates upon this in the MOH report of 1970:

> With regard to genetic endowment there is a moral responsibility in certain instances for the community to provide not only general information but family planning and genetic counselling and a similar responsibility rests with parents to balance their family in accordance with this advice to ensure minimal handicap to their offspring.[7]

The MOH's argument relies upon a simple logic and starts off uncontroversially. However, the placing of the comment about intelligence at the end of the sentence (in the first extract) suggests that it is the most important, and, perhaps, that this is the real nub of the argument. It is also reminiscent of both the RCP's and the Beveridge Report's oblique reference to class in commenting on differential birth rates (see previous chapter). What precisely is meant by 'genetic counselling' is unclear, though we can speculate that 'handicap' here may have a wide rather than a narrow meaning.

Aside from any connections with the findings of the RCP, the selection, presentation and detail of demographic statistics in these boroughs are of interest in themselves. Perhaps most striking is the differentiation in the MOH reports between legitimate and illegitimate births in both birth rates and infant mortality rates. This is interesting in a number of ways. Firstly, in Table 3.3 we can see that rates of infant mortality are consistently higher (with only one exception, in Greenwich in 1946) in both boroughs amongst illegitimate births. In this five-year period, where figures are given, the average rates for Greenwich are 33 (legitimate) and 45.6 (illegitimate), and for Woolwich they are 30.5 (legitimate) and 50.75 (illegitimate). Secondly, we can see that while the infant mortality rate for legitimate children falls steadily throughout this period, the rate for illegitimate children is erratic (though this may be to do with the relatively small numbers involved). Thirdly, we might ask why the MOHs saw the need to differentiate their findings in this way.

Given that the rates of illegitimate infant mortality were generally higher, if it was only rates of infant mortality which were differentiated in this way this may not need much explanation. It could be assumed that the MOH intended to highlight this difference, maybe as an acknowledgement of concern over the higher figures for illegitimate children. The difference in mortality rates is, however, not commented upon, and furthermore, birth rates are similarly divided into legitimate and illegitimate births at this time.

This lack of comment, taken with evidence elsewhere may suggest that it is illegitimacy itself which is the issue of concern for both local authorities in the 1940s. For example, both councils agreed in 1945 to participate in a Ministry of Health initiative on the care of illegitimate children. This involved cooperation with and a reinforcing of the work of moral welfare associations already in existence within the two boroughs through increased financial assistance to these voluntary organisations. In addition to this, a 'special worker' would be appointed to administer the scheme. Perhaps unsurprisingly, this worker is gendered as female, with the Metropolitan Borough of Woolwich Maternity and Child Welfare Committee noting the need for the worker to be 'experienced in the special problems which *she* would have to handle'.[8] There is a similar gender implication in the second main proposal for the scheme, that guaranteed payments to foster mothers (not parents) should be made. Thus 'unmarried mothers, on the advice of welfare workers or otherwise, would apply for their children to be fostered'.[9]

The natural mother would be expected to make a financial contribution towards the upkeep of the child, according to her means.

Illegitimacy does begin to be commented upon in the MOH reports for the London Borough of Greenwich, which start in 1965. In that year, the MOH comments that

> it would appear generally to be the case that illegitimacy is greatest when social standards, cultural and material, are low and collectively, factors such as an insecure family life, poor and over-crowded homes, lack of direction and personal drive in life etc. seem to be implicated.[10]

It is also argued that illegitimacy may be more common in London than in other parts of the country for two reasons: because women who are pregnant with illegitimate children may be attracted to the anonymity of the large city; and because of the superior facilities in ante-natal maternity and welfare fields which the city offers.

Later still, comment becomes directed at bringing about change, as can be seen in this extract from the MOH report of 1970:

> In future we must try to do more for the unsupported mother, both in relation to encouraging early and consistent pre-natal care and in the provision of adequate hostel accommodation for those in need.[11]

Also at this time in MOH reports, unmarried mothers are referred to somewhat more sympathetically. In 1965, the MOH explains how 'unsupported mothers' are normally 'put in touch with Moral Welfare Workers who in most cases arranged for admission to a Mother and Baby Home prior to hospital confinement'. Some expectant mothers did approach the Children's department asking for their children to be considered for adoption, but 'wherever the mother decides to bring up her own child, every assistance was given by the health visitor and, whenever possible, priority admission of the child to a day nursery was arranged when the mother returned to work'.[12] Although, given the fact that only ten such places were reserved for Greenwich residents in the Lewisham day nursery,[13] this promise rings somewhat hollow, nevertheless the non-judgemental tone is worthy of note.

Another group which is specifically monitored by the borough is those who are designated problem families. These are defined in the 1965 MOH report as

> those families which, for various reasons, are unable to cope with the difficulties and stresses of life and who need a great deal of support and some material help. Often they are large families and, usually, the mother has a number of children under five years to manage.[14]

A regularly updated index of such families is kept by the borough councils. Families on the index are frequently visited by health visitors who have the power to call in other specialist help, cooperating especially with social workers 'to provide the best available means to rehabilitate these families'.[15]

It is possible to argue that the monitoring of the population, with the increases in the scope of monitoring and the identification of problematic citizens, is evidence of a particular kind of social control at work. Given this (and bearing in mind the widening of the scope of state intervention in families, discussed in Chapter Two) it is further possible to argue that such developments in this period amount to an extension of the social control function of the state. Critiques of social welfare, especially those influenced by Foucault, frequently point to surveillance, regulation, proscription and prescription in relations between families and the state.[16] Certainly, the identification of 'problem families' and the various interventions available to facilitate rehabilitation would seem to be clear examples of local authorities exercising social control.

There are areas of ambiguity in this relationship between families and the state though, as is suggested by Janet Walker's recent observation that

> social welfare incorporates policing, paternalism and participation: the surveillance of families in danger or out of control; the provision of kindly help and advice to those in trouble; and a desire to work *with* families, facilitating their ability to determine their own destinies.[17]

As well as monitoring in a controlling way, social welfare also incorporates what may be generally agreed to be improvements in the quality of day-to-day life, and it is here that the sense of progress, integral to the presentation of statistics in the MOH's reports, needs to be remembered. Monitoring the population can also be about observing increases in the incidence of particular diseases, of domestic overcrowding, or of maternal or infant mortality, and taking action to counteract such trends. The MOH reports for both the metropolitan boroughs of Woolwich and Greenwich resonate with this sense of concern to improve the living conditions of local people.

This ambiguity within social welfare is illustrated in oral evidence given by a former employee of Greenwich council who was involved in this area of the council's work.[18] Both Greenwich and Woolwich borough councils are remembered as having their particular areas of expertise. Woolwich was especially proud of its maternal and child welfare provision, while in Greenwich it was the council's geriatric service which was particularly strong. Greenwich council is remembered as 'avant garde', particularly in the provision of welfare services for the elderly where it pioneered chiropody and incontinent laundry services. There is, it must be said, a paternalism and a concern for monitoring within the description of the provision of these services. We are told that 'in effect anybody who was over sixty-five was known to us – everyone of those had at least two visits a year, whether there was anything wrong with them or not', and more generally,

> if we can teach people to live properly, exercise properly, look after their health and be aware of things so they don't pop round to the doctors for a couple of aspirins . . . they don't overload the doctors. The doctors themselves don't overload the hospitals and really and truly if you are going to get down to basics looking after the family you have got to start at the beginning. You have got to get to the mums and you have got to get to the children and you have got to get to the family.[19]

This tension between improving living conditions and exercising social control is arguably characteristic of these local welfare services in this period.

A mood of optimism that social problems could be tackled effectively and eradicated, which Janet Walker has suggested characterised the early postwar welfare state,[20] is clearly in evidence here, and the success of these local authorities (in conjunction with national government) in combating post-natal mortality, disease, premature death and in promoting the welfare of local citizens needs to be remembered alongside the paternalism and increased potential for social control. The new welfare services were framed within a particular discourse of the family though, and in the discussion of services which follows below, this clearly had an impact.

Family planning

Considerable discussion about the provision of family planning advice is in evidence in the new London Borough of Greenwich. This service was initially provided by the Family Planning Association without financial aid from the old borough council. Reference is made to a women's special clinic in the old borough's MOH report for 1956, though it is unclear if the council is supporting the clinic financially. By the time of amalgamation with Woolwich, the MOH reports are addressing the issue of family planning much more directly, even though the statutory powers of the council were yet to be extended by the NHS (Family Planning) Act 1967. The 1965 MOH report notes extensions to the family planning service (still run by the Family Planning Association) in May and November of 1964. In 1966 the MOH reported its support for further provision of family planning, arguing that perinatal and maternal mortality tended to increase after the birth of the third child and that the children of spaced and limited families tended to be healthier, while the tranquillity needed for the very young to develop stable personalities could be threatened by unexpected pregnancy. It also suggested that family planning could lead to relief from the economic consequences of too large a family as well as relief from 'the tensions, ill-temper, neuroses and mental disability born of fatigue, frustration, anxiety and depression'. The other practical advantages accruing from the adoption of family planning were seen to be 'less problem families and a corresponding reduction in demands made on the local health and welfare services'.[21]

In the following year, when the new family planning law came into effect, its virtues were further set out by the MOH:

> Planned parenthood tends to strengthen family life, prevents marital disharmony, ill-health and social breakdown and its aim is the enrichment of all human life. There should be no lack of support for such a measure the objective of which is to prevent the mental, physical and social disasters revealed in the overburdened homeless families units, reception centres, foster homes, hospitals, remand homes and prisons.[22]

In 1969 the MOH could report a 40 per cent rise in the use of family planning clinics. It also reported venereal diseases (VD) rising 'at an alarming rate', especially amongst the young. The council had therefore been persuaded to establish a special clinic for people aged over 16 to discuss emotional, moral and sexual problems as a way of combating VD.[23]

Housing

The normative impulse displayed in the literature considered so far is repeated in much of the available source material on housing. This can be clearly seen in examining aspects of both councils' housing policy in the late 1940s. A prime example of this is the way in which Woolwich Council formulated its points system to ascertain council housing need (Figure 3.1). While it may well have been the case that most applicants were married and formed part of a 'family', it is nonetheless significant to note the way in which the language is exclusive and that marriage and conventional family life are implicitly prioritised. Consideration of housing applications is 'confined to those families who were living in the Borough in September, 1939'; points are awarded 'For each member of the applicant's family'; extra points are given for an 'Applicant, wife, or member of family suffering from Pulmonary Tuberculosis'. Nowhere in this scheme is there any acknowledgement that people can and did live in anything other than a 'family household'. There is, not surprisingly, an assumption that the applicant is a married man.

Similar examples are to be found elsewhere. In Metropolitan Borough of Greenwich *Report of the Medical Officer of Health for 1945*, population statistics

9. **Revision of "Points Scheme" for Selection of Applicants for Accommodation.**
The Council, at its meeting on the 13th June, 1945 (*see* paragraph 6 of this Committee's Report of the 17th May, 1945), adopted a "Points Scheme" for the selection of applicants for accommodation, when the Committee reported that it proposed to review the scheme in six months' time.

The scheme has accordingly been reconsidered, and from the experience gained certain alterations and additions therein are proposed to give increased points according to the degree of need for rehousing.

The revised scheme is as follows:—

Number of Points

(1) For each member of applicant's family 1

(2) In respect of applicant's present accommodation:—

    (*a*) .. .. .. $5 \times \dfrac{\text{Number of persons in applicant's family}}{\text{Number of rooms occupied}}$

    plus

    (*b*) .. $5 \times \dfrac{\text{Total number of persons in house, including applicant}}{\text{Total number of rooms in house}}$

    Where family compelled to live separately due to lack of accommodation, *no points under (b)*, but allow 5

(3) Where applicant previously had accommodation in Borough which could not be retained due to:—

    (*a*) Compulsory transfer to another area on work of national importance 8

    (*b*) Evacuation of family on Government advice 3

(4) Applicants who lost their former homes as the result of enemy action and are without adequate accommodation 10

(5) Applicant (or late husband in case of widow) has served, or is serving, in H.M. Forces (including Merchant Navy) since 1939 10

(6) Disablement .. .. up to 5

(7) Applicant, wife, or member of family suffering from Pulmonary Tuberculosis 5

(8) Where existing accommodation unhealthy or in bad state of repair up to 5

Points to be awarded under only one of the items 3, 4, or 5 should they come within two or more of those categories.

Except in exceptional circumstances, consideration at present be confined to those families who were living in the Borough in September, 1939.

For the purpose of allocation, applications to be divided into two main groups:—

    Group 1—Forces' cases and homeless.

    Group 2—Other cases.

Accommodation available for letting to be apportioned between the two groups on a basis to be fixed from time to time according to prevailing conditions, and in the first instance to be 5 to 4 respectively.

The Committee

RECOMMEND—

That the revised "Points Scheme" set out above be adopted in substitution for that approved by the Council on 13th June, 1945.

Figure 3.1 Woolwich council's points system for selection of applicants for accommodation, 1946.

Source: Metropolitan Borough of Woolwich, *Minutes of Proceedings*, 9 January 1946. By permission of Greenwich Local History Library.

are given which include figures for the number of inhabited houses and 'the number of families or separate occupiers'. A similar report three years later, which comments on the extent of new accommodation provided by the council in that year, notes that 'excluding the families accommodated in requisitioned dwellings, the total number of dwellings provided since the termination of the war is now 2,061'.

The normative drive behind assumptions about housing can again be seen in the *Municipal Tenants' Handbook*, produced by the Metropolitan Borough of Greenwich in the 1940s and 1950s. In a 1953 version of this document, the borough's chairman of the housing committee introduces the handbook with the message that 'For many years the Greenwich Borough Council have been actively engaged in providing homes in which families can establish a normal family life'[24] (see Figure 3.2). This concern to centre discussion of housing need around families did not end in the 1940s. Roy Parker, writing in the 1980s, noted how 'local authorities' housing programmes have concentrated for long periods on supplying dwellings of a size to suit the family with two or three children, and the allocation of council houses has similarly given preference to applicants with children'.[25] Indeed, the newly formed London Borough of Greenwich Housing Committee commented in April 1965 that house-building had tended to be almost exclusively for specific projects such as slum clearance and that what was really needed was the creation of a pool of houses available for families needing them but not included in priority cases.[26]

In one sense, this concern with families is unremarkable. The evidence suggests that a majority of housing applicants were applying on behalf of families, and so for this to feature in the council's creation of policy makes sense. However, two things are significant here. Firstly, it seems that a particular kind of family – two-generational, with two or three children and a male head of household – is perceived as the norm. Secondly, the emergence of such norms in public policy through the use of implicit language and terms of reference centred around the family has an impact on those outside of that norm. What this impact might be is difficult to ascertain, but clearly there is evidence here of the marginalising of certain groups. These themes will be returned to in the analysis of oral evidence in Chapter Five and also in Chapter Six.

Later in the period, particularly in the second half of the 1960s, concerns begin to be raised about the type of new housing provided by the councils. This passage from the London Borough of Greenwich's MOH report for 1966 is perhaps influenced by, and certainly echoes, Wilmott and Young's classic account of housing in Bethnal Green and the policy of rehousing in new estates:

A Message from the Chairman of the Housing Committee

EVER since the end of the First World War, the Greenwich Borough Council have been providing houses and flats for the citizens of the Borough. They are not, however, satisfied with merely providing places in which to live; they want to see happy homes established, and are only too anxious to co-operate with their tenants to this end. The prime responsibility for home-making rests of course with the family, but the Council feel that, by publishing this handbook, they can assist in promoting that sense of civic consciousness, responsibility, and good neighbourliness, which is so essential to a community. I hope that you will accept this booklet as evidence of the fact that the Housing Committee and the officers of the Housing Department are interested in your welfare and are keen to see that, so far as lies within their power, the Council's housing estates become pleasant places in which to live.

A.G.E. Woolven.

The OLD TOWN HALL

A Message from the Chairman of the Housing Committee

FOR many years, the Greenwich Borough Council have been actively engaged in providing homes in which families can establish a normal family life. Despite the continued difficulties encountered with regard to the supply of both materials and manpower, together with the diminished number of suitable sites which remain available to us, the continued building programme will make further provision for applicant families who qualify under the Council's letting policy.

By the publication of this handbook, the Council again seek your close co-operation in maintaining the high standard of occupation associated with all properties and the preservation of all amenities, especially lawns, flower beds, shrubberies, trees and communal services like laundries, passenger lifts and so on.

I am sure you are all conscious of your civic responsibilities in these matters and of your desire to maintain good relations with your neighbours.

I hope you will receive this second edition of the handbook with the assurance that the Housing Committee and Officers of the Housing Department are sincerely mindful of your welfare and anxious to ensure that the Council's housing estates will continue to maintain the high standard of homes essential to the well being of the nation's families.

A.E. Rutter

HOUSING DEPARTMENT OFFICES: OLD TOWN HALL
141 GREENWICH HIGH ROAD, S.E.10 *Telephone* GREenwich 4311–3

The OLD TOWN HALL

Figure 3.2 Top picture: Message from the Chairman, Councillor A.G.E. Woolven, *Tenant's Handbook* 1949–50. Bottom picture: Message from the Chairman, Alderman A.E. Rutter, *Tenant's Handbook* 1953–54. By permission of Greenwich Local History Library.

Some neuroses are precipitated by modern environmental conditions found in some satellite towns and at some new housing estates. In the quest for higher density housing, wholesale destruction of older and more mellow houses occurs which breaks up thriving communities and isolates the displaced families in unfamiliar areas among complete strangers . . . Moreover multi-storey dwellings are producing family isolation and a neurosis in mothers who are cooped up in small self-contained flats, insulated from normal sights and sounds of everyday life, deprived of the daily neighbourly 'chat' and cut off from easy contact with friends and relations.[27]

These concerns about housing are clearly connected to some of the concerns which begin to be expressed about the care of the elderly, especially from the mid-1950s onwards and which will be considered later. There is also here a concern for the connection between family and community.

Relief from domestic work

Another major area of consideration are welfare services where the local authorities provide some public relief from domestic work for those most in need. This is an area which expands greatly over the 1945–70 period and comprises chiefly the provision of child care, care of the elderly and the development of the Home Help Scheme.

The home help service

The home help service, which the Ministry of Health empowered local authorities to develop in 1945, originated as a Home Help Scheme to assist in cases of confinement. This service was expanded after the war to provide assistance in cases of illness and to include the aged and infirm. Within the provision of this service we can see a set of gender-bound ideas in operation. This is as true for clients of the system as it is for those employed through it. In the home, aside from in cases of childbirth, the Metropolitan Borough of Greenwich was able to offer domestic help 'where the housewife falls sick or must have an operation'; 'where the wife has suddenly to go away to visit her husband in hospital' and there is no one else to look after the children; or where several members of the family are sick at once, for example during a 'flu epidemic. Woolwich cites similar, though less specific, grounds in offering the scheme in cases where 'the housewife is incapacitated'.[28] Furthermore, an Order in Council empowered the Metropolitan Borough of Greenwich 'to employ women to provide such help',[29] while recommending seeking the help of women's voluntary organisations in bringing cases of need to the council's attention.

The home help service changes over time and reacts to new circumstances in the boroughs. In the 1940s when it was introduced primarily to provide assistance in confinements, the norm in the boroughs was for births to take place in the home. By the mid-1960s the trend had reversed, and home births were in decline as hospital births came into favour. This, coupled with the rise in demand for the care of the elderly, means a redirecting of the home help service towards assisting the 'aged infirm and chronic sick'.[30]

Nursery care

A more controversial example of relief from domestic work can be found in the provision of nursery care. The debate over the closure of the wartime day nurseries is significant here. Denise Riley has argued that although the closure of day nurseries has often been seen as part of government policy to reconstruct the family after the war, policy differences between government departments and the apparent absence of a coherent overarching strategy undermine this view.[31] This may well be so. Evidence from local government papers suggests that in some cases there was governmental pressure to maintain, at least in part, the provision of day nurseries in the area, and that where closure was recommended, a change from day nurseries to nursery schools was suggested and carried out. Woolwich council minutes for 3 April 1946 stated that the Ministry of Labour

has emphatically stated that the four day nurseries in the borough will still be required, and that they should continue to be open as at present from 7 am to 6.30 pm, that war conditions still prevail, and that the services in industry of younger women, particularly in view of the requirements of the Government as to increasing export trade, are still required.

This may be connected to the occurrence of work of national importance in the borough, especially in the Woolwich Arsenal, which employed large numbers of women. When the central funding for day nurseries was withdrawn at the end of March 1946 (in a joint circular from the Ministry of Health (221/45) and the Ministry of Education (75)) what emerged is not so much the proposal to close these nurseries as the proposal to change their use. The circular requests that welfare authorities and education authorities formulate schemes to take over existing day nurseries and promotes the development of nursery schools through the provision of funding under the Public Health Acts.

Both Woolwich and the Metropolitan Borough of Greenwich were keen to support this development of nursery school education, and through negotiations the LCC took over the day nurseries in the two boroughs, turning these into nursery schools. This decision may well have been influenced by the Metropolitan Boroughs Standing Joint Committee's report on the continuation of day nurseries after the war, presented at its meeting held on 30 July 1945, which stressed the educational and welfare benefits that these nurseries had for children:

> In the Committee's opinion the war-time day nurseries serve a very useful purpose both from the point of view of the mother who finds it necessary to work and the care, attention and guidance which children attending the nurseries receive.

The provision of education in nursery schools was to be for children in the 2–5 age range. This meant that some women, who had children under the age of 2, would no longer have access to child care. This was recognised by the two boroughs and some attempt was made to remedy this with the introduction of daily guardian schemes, where the councils would pay part of the cost of individual child care with recognised carers. It is important to note that this was not a scheme intended for use by any woman who wanted to use it. Both councils were very clear about the kinds of women whom they thought would need to use it and the circumstances in which a woman might find herself in order to be eligible. There may have been no overarching coherent policy to return women to the home after the war, but here, in the boroughs of Woolwich and Greenwich, we can see how support for the continuation of nursery provision operates within a very particular set of ideas.

Woolwich council's Maternity and Child Welfare Committee minutes of 12 February 1947 show that

> in connection with the closing of the Council's Day-nurseries the committee considered a report on the establishment of a daily guardian's scheme to provide in the first place, for the care of children attending the day-nurseries whose mothers must work from economic necessity.

Later, once the scheme was up and running, the committee resolved to allow some children on to it even if they had not been in a nursery before. This could be done only where 'the mother has a gainful occupation in order to prevent hardship'. The medical officer of health was to be the judge of this.[32] Thus women were not to have the *right* to child care; it was to be provided where it was deemed necessary. In Greenwich, where the council decided to maintain only one day nursery this was primarily intended for babies of mothers who are on full-time work of National or Industrial importance. Cases are accepted on compassionate or hardship grounds from non-working mothers provided there are vacancies.

After this period, recorded debate about the provision of nursery care seems to diminish. In the MOH report for the new London Borough of Greenwich in 1965, the MOH notes that the new borough did not inherit a day nursery, but instead relied upon the reservation of ten places in a day nursery in the new London Borough of Lewisham. Again, priority in these was to be given to 'unmarried mothers and widows who needed to work'.[33] A hope to extend the provision of this service is expressed, but is connected not to extending the possibilities for women working outside of the home, but to providing 'handicapped and deprived children' with the opportunity of enjoying the company of others in their age group. This would supplement the council's Occasional Creche Service, provided at the borough's two welfare centres, which offered child-minding for children under the age of 5 'while their mothers visit hospital, attend to shopping and other domestic duties or take part in activities at the centre at which the creche is held'.[34]

Care of the elderly

The issue of the welfare of elderly people is one to which increasing time and resources are devoted over the period 1945 to 1970. The evidence suggests there is an upsurge in the demand for services particularly from the mid-1950s. An insight into this can be gained from both the increase in space devoted to reporting on the care of elderly people in the MOH reports and the increase in the range of services offered by the local authorities. Such increases are often accompanied by accounts of an upturn in demand from the users of services.

The Metropolitan Borough of Woolwich sets out its overall philosophy on the care of the elderly in the report of the MOH validated by the council in 1956. The policy is to help maintain older people in their own homes through the provision of nursing and domestic help.[35] It also seeks to aid and support voluntary sector support for the elderly, through initiatives like the Friendly Visitors scheme in which volunteers make regular social visits to elderly people to address the problems of loneliness and isolation, or, the Women's Voluntary Service's organisation of donations of clothing to the elderly.

Throughout the 1950s and 1960s there are a number of trends in policy towards the care of the elderly which can be noted.[36] Firstly, more domestic help for older people became available. Woolwich council established its laundry scheme 'to assist aged persons for whom no other arrangements for the laundering of soiled linen were possible',[37] an initiative matched by the Metropolitan Borough of Greenwich. Its Incontinent Laundry Service was expanded due to demand in 1961 and 1962 and was continued by the London Borough of Greenwich after amalgamation. The provision of a mobile meals service (later named Meals on Wheels) is further supported and expanded in this period as are the lunch clubs which developed in the boroughs for the provision of meals and company for older people. The home help service – which had been primarily intended for assistance in domestic childbirth – was able to turn its attention to the care of the elderly as the proportion of hospital births grew steadily throughout the period. The consolidation of training for workers in these areas is another theme with for example, home help workers being sent on short courses from 1965.

Collaboration with voluntary agencies was maintained and expanded upon as voluntary agencies were given grants to carry on good works and to develop the provision of services further. In 1956 the Woolwich council gave its first grant to the Woolwich Council for Social Services (WCSS) for the coordination of voluntary organisations engaged in helping the elderly. The following year it established on a more permanent footing the Mobile Meals Service which was operated jointly by the Women's Voluntary Service (WVS) and WCSS with a grant from the council. The Metropolitan Borough of Greenwich continued to financially assist the Meals on Wheels service, which was run by the Red Cross in Greenwich, and supported the establishment of the Greenwich Old People's Welfare Association in July 1954 to coordinate the various clubs and societies for older people in the borough.[38]

Finally, there were attempts to establish a 'comprehensive old people's welfare service' which involved the creation of new formal council committees and the central monitoring of all older people by the borough councils. The new powers acquired by local authorities in 1962 under the National Assistance (Amendment) Act to provide meals and recreation for older people, either directly or through the assistance of voluntary agencies, placed existing services within the two boroughs on a new footing and led Woolwich council to set up a new Old People's Welfare Committee with responsibility for a wide range of services for the elderly. Two sub-committees were also established with responsibility for the Meals Service and coordination with voluntary organisations. The Old People's Welfare Committee was charged with compiling a central register of the elderly and enabling the interchange of information between the various branches of welfare services. It was also to establish a central enquiry office for the use of older people and to organise publicity for the services and assistance available to older people in the borough.

Local authority and voluntary agency interaction

Before the 1940s, much social provision of welfare had been undertaken by voluntary agencies with philanthropic, moral or religious concerns. In Woolwich and Greenwich this network of voluntary associations was well developed and included the Women's [Royal] Voluntary Service, Woolwich Invalid Children's Aid Association, Woolwich Parochial Almshouses, and local branches of the National Council for Maternity and Child Welfare, the Child Guidance Council and the Family Welfare Association.

As we have already seen, voluntary agencies were integrally involved in the provision of social welfare – from family planning to the care of the elderly – in the 1945–70 period. Yet the idea of a welfare state can be seen to be at odds with this kind of social welfare, and the ways in which voluntary agencies were involved in the provision of social welfare was constantly under review in this period by both the state and the voluntary agencies themselves. Developments in the relationship between the state and the voluntary sector in the provision of welfare were complex, not least because ideas about statutory welfare provision altered radically between the early days of the welfare state in the 1940s and the structural changes in the provision of welfare services which accompanied the reorganisation of local government and the reports of the Seebohm, Ingleby, and Maud Committees in the 1960s.[39]

Whatever changes took place in this relationship between statutory and voluntary bodies, the voluntary agencies (certainly in the Woolwich and Greenwich areas) remained vital in providing welfare services. Consequently, voluntary agencies had important impacts upon ideas about the family, both directly in their practical interventions into people's lives and more generally in their contribution to official discourse on the family. To illustrate this more clearly I will be looking in detail at the Charity Organisation Society (COS, renamed the Family Welfare Association, FWA, in 1946) as a case study. The COS/FWA has been chosen for a number of reasons. The FWA has both clearly stated views on the family and an active role in practical interventions. It produced a considerable amount of published and unpublished written material, much of which has been preserved and is accessible to the researcher. Furthermore, the FWA is London-based, with a branch in Greenwich, but it also has a national role participating, amongst other things, in major national enquiries related to the family. A study of the FWA therefore provides an opportunity for consideration not only of the ways in which local authorities interact with a voluntary agency but also of how the national and the local are related. So, the analysis will involve consideration of the ethos of this charity as a national institution and the specific casework of its local division in this part of south-east London. The main COS/FWA archive is held at the London Metropolitan Archive. Here, national and local annual reports are available for the period up to 1965. A substantial number of closed-access documents are also held. These include local Area Committee minutes which are closed until 2018 and case notes which, though usually closed, were made available to me with permission from the FWA.

In 1945 the COS was a well-established charity. It had been involved in establishing the Citizens' Advice Bureaux (CABx) just before the war, and reports from the CABx were included in the COS/FWA annual reports of the 1940s and 1950s. After the war, the FWA opened its Marriage Guidance Centres (later renamed Family Discussion Bureaux). Its work was influential at both national and local level in the discourse on the family.

The COS had been set up in 1869 to address two needs: to help and encourage self-respecting families who were struggling to avoid destitution; and to coordinate and organise existing charities to make best use of resources and in particular to reduce any overlap in the provision of help. Although it developed a national casework department, the COS, and later the FWA, was primarily a London charity in this period, subdivided into local committees covering areas roughly commensurate with inner-city London boroughs. In her history of the COS, Madeline Rooff characterises it as an 'essentially upper middle class' organisation to which professional men gave time and money.[40] The early philosophy of the COS was very much influenced by the idea of self-help, with perhaps a Smilesean inflection. The COS was not broadly in favour of state intervention, believing that voluntary agencies were best at organising social welfare.

These attitudes were clearly at odds with the prevailing sentiments of Beveridge and the postwar settlement, and the COS did indeed officially reverse its attitude to state intervention in the early postwar years. This change in outlook was to be signalled by the adoption of the new name, the Family Welfare Association. Despite this official change in philosophy, it is clear from the records of the FWA at both a national and a local level that the older philosophy remained popular amongst many members and can be seen to have influenced the work and tone of the organisation throughout the period under consideration. It was also argued by the association in this period that in spite of some differences, its essential beliefs were at one with the welfare state. A pamphlet produced between 1952 and 1957 argued that

> throughout its long life [the FWA] has pressed for and been successful in initiating, legislation on outstanding social problems. Even the Welfare State bears witness to the Association's pioneer work, for the public welfare services

are modelled on facilities previously offered by the Association and other voluntary societies, and operated in the light of their long experience of social work. The very conception of the Welfare State, too, springs from that social conscience which the Family Welfare Association has done so much to develop.[41]

Up to 1948 the COS/FWA operated in the local area through its Deptford and Greenwich branch. This was later expanded to include Lewisham and renamed Area 6. At a later date the local branch of this organisation metamorphosed into the Greenwich Council for Social Services (GCSS) which was in operation until 1973. The demise of the GCSS coincides with the creation of a social services department at the London Borough of Greenwich.

Some of these developments reflect a changing role for the FWA as the welfare state itself develops. In successive annual reports of the Council of the Family Welfare Association, we can see how the FWA responds to the new welfare legislation. There are two main themes here. Firstly, the FWA sees its role in alleviating material deprivation diminishing, leaving more time and resources for 'personal services' or family casework. However, while the increase in state welfare is seen to be a good thing, it 'bring[s] a measure of material relief, but [it] will never sweep away the infinite number and variety of individual human problems that always face and endanger happy family life. It is here that the Association will continue to find a field of work'.[42] This is prefigured in the Deptford and Greenwich COS and CAB annual report of 1946 which asserts the idea that there is work of a more personal nature which the voluntary agencies can do and which statutory bodies cannot.

This reassessment of the function of the FWA involved a further reassessment of its relationship with local government. The annual report of the national council of the FWA saw this as a 'new alignment between governmental and voluntary agencies' and was pleased to report 'a close and happy co-operation with the officials of Central and Local Authorities'.[43] Indeed, the Association's annual report of 1950 claimed that 'one of the functions of a voluntary agency is to seek new ways in which it can co-operate with the State Social Services'.

Similarly, the Greenwich and Deptford FWA reported in 1948 that more and more cases were 'problems of marital and family disharmony where financial difficulties play little or no part' and that these cases were 'frequently referred to us by discerning statutory officials who, having relieved the material need, realise that much is still necessary if the unity of the family is to be preserved and the disaster of a broken home averted'.

This relationship was to change further as the local authority extended its family casework with the reappraisal of social services that took place throughout the 1950s and 1960s. In 1960 the report of the Ingleby Committee noted the lack of a statutory family service for relieving family distress, preventing breakdown and re-establishing family life. The report of the Younghusband Committee in 1959 had also suggested that local authorities might take on more family casework in the future. The FWA responded to these by reiterating the value of the work it was already doing and confirming the policy of working closely with local authorities. It did not see itself as becoming redundant in this period: 'The growth of the statutory services has rather served to indicate the place that the Association should occupy than to suggest any diminution in the need for the fund of skills and experience which it has to offer'.[44] As the London Metropolitan Archive's holdings of the FWA annual reports end with the year 1964–65, it is unclear how the Association responded to both the reorganisation of London local government in 1965–66 and the introduction of unified social services in 1970.

The FWA not only responds to but also helps *shape* the public discourse of official committees. Both the Royal Commission on Population and the Royal Commission on Marriage and Divorce take evidence from the Association, and in many ways the ideas of the FWA can be seen to be in line with those of such public discourse. Given the fundamental aim of the FWA in this period – to work for social improvement in and through the family and to seek to restore the family as 'the true basis of civilised society'[45] – it is unsurprising that the ideas about the family being expressed by the COS/FWA at a national level in the 1940s and 1950s should correspond with those in the main state sponsored reports. In 1945 the COS national annual report claims that 'most of our post-war social problems can be traced back to two fundamental causes: housing and family disintegration'. It goes on to suggest

it is with the second problem, of family disintegration, that our future work will be chiefly concerned. The war has certainly thrown family life off its balance. The fact of long separation, the direction of women into the Services and industry and the transfer of young persons have all played a part in adding to the problems of family disintegration. The war has neither abolished the family, nor relegated it to an unimportant position. The physical homes of many thousands of families have been destroyed and until these have been rebuilt the work of this Association and its endeavour to re-integrate the family is of first importance to the family.

This idea of rebuilding the family is reiterated a year later in a report which foreshadows the Royal Commission on Population report which was to appear three years later. Here the FWA chair argues,

it is upon the stability of the family that the future peace of the world will depend and the work of the Association therefore becomes of the highest importance to the life of the Nation. Family life suffered as a major casualty of war.

The situation had failed to improve for the FWA national chairman, Sir Colin Jardine, by 1950 when the national annual report saw that 'the tensions confronting family life are greater than ever before, and . . . we are living in a world of danger such as humans have never lived in before'. The idea is again asserted that

> the Association believes that the family is the nation's primary institution, and that family life is the most important undertaking in our society today. In it lies the key to the whole business of civilisation, and from its unity of strength, based on trust and mutual understanding, springs our hope for a peaceful, united world.

This is the dominant view of the Association as late as 1955 when the goal of all branches of the Association's work is described as 'the preservation and maintenance of that high standard of family life upon which the future of our civilisation must depend'.[46] Finally, the FWA as a national organisation affirms the finding of the Royal Commission on Marriage and Divorce, quoting directly from the Commission's report that 'the nation's well-being depends largely upon the quality of married life among its members' and commenting that 'these words . . . aptly restate and reinforce the principles which have guided the work of the Association since its inception some 87 years ago'.[47]

The purpose of the FWA in this period is also clearly set out, and is perhaps indicated by, the change in name from the Charity Organisation Society. The need for the organisation of disparate charity work had diminished as the FWA's role changed from one primarily concerned with distributing financial help to the deserving poor to one concerned with ongoing family casework. By the 1950s the Association announced:

> This, then, is the fundamental aim of the Family Welfare Association: to work for social improvement in and through the family; to seek, with every means at its disposal, to restore the family as the true basis of civilised society . . . The aim is one likely to command universal assent.[48]

There is in this a sense of crisis in the family, of a need to *restore* the family to a previous state of being which sits uncomfortably with the supposed universality of sentiment. Later in the same pamphlet, the FWA suggests this crisis is one of industrialism:

> Before the Industrial Revolution the family provided its own social service. It was helped, in emergencies, by the church and the charitably-minded; but

ultimately it was on the three-generation family unit that all social security was based. The Industrial Revolution smashed this structure. It created new forms of mass employment – and unemployment; mass living – and mass dying; and in the society so based the family, as a means of social service, became largely ineffective. Industrialisation brought into being a new submerged class of paupers in the great industrial cities; at the same time, to many millions of working people, the essentials of life came to depend almost entirely on the continuance of factory employment which developments in countries thousands of miles away could remove at one stroke. For those millions the threat that they themselves might become submerged was the one basic fact of life.

It is clear from the content and tone of these annual local (and national) reports that a particular sense of the family is central to the COS/FWA's thinking in the late 1940s. Immediately after the war, the Deptford and Greenwich FWA predicted an increase in casework involving matrimonial problems 'of every kind':

> There is already a disturbing amount of infidelity and of unmarried motherhood and it is probable that the return of large numbers of men after such a long time abroad will bring about a crisis in a number of tangled relationships that have so far drifted on, either undisclosed or tacitly accepted.[49]

There are no real surprises here. Extra-marital sex is seen to be disturbing, and predictions of marital disharmony in postwar reunions echo ideas expressed elsewhere and discussed in previous chapters. What is interesting though is the way in which potential clients are viewed when contacting the COS in this connection:

> There are those who drop casually into the CAB to make enquiries about divorce because they think that a change of husband might suit their peacetime plans better. They can often be persuaded that it is not a simple matter as the public seems to think. There are the really tragic cases where one or often two homes are already wrecked, and it requires much skilled help to bring some sort of stability to the lives of those involved.

Over the period 1945 to 1970 there are subtle but distinct shifts in tone. Examples discussed in national annual reports suggest a move towards a more counselling approach to family casework, while the introduction of jargon from counselling and psychotherapy is in evidence. A case from the annual report for 1959–60 records a widower, sick and unable to work, with unruly children who seem to think he is shirking. In the course of her work, the FWA caseworker 'became aware that Mr Sawyer . . . was grieving for his wife who had died four years earlier'. The caseworker began weekly visits, over which time Mr Sawyer would 'express slowly and painfully his grief over the death of his wife and talk over his anxieties concerning his health and the care of his children, who are still very important to him'. There were seen to be possible connections between Mr Sawyer's emotional stress and his symptoms, though Mr Sawyer himself 'fears such ideas and so resists them'.[50]

A sense of the potential universality of family casework is highlighted in the annual report of 1962–63, where the chairman of the Association reminds members that in their work there should be no sense of ' "us" and "them" ' – expressing the view that one day anyone could become the subject of casework as a result of illness or misfortune. These changes of tone in the official publications of the Association were not, however, always as clearly in evidence in the casework notes of its workers and volunteers.

Before going on to look at casework, we might pause to consider who exactly it is that is involved in the FWA in Greenwich and Deptford. The committee – who meet on a weekly basis and who make decisions on individual cases – is almost entirely female and comprises representatives from the School Care Committees, the Red Cross, the Women's Voluntary Service, the Invalid Children's Aid Association, and the Diocesan Moral Welfare Worker. In contrast, its figurehead presidents were, in the late 1940s and 1950s, the Bishop of Woolwich and the Astronomer Royal. In other words, not an unsurprising combination of religious/establishment male titular leaders with predominantly middle-class women running the organisation on a week-by-week basis. As we shall see, from the tone and content of the case notes, we can infer that the caseworkers are respectable, almost certainly middle-class women. The annual reports tell us that these caseworkers will have received training from the FWA and are either paid workers or volunteers.

The 94th annual report described the role of the caseworker using the metaphor of the mechanic. It suggested families were sometimes in need of help

> to function more adequately and this cannot be achieved unless the family
> is integrated; a machine will not work properly or smoothly unless each of
> its component parts is doing so, and a damaged or faulty machine will not
> always 'right' itself, so the mechanic is called in.[51]

Elsewhere, family casework is described as

> a form of social science based on the belief that it is the man himself, and not
> his symptoms, which needs help. Symptoms can be relieved mechanically,
> almost automatically. But if the man himself is to be healed of his social

disorder, then it is a question of growth over a long period, a growth which can spring only from a human relationship itself maintained over a long period. It is a matter for distilling self-reliance in those with no confidence, and self-discipline in the undisciplined – in a word to help the defeated to help themselves.

The processes this involves are described as: (1) investigation, (2) diagnosis, (3) the exploitation of all possible sources of help, and (4) treatment.[52]

It seems likely that caseworkers were encouraged to make an initial assessment of the character of those people coming to or referred to them for help. In the margins of case notes there is usually an early subheading 'Impressions', and here a detailed account of the early impressions of the clients' appearance and character is given. This practice carries on at least to the late 1950s when the holdings of new case notes in the London Metropolitan Archive end. These examples are from the mid-1940s and relate to cases of financial hardship due to desertion:

> I feel that Mrs A is a very well-meaning person who has been used to a rather higher standard, but I wasn't very impressed with her tidiness and the kitchen or her own appearance.[53]

> Fairly pleasant appearance . . . facing her position fairly well . . . visited before 10 o'clock and the door was opened by Mrs B [senior] with grey hair still in curlers but otherwise very clean and respectably dressed.[54]

The following are from the late 1950s and relate to a case of hardship following mental illness and a case of rent arrears due partially to unemployment:

> Mrs C is an untidy sort of person and not at all houseproud and rather slovenly. Mr C is cleaner and makes a better impression . . . Mrs C is a stout, rosy-cheeked, untidy-haired woman, not very well dressed, but there is something about her speech which makes one think she has had a good upbringing, although she does tend to use rather grand words slightly out of place.[55]

> a rather untidy looking woman and although she had a fresh complexion, she looked I thought considerably older than 35 years. She smelt rather offensively.[56]

It is clear from the outcome of cases that these impressions are usually influential in decisions that are made at FWA committee meetings about whether and how to offer financial or other assistance. The highly subjective nature of these impressions is illustrated further by the following case from the period 1947 to 1952 in which different caseworkers become involved over a period of time. The first caseworker describes Mr D as 'very big and dark and slightly unpleasant looking with rather slitty eyes and a not too gracious manner . . . Miss Roberts agreed with me that Mr and Mrs D were anything but a desirable couple but blamed Mr D and said he is a horrible jellyfish sort of a man and she thought it unlikely that he would keep straight'. At a later point another caseworker reports the same Mr D being 'a very quiet young man . . . possibly a little shy. I did not find him sullen and obstructive in the way that Miss Walter found him'.[57]

This subjective analysis is at odds with the scientific approach to casework which is described above. The concern with appearance and cleanliness – tidy/untidy, respectable/unrespectable – as well as a concern for clients to be facing up to their situation is, however, very much in keeping with the original precepts of the COS: the need to distinguish between the deserving and undeserving poor, the respectable who can be helped over temporary adverse circumstances, and the unrespectable for whom help would have no long-term benefit. In practice, there is some compromise between the two.

A case from 1958–63 involves a family who presents with the problem of rent arrears. In the course of casework, the caseworker decides there are some genuine or respectable reasons for the arrears – the husband and father of the family has been in irregular employment as the result of an accident in 1951. The family do have a long history of problems in paying the rent which dates back to before this accident, though, and on a home visit the caseworker notices a television in the front room which she feels is at odds with their stricken predicament. The caseworker forms the opinion that though their circumstances are unfortunate, the family are partially complicit in the situation and therefore a degree of discipline needs to be injected into the family's handling of the situation for their own good. The FWA refuses to give or lend the money to clear the rent arrears, but instead intervenes in a number of ways to influence the situation. They negotiate with the rent collector; encourage Mr E to find work; encourage the National Assistance Board to provide extra money for one week and intervene with the children's school to provide help with clothing. Once the immediate problem of the rent arrears is successfully resolved, the family case is left open for potential further help in the long term.[58]

The practice of involving many different parties in the resolution of case-work is similarly carried out within families wherever possible. Members of extended family are sought out with a view to providing financial assistance, further assessment of the character of the client and confirmation of details of the case supplied by the client. Part of the initial assessment of a client's situation involves finding out the names and circumstances of extended family members. An example can best show this. In the autumn of 1947, a Mrs M was referred to the local FWA by a 'lady supervisor' at Siemens, where Mrs M worked. Mrs M was 19 years old, had been married for nine months and was seven months pregnant. She and her husband had set up home in a temporary building on heathland, but soon afterwards her husband had deserted her. Mrs M came to the FWA for help and advice. She would soon have to stop work at Siemens and was anxious and uncertain about her future.

The FWA caseworker took details about Mrs M's wider circumstances. It seems her mother had died and her father was living in a northern city, where Mrs M had lived until joining her husband in London after his demob. Mrs M had parents-in-law who lived in the Metropolitan Borough of Woolwich. After initial assessment, the caseworker suggested that Mrs M should try to move in with either her father or her parents-in-law. Mrs M replied that this would be problematic in that her father had no spare room in his house, each room other than his own already being sub-let. Furthermore, relations with her parents-in-law were difficult. The caseworker maintained that one of the few options open to Mrs M would be to attempt a reconciliation with her parents-in-law. The caseworker wrote to Mrs M senior asking if it would be possible to call round to discuss the matter with her. The caseworker records her initial impressions of Mrs M senior and tries, successfully, to convince Mrs M senior to take in her daughter-in-law.[59]

Later in the case, Mr M junior is located (perhaps with the help of the police, who have been alerted by the FWA of his desertion) but he has nowhere to stay and the caseworker again intervenes, inviting Mr M junior to meet and talk about the situation, and to mediate between him and an elder sibling who has room to spare. There is also now the issue of raising money to buy a pram for the baby. The FWA are initially keen on lending the M family some of the money, expecting Mrs M senior also to contribute and her son to make regular repayments. A delay to the start of these repayments is agreed when the caseworker writes to Mr M's brother asking for confirmation that Mr M has a debt of £10 outstanding to his brother.

There are a couple of other points that can be made about this case. The case illustrates how it was accepted within the FWA that extended family members should be involved in individual cases. In Mrs M's case, the involvement of many members of the extended family – from her husband's as well as her own side – is striking, and the contrast with our contemporary ideas about confidentiality is marked. What may also be striking to twenty-first century eyes is the involvement of outside agencies – the employer and the police – in attempting to resolve this deeply personal issue.

At this point it is useful to turn once more from the specific to the general. In these past two chapters the focus of attention has changed from Royal Commission reports, through policy and legislative change, to the case notes of individual people and families. This has involved consideration of the interplay between voluntary and statutory organisations, and between national and local concerns. We have seen that the relationship between the centre and the locality is far from simple, and that a straightforward model of ideas coming from the centre to the locality is unsatisfactory. The implementation of national policy is mediated by local conditions and particularities (for example, the central concern to keep open day nurseries in Woolwich runs against the grain of national policies to phase out day nurseries, perhaps because of the occurrence of work of national importance in the borough). Furthermore, some issues which achieve a high profile in national debates (for example, the decriminalisation of homosexuality and abortion) do not appear to have been of much concern to the local authorities, or at least are not discussed in what sources are available from local committees and enquiries.

The interaction of the voluntary and statutory agencies is also important in understanding how the formal provision of welfare is organised. Furthermore, the example of the FWA shows how the experience of local casework can inform opinion in the central organisation of voluntary agencies (in this case through the use of individual case histories in national reports), which in turn is drawn upon in the formation of policy proposals by Royal Commissions and government departmental committees (as was shown in Chapter Two).

One further point needs to be made. All of this discussion relates to the kind of welfare provision which is visible and well documented. The informal, less visible care offered by family members and neighbours needs also to be considered. As Adrian Webb and Gerald Wistow have argued, the complex and interactive nature of relations between centre and locale in the provision of social welfare is further complicated by the continued importance of voluntary provision and informal care within families. As they have argued elsewhere, the stereotype of voluntarism as cultural imperialism is found wanting when informal rather than formal volunteering is taken into consideration. The middle classes may have predominated in formal volunteering, such as with the FWA, but in working-class neighbourhoods informal care networks, often invisible to the researcher, may account for equal if not greater participation of working-class people in voluntary welfare.[60] The invisibility of neighbourly care networks is something which can be addressed by oral history work. It is therefore suggested that evidence presented in Chapter Five needs to be read in conjunction with evidence presented here.

CHAPTER FOUR

'Family viewing'
Family, popular culture, representation

History, mass media, methodology

Mass media as historical source

The second half of the twentieth century is a period of mass society and mass communication, in which the media has come under intense scrutiny. Developments in communication theory, media studies and cultural studies articulate sophisticated understandings of the production, consumption and reproduction of meaning in mass media. The media is also commonly blamed in public debate for depicting/promoting certain ideas and actions, whether these be connected to violence, immorality or stereotypes of groups of people. Between these academic and popular interrogations of the media, there is a common understanding that mass media forms are powerful conveyors of ideas. Historians look to the available sources for their period of study; and for historians of ideas in the contemporary period it is clear that where they are preserved and are available for study, sources from the mass media offer a very useful – and for this study arguably an essential – addition to historical evidence. Official publications and public policy offer one major source of public discourse on the family; the mass media offers another. Furthermore, because of the different circumstances in which the examples from official publications/policy and the mass media are produced, it is possible to make comparisons between the different strands of sources which illuminate them both, and which add to our general understanding of ideas about family in this period. This will be done in the Chapter Six which will consider the analysis of popular media in the present chapter alongside the analysis of official discourse and policy from previous chapters, and the analysis of remembered experience which follows in Chapter Five.

The primary focus of this book is not the media but ideas about the family. This chapter will not therefore seek to offer a comprehensive account of the representation of the family in all media in the 1945–70 period. Instead, it will offer an analysis of some of the most significant representations of the period focusing on one important medium, film, as the main primary source. There are practical reasons for this. A wide range of film from the period is readily available to the researcher and the transference of film to video enables close readings. The range of film available on video or from videoed television transmission means that examples from this one medium can be charted across the whole period. Furthermore, film is a truly popular medium in this period, even though the 1950s and 1960s are ordinarily spoken of as a period of decline in cinema attendance. Although by 1964 the total number of cinema admissions in Britain had fallen to 343 million a year (compared with over 1 billion in 1950[1]), this is still a substantial figure given a total population of around 50 million. This leads me to argue that film is still an important medium at this time despite a general decline in cinema attendance. It is also an especially democratic medium as no particular skills, such as reading, are usually required in watching. Where films are major box office successes, it is assumed that they have a certain cultural resonance. The feature films considered here are all mainstream and commercially successful.

The situation with television is different for researchers. For the earlier part of this period, up to the mid-1950s, television was not a significant presence in British homes. Only 350,000 homes had television in 1950[2] and television only replaced radio and cinema as the standard form of popular entertainment in the 1960s.[3] Programmes were not recorded before 1952, and then only intermittently until the end of the decade.[4] Work is only now beginning to be done which turns to the questions raised by these absences.[5] Where recordings of programmes have survived, access is severely limited. The BBC archive is not intended for outside researchers. Other institutions which do offer a screening service – such as at the British Film Institute – are prohibitively expensive. A selection of television programmes does exist on video, but this selection is limited. I have therefore used some television programmes in this research, but they play a supportive rather than primary role. Other supporting sources, including literature and print media, will similarly be used. Print media from the period is readily available but has already been extensively researched, especially in the area of women's magazines.

I have restricted my film research to the particularly relevant genres of the period – family melodramas of the 1940s; early social comedies of the family; the social problem film and the British New Wave or working-class realism of the late 1950s and early 1960s; and the 'Swinging London' films of the late 1960s, along with the 'anti-Swinging London' films that they inspired. Each of these genres has a set of narrative themes which connects directly to ideas about family and which foregrounds the domestic and interpersonal relationships. While other genres – horror, detective, cartoon etc. – may have something to offer in the way of ideas about family, these tend to be tangential to their central narrative themes. Furthermore, it is possible to build upon other researchers' work on the chosen genres (in which the unifying narrative themes are identified) through close readings of selected films in which the unifying narrative themes are exemplified.

Analysis of films

As discussed in the opening chapter, Stuart Hall has written of a process of encoding and decoding in the production, circulation, consumption and reproduction of meaning in visual discourse, an analysis which allows him to insert semiotic theory into actual social existence.[6] Within this argument he is particularly concerned with the processes by which codes or signs become naturalised, and what this process of naturalisation has to say about dominant ideas:

> Certain codes may, of course, be so widely distributed in a specific language community or culture, and be learned at so early an age, that they appear not to be constructed – the effect of an articulation between sign and referent – but to be 'naturally' given. Simple visual signs appear to have achieved a 'near-universality' in this sense . . . However, this does not mean that no codes have intervened; rather that the codes have been profoundly *naturalized*.

He argues that such naturalised codes demonstrate the degree of habituation produced when the encoding and decoding sides of an exchange of meanings are aligned and reciprocated. In connection with ideology he goes on to argue that signs appear to acquire their full ideological meaning at a connotative level, 'for here "meanings" are *not* apparently fixed in natural perception (that is, they are not fully naturalized), and their fluidity of meaning and association can be more fully exploited and transformed'. Although written about in connection with televisual discourse, this argument is pertinent also to film and can be usefully drawn upon in analyses of representation. One aim of this chapter is to examine naturalised codes in the representation of the family.

In *The Matter of Images*, Richard Dyer writes about the ways in which work on the cultural representation of social groupings has grown since the 1970s. He describes how this 'images of' analysis started with work on the representation of women and black people, and how this then spread to work on different oppressed or minority groupings. More recently, this focus has turned on dominant or majority groupings, such as men and white people in western cultures.

Dyer sees a political impulse behind the desire to produce this kind of analysis, as representation is directly related to the ways in which people are able to live out their lives:

> How a group is represented, presented over again in cultural forms, how an image of a member of a group is taken as representative of that group, how that group is represented in the sense of spoken for and on behalf of (whether they represent, speak for themselves or not), these all have to do with how members of groups see themselves and others like themselves, how they see their place in society, their right to the rights a society claims to ensure its citizens. Equally re-presentation, representativeness, representing have to do with how others see members of a group and their place and rights, others who have the power to affect that place and those rights. How we are seen determines in part how we are treated; how we treat others is based on how we see them; such seeing comes from representation.[7]

It follows that negative images and associations can be produced or shored up by particular representations while, alternatively, positive images can be reinforced, affecting both the thoughts and the actions of those seeing the representations.

This, then, is what is commonly meant by work on representation. It is possible to consider these sorts of issues in relation to particular groups within the family. For example, how are women represented in images of the family and in what contexts? Do black families figure significantly in representations of the family and, if so, how? What class issues arise? And how do non-heterosexual people feature in images of the family, if at all? Similarly we can ask how dominant or majority groupings appear in representations of the family.

I will be aware of these kinds of questions in this chapter, and could therefore locate this study within the context of the kind of 'images of' analysis which Dyer describes. However, I want to do something more than this, as little or no work on representation has been done which focuses conceptually on 'the family' rather than on examples of its constituent parts. There is, for example, much feminist work on how women are represented within the family, but virtually nothing on how 'the family' itself is represented. Given the ways (discussed in the first chapter) in which 'the family' is commonly unproblematised conceptually, this would seem to be an aspect of representation in need of further attention. In this chapter I attempt to do this by taking the 'images of' analysis which Richard Dyer talks about and turning its focus not just on 'social groupings' as he suggests, but on 'the family' as a cultural formation.

There are many potentially diverse ways of reading these films, and we cannot be certain about how contemporary audiences may have read them. Although my reading of them may only be one amongst many, it is informed by a training in history which allows for films, as historical sources, to be interrogated in much the same way as any other historical source. For this book, a system of analysis has been developed which has been applied to all films considered. The analysis includes looking at the relationships between characters; consideration of that dialogue which directly or otherwise addresses ideas about family; observations about gender difference; and the presence or absence of family rituals and interaction in the narrative.

The analysis of films here also draws upon the critical vocabulary of film studies. Narrative structure is closely analysed and particular attention is given to the opening and closing of the narrative, as narrative theory suggests these have a heightened importance in the film's meaning. Point of view – the position from which something is seen – is considered, both in the sense of from whose perspective the film is seen and in the sense of the point of view the narrative directs at its subject. Attention is also paid to the film's construction of character, and the *mise en scène* – all that is put in front of the camera. There is also some consideration of the composition of the film, the setting up of particular shots and sequences and what meanings can be deduced from these.

Structure of chapter

As well as being organised around genres, the chapter was originally conceived chronologically, as this seemed the most obvious way to assess the changing nature of representations of the family. It has been rearranged to begin with a consideration of the films of the British New Wave (and the associated 'social problem' films of the period) for a number of reasons: the films are usually described as pivotal, a new aesthetic which found new subjects and new ways of representing interpersonal relationships. For John Hill these are amongst the first 'politically serious representations of working-class life'[8] and for this reason relate to what is a pivotal moment in the wider British culture. These films are on the cusp of two cultural periods with distinctly different images: the 1950s of Dixon of Dock Green, austerity, the coronation and the Festival of Britain; and the 1960s of permissiveness, representations of working-class life, women's liberation and Swinging London. If it appears odd that such films should come from film-makers who took up essentially oppositional standpoints, it should be remembered that something of this polarity was beginning to enter the mainstream at that time. The later legislation of consent was enacted after a period of public debate of which the films of the British New Wave and 'social problem' genre were intrinsically a part. In Raymond Williams's terms, this can be understood as a period in which the emergent structure of feeling strengthens and begins to eclipse the existing dominant structure of feeling.[9] In this way, this set of films can be seen as transitional documents.

In order to more fully understand the nature and limits of this change in the representation of the family, the chapter proceeds by placing this set of films in context. Analysis is made of and contrast drawn with earlier and later film genres, beginning with the melodrama and social comedy genres of the 1940s and 1950s and concluding with the 'Swinging London' films which appeared after the brief moment of the British New Wave. Further contexualisation is made in these sections through comparisons with other media and broad developments in social mentalities.

British New Wave and social problem films

The films of the British New Wave grew out of the collaboration of a small number of directors and producers who were involved in the *Sequence* film journal in the late 1940s and the Free Cinema group in the 1950s. Connections can also be made with the documentary film movement of the 1930s and the 'New Wave' film-making in France, Poland and the United States. Whereas the films of the British New Wave were shown in art house cinemas in the United States,[10] in Britain itself they were mainstream successes (in many cases being amongst the handful of most popular films of their year), striking a chord at the Ritzys and Odeons across the country. Although the film-makers may have taken up broadly oppositional positions, the films were produced, released and distributed through the mainstream industry and we can deduce from their huge popularity that the concerns of the films were in some way connected to the wider social experience of audiences. Janet Thumim has argued that in such films there are points of intersection between the fictional and wider social experience, exemplified in the films and the audience respectively and evident in the themes which appear concurrently in different films.[11] That different themes occur at different moments would seem to strengthen this argument.

I will start with a brief synopsis of the main films under consideration in this section. Chronologically, the films are *Room at the Top* (dir. Jack Clayton, 1959), *Look Back in Anger* (dir. Tony Richardson, 1959), *Sapphire* (dir. Basil

Dearden, 1959), *Saturday Night and Sunday Morning* (dir. Karel Reisz, 1960), *A Taste of Honey* (dir. Tony Richardson, 1961), *Victim* (dir. Basil Dearden, 1961), *A Kind of Loving* (dir. John Schlesinger, 1962), *The Leather Boys* (dir. Sidney J. Furie, 1963) and *Billy Liar* (dir. John Schlesinger, 1963).

I have found it useful to group together some of the films due to similarities in plot or point of view. The largest group includes *Room at the Top*, *Look Back in Anger*, *Saturday Night and Sunday Morning*, *A Kind of Loving* and *Billy Liar*. A contemporary critic made connections between some of these films at the time. Ian Wright, writing in the *Guardian* on the release of *Billy Liar*, observed 'we've seen it all before – "A Taste of Loving on Saturday Night at the Top". We've seen the dreary town, Billy's useless defiance, the office where he works and the men who bully him. We've seen his girlfriends and his parents and we have got a pretty good idea of what they are going to say next.'[12] I would remove *A Taste of Honey* from Ian Wright's list. In the other films – as also with *The Loneliness of the Long Distance Runner* and *This Sporting Life* – we predominantly enter into the world of young, educated or prosperous working-class men, sometimes seeing that world from their point of view, but always with their concerns as central. The narratives centre around the possibilities of their lives and in particular around a number of relationships they have with women. The women's world tends to be marginalised. Ian Wright's review highlights the fact that with Billy Fisher – as well as Arthur Seaton, Joe Lampton and Vic Brown – we see 'his girlfriends', rather than 'their relationships'.

Room at the Top is usually seen as one of the first of the new genre of working-class realism in film. Adapted from John Braine's novel and taking advantage of the shake-up in censorship regulations, this new X-rated film was seen by contemporary reviewers as 'an eye-opener'[13] and 'one of the bravest and best British films in years'.[14] Arthur Knight, writing in the *Saturday Review* heralded it as a new kind of film, saying he felt the 'shock of recognition, the shock of recognising ordinary, tawdry people on the screen . . . and the shock of realizing how rarely this had happened before'.[15] The nature of the realism will be questioned later, but for now here is a synopsis. The narrative centres on Joe Lampton, a working-class grammar-school boy who manages to secure a clerical job with the council in the nearest city, and his determination to marry a local factory owner's only daughter, Susan, as a means to get to 'the top'. The narrative deals with various obstacles in his way, including the disapproval of Susan's parents, the presence of Susan's fiancé, the scepticism and lack of similar ambition amongst his friends and colleagues, and a diversionary affair with another woman, Alice Aisgill, played by Simone Signoret.

Look Back in Anger is another film adaptation which centres on a grammar-school boy, Jimmy Porter (played by Richard Burton), his emotional and psychological make-up and the impact of this on his relationships and his life. Again, two relationships involving the main protagonist are highlighted – Jimmy and his wife Alison; and Jimmy and Helenna, his wife's friend. With *Saturday Night and Sunday Morning*, something of a pattern begins to emerge. Here again the film is built around a young working-class man, Arthur Seaton, this time a man not highly educated, but prospering in the postwar boom. The narrative is again structured by two relationships featuring Arthur with Brenda, wife of a colleague, and Doreen a young woman who lives with her mother and hopes to marry Arthur. Arthur's discontent with what seems possible in his life and attempts to resist the lifestyle of his parents are foregrounded.

A Kind of Loving sits easily with *Room at the Top*, *Saturday Night and Sunday Morning* and *Look Back in Anger*. Although not strictly seen from Vic's point of view, it is his world that we enter in the film and his concerns that are paramount. Vic (played by Alan Bates) works with Ingrid (June Ritchie) where they meet and form a relationship. We learn from Vic that he is half-hearted about this, but he agrees to marry Ingrid when she tells him that she is pregnant. After the wedding, the couple live with Ingrid's mother, Mrs Rothwell (played by Thora Hird). Where it is shown, Ingrid and her mother's world is seen to revolve around the new consumerism of television and shopping. Vic and Mrs Rothwell do not get on, and in the course of the narrative Vic leaves the house and the marriage. He and Ingrid are ultimately reunited after it is agreed that they will both move out of her mother's house and live on their own.

Billy Liar incorporates many of the elements of realism in the films outlined so far, but is also much more of an invitation into the fantasy world of Billy Fisher. Billy is discontented at work, his family do not understand him, and he is juggling relationships with at least three women. It is, like most of these films, seen largely from the perspective of the central male protagonist. The narrative is mostly concerned with Billy's attempts to get away from all this and to become a scriptwriter in London.

A Taste of Honey stands out from the other working-class realism films. Its central protagonist, Jo, is female and her point of view frames the narrative. Also, despite becoming pregnant, Jo does not seriously consider marriage in the film. Jo sets up home temporarily with a young homosexual[16] man, Geoffrey, before her mother intervenes on hearing that Jo is pregnant. Helen, Jo's Mother, is forced to leave a brief marriage with Peter and decides to replace Geoffrey as Jo's flatmate.

I have also grouped together the social problem films of Basil Dearden and Michael Relph – *Sapphire* and *Victim*. The issue at the heart of *Sapphire*, the racism surrounding the recent wave of immigration, is framed within a classic murder mystery plot. A young woman (Sapphire) is discovered dead on Hampstead Heath and the central character of Superintendent Hazard (played by Nigel Patrick) is sent to investigate. As the narrative unfolds, the families of the victim and more so of her fiancé, David, take on a central importance and ultimately Sapphire's relationship with David and his family provides the means for understanding her murder.

Victim centres on the plight of homosexual men in London of the 1950s, and is particularly concerned with the 'blackmailers' charter', or the Labouchere amendment to the Criminal Law of the 1880s, and the debate about reform of the law which had been spurred on by the report of the Wolfenden Committee. Like Dearden's other 'social problem' film, *Sapphire*, it is structured around a classic crime/mystery plot. The film stars Dirk Bogarde as a blackmailed barrister, Melville Farr, who takes on the blackmailers and wins. Although evidently emotionally involved with at least two men, Melville Farr is married and thus occupies an unusual position both within the family and the operation of the law (as married person and barrister) and also without (as man blackmailed over his sexuality and person privately pursuing the central criminals without police help).

The Leather Boys has also been described as a social problem film[17] but can equally usefully be seen as another example of (male) working-class realism and as such can be grouped either with *Victim* and *Sapphire* or *Room at the Top, A Kind of Loving* etc. Initially it seems to be a film about the problems of early marriage, and can be seen to be addressing the trend towards early marriage which had appeared in analysis of demographic statistics. Dot (played by Rita Tushingham) and Reggie (Colin Campbell) are married on Rita's sixteenth birthday. They set up home in a small flat. Reggie goes out to work while Dot takes on the role of the housewife, except that problems arise in their relationship as Dot is seen to become too wrapped up in consumerism. She spends much time and money on her hair and clothes as well as magazines and other entertainment. Reggie becomes discontented and begins to form a friendship with another biker, Pete (Dudley Sutton). Reggie leaves the flat to live temporarily with his grandmother. Pete, who seems to have few connections, goes to stay with them. An attempted reconciliation with Dot fails after Reggie finds her at the flat with another man. He then resolves to go away to sea with Pete, though this plan falters when Pete's homosexuality finally becomes clear to him.

Turning now from synopsis to analysis, rather than analyse each film in turn, I will instead draw out a number of themes to do with ideas about the family and the way in which families are represented. These themes are firstly the central position of marriage or marital conflict within the narratives; and secondly the appearance and representation of non-nuclear families which will include discussion of the representation of extended families and an analysis of the fate of non-conventional families and interlopers into the family.

To turn to the first of these, the central position of marriage or marital conflict in the narratives, we can begin by noting how marriage is something which most (though not all) of the young characters in these films aspire to almost unquestioningly. Early on in *A Kind of Loving*, Ingrid makes clear her need to marry soon even though she is only 19. She tells us that all the girls she went to school with are married or settled into a steady relationship. Dot and Reggie stumble rapidly into marriage at the start of *The Leather Boys*, while the expectation of marriage suffuses the young men's conversations in *Saturday Night and Sunday Morning* and *Room at the Top*. In *Saturday Night and Sunday Morning*, Arthur's cousin Bert tells him 'you've got to get married sometime . . . that's how things are, Arthur, there's no use going crackers over it'. In a different way, the narrator in the contemporary documentary film *We are the Lambeth Boys*, also directed by Karel Reisz, supposes marriage to be inevitable for one of the young women, Beryl, who works in a food factory. 'She will probably work here until she is married', he tells us. In this case, Beryl's views are not shown.

This can be related to a particularly relaxed view of marriage which is shown by a number of older characters. Dot's mother seems to have no qualms about her daughter's impending marriage (to take place on her sixteenth birthday), while Arthur's aunt in *Saturday Night and Sunday Morning* asks him, 'why don't you marry [Brenda] then, if she's a nice girl?' Caution about marriage tends to focus on whether the young people are marrying for the right reasons – Joe Lampton's aunt and uncle in *Room at the Top* are anxious about his interest in Susan: 'Are you sure it's the girl you're interested in and not the brass?' In all of these films, with the exception of *A Taste of Honey*, when pregnancy becomes a factor in a relationship and neither character is already married, there is an expectation amongst the characters' families that they will marry. This expectation of marriage seems also to be present amongst the characters themselves, although this is not without its tensions. Vic Brown instantly proposes marriage to Ingrid in *A Kind of Loving*, and yet later berates his family for their unquestioning acceptance of this.

Yet there is a distinct tension in evidence between the desire for marriage and the desire for sex. 'You can't get sex these days until you've married them', Arthur's cousin tells him in *Saturday Night and Sunday Morning*, while Billy Fisher in *Billy Liar* makes offers of engagement to both Rita and Barbara in the hope of persuading them to have sex with him. When he is found out, Rita tells him that he cannot 'handle the goods' if he doesn't 'intend to buy'. That sex and marriage are very clearly linked for Vic's younger brother in *A Kind of Loving* is shown by his reaction to discovering Vic's soft porn magazine: 'Bet you wish you was married to her!'

More practical concerns are discussed in *Room at the Top* by Joe and Charlie. Joe's theory is to carefully control the kinds of women he will allow himself to fall for – and he intends to aim high. Charlie initially dismisses June as a suitable candidate for marriage, noting that anyone who married June would also be taking on an invalid mother. Although these views are well aired in the film, ultimately the characters are shown either to ignore these more practical considerations in order to find a fulfilling relationship (Charlie overcomes his fear of 'taking on' June's mother and they seem destined for a happy marriage) or they ignore this at their peril (Joe in facing up to his love for Alice and his attraction to Susan's money chooses the latter to his cost). It is, I think, important to look at what happens to the main characters and their marriages as the narrative draws to a close.

Joe's fate is clearly juxtaposed with Charlie's at the end of *Room at the Top*. Joe, in rejecting Alice and accepting an emotionally and physically unsatisfying relationship with Susan, is clearly represented as having made the wrong choice. He has abused the institution of marriage. Charlie, on the other hand, has rejected his earlier, more calculated approach to marriage and seems destined for a contented marriage with June. The narrative structure of the film shows Charlie 'growing up' and adjusting well to adulthood. The significance of marriage – seen notably at the start or end of a number of these films including *The Leather Boys* and *A Kind of Loving* – is signalled here by the closing of the film on the scene of Joe's marriage to Susan.

In one sense, Joe and Susan's marriage at the end of the film conforms to the narrative norm of mainstream cinema with the heterosexual couple being ultimately reunited after difficulty or separation. But their reunion is troubled and does not offer the same message as Vic and Ingrid's reunion in *A Kind of Loving*, where there is far greater hope of a happy outcome away from the interference of Ingrid's mother. In *The Leather Boys*, the narrative drive seems to be leading towards a similar reunion for Dot and Reggie and briefly they are reunited. However, this is short-lived and the film ends with Reggie leaving Dot, attempting to flee to America with Pete (a good old-fashioned ending) only finally to have Pete's homosexuality revealed to him, prompting an inconclusive ending where Reggie walks off to nowhere in particular. Here cinematic convention is undermined in that no solutions are offered.

The troubled reunion of the heterosexual leads is most bizarrely acted out in *Victim*, though it must be said that the representation of the Farr's marriage is not untroubled before the disruption of events in the narrative. Although they are an attractive and materially successful couple, there are clear indications that all is not well. Most strikingly, the couple have been married for a number of years and yet they do not have any children. Laura certainly has an affinity for children as is demonstrated in her choice of part-time work with disturbed children. This choice, as well as the disrupting and unsettling presence of the children, would seem to emphasise the lack of children in the marriage. (Indeed, Richard Dyer has referred to children as the 'structuring absence' of the film.[18]) Furthermore, Laura seems uncertain about the success of their marriage. When her brother questions her, she is not sure if she has discovered 'real love' with Mel. There is little indication of any physical intimacy between them, though an emotional bond seems to exist. In this respect their marriage is not a sham in the sense of merely being a cover for Mel's sexuality. In fact, Mel is shown to believe that the marriage would enable him to control his sexuality, though this turns out to have been unsuccessful.

Towards the end of the film, when Mel has decided to go public to end the blackmail and get justice for Boy's death, there is doubt cast over the future of the marriage by both partners. Though he tells Laura that he will need her more than ever once the publicity and humiliation are over, Mel imagines that she will be unable to bear it and he cannot expect her to stand by him. Laura also has doubts about Mel's desire to continue in the marriage. In the closing scenes they are, however, reunited.

I will return to the analysis of marriage and its representation later, particularly in making comparisons with the ways in which marriage is discussed and represented before and after the films of the British New Wave. Before doing this I want to turn to consider the second theme of this section, which is the appearance and representation of non-nuclear families in British New Wave film.

One thing that is noticeable about the films discussed so far is that extended families are represented in some form in all of them. That this happens, and the ways in which it happens, offers insights into ideas about the family within this genre. If the extended family is considered at all in discussion about these films, it is usually the intergenerational conflict between parents and adult/adolescent children or children-in-law that is focused upon. As these films are often understood as being concerned with the conflicts between an older, more settled way of life and the young people (men?) who are struggling against its confines, this is probably unsuprising. Certainly we can find evidence of this kind of interaction in the extended family – though in some cases, like *A Kind of Loving*, the central protagonist, Vic, is shown to be generally untroubled by his parents who form a benign presence in the film. In *Saturday Night and Sunday Morning* however, Arthur speaks of his father being 'dead from the neck up'. He seeks to reject the drab and compliant lives of his parents and to live life on his own terms. Jo in *A Taste of Honey* is in perpetual conflict with her mother and her short-lived stepfather, Peter. Billy Fisher's existence is framed by the stifling presence of his parents and grandmother whom he ridicules and defies. Parents-in-law fare no better in *Look Back in Anger* and *A Kind of Loving* where both Jimmy Porter and Vic Brown are in conflict with their wives' parents.

Looking beyond these conflicts to the margins of the narratives, the extended family – about which I have been able to find nothing written in this context – is often shown in a different light. In particular, members of the main protagonists' extended families are, on the whole, shown in supportive roles, offering help and advice to the younger family members and often being sought out for exactly this purpose. Furthermore, extended family members help the narrative along through their advice and practical support, providing a means by which morality can be explored and difficulties can be faced and resolved. The ways in which extended families are working here are in sharp contrast to the intergenerational conflicts for which these films are most remembered and seem instead more to do with the kind of family/community interaction which was a concern of contemporary sociological writing and which Michael Young and Peter Wilmott spoke of in their *Family and Kinship in East London* (1957).

When, for example, Brenda tells Arthur she is pregnant in *Saturday Night and Sunday Morning*, it is his aunt that Arthur goes to for advice and practical help. The aunt is reluctant to help with an abortion, but does so because Arthur is family. She is represented as approachable and understanding while offering a degree of moral guidance. The role of confidante is similarly acted out by Christine, Vic Brown's sister in *A Kind of Loving*, though her presence is felt most strongly when Vic goes to her for support after leaving his wife to find that Christine will not support his actions and, instead, urges a speedy resolution to the situation and a return to the marriage. Ultimately, Vic follows this advice. In *Room at the Top*, it is Joe Lampton's aunt and uncle who offer moral and practical guidance over his relationship with Susan, and it is his ignoring of their advice that leads to his downfall. In this way, Joe's aunt and uncle give voice to the moral message of the film – that marriage should be about love, not money.

If Billy Fisher's grandmother is a figure of ridicule in *Billy Liar*, Reggie's grandmother in *The Leather Boys* has a close and loving relationship with her grandson. While the rest of his family seem uncaring or unwilling to take much interest in the old woman, Reggie – in many ways the archetypal rebel – is determined that she will not be forced out of her home and into residential care. He takes the time and effort to find out what it is that she wants, and enables her to achieve this by moving in Pete as a lodger and by his own regular visits to her. She in return offers him the space to be able to consider the future of his marriage.

The kind of familial relations just described tend to take place at the margins of the narrative. Alternatives to conventional nuclear families are, however, occasionally represented in the mainstream of the narratives. It is useful, then, to see how alternatives are represented and how ultimately they fare. *A Taste of Honey* is especially interesting here. In the course of the film we see five different domestic arrangements, starting and ending with Jo living with her mother, Helen. In between we see Helen with her new husband, Peter; Jo living on her own; and Jo living with her friend, Geoff. Of all of these different domestic arrangements, only this last one, Jo's living with Geoff, is seen to be successful. The film starts with Jo and her mother living in a dingy bedsit, preparing to make a hasty exit as they cannot pay the rent. Their next home is cramped, damp and equally unpleasant, and mother and daughter do not get along well. Helen is shown to be a feckless and irresponsible mother. Jo is an unhappy and resentful daughter. When Helen finally marries Peter, it is made clear that it is impossible for Jo to live with them.

Meanwhile, Jo finds herself a job and manages to secure the rent on a flat. She is, however, lonely and not very domesticated until she meets Geoff, an arts student in what Richard Dyer has called the 'sad young man' mould,[19] ultimately allowing him to move in with her. By this time Jo is pregnant from a brief encounter with a sailor. As Geoff moves in they both start to plan for the birth, and a successful, if unusual, alternative family is set up. This is the only domestic arrangement with which Jo is seen to be happy and content. In fact it could be that this, rather than her brief affair with the sailor, is her 'taste of honey'.

As this is the only successful 'family' shown in the film, it is intriguing to see how this is finally dealt with in the narrative. Only months after her marriage to Peter and their move to suburbia, Helen is thrown out, the marriage deemed a failure. She returns to Jo in the hope that Jo will allow her to live with her. In order to achieve this, Helen sets about arranging the removal of Geoff. Helen suggests that in her condition, Jo needs her mother, and although Jo tells Geoff 'it's you I need, not her', Geoff literally wilts away after a confrontation with Helen. It is as if he (and perhaps the viewer, too) knows that he has no right to be there. The successful domestic arrangement is unceremoniously disbanded and the previously unharmonious domestic arrangement between mother and daughter is reinstated.

There is a similarly brief alternative to married domesticity in *The Leather Boys*, where Pete and Reggie temporarily live together at Reggie's grand-mother's house. From Reggie's point of view, this may not be a serious alternative, as he clearly considers this a passing situation. He might go back to his wife, Dot, or he might move on elsewhere. For him there is no clear sense of having set up home with Pete (though this sense is much stronger in the novel on which the film is based). For Pete the situation is different. He is far more deeply involved in the situation, and his feelings come to a head when Reggie decides to leave. He does not seem able to understand why Reggie would want to go back to his wife. He asks if they have not been happy enough together, and if so, why Reggie would reject this new domestic arrangement. For Pete there seems to be no question that they have indeed set up home together, and that this arrangement could or should be as valid as Reggie's previous domestic arrangements with Dot.

Perhaps both of these alternative domestic idylls are doomed to be short-lived in the contexts in which they are shown. In terms of narrative convention they both exist as the disruptive elements in troubled relationships, offering a temporary dislocation before the main characters are returned to their previous positions. In the internal logic of the films, the alternatives are made impossible. It is interesting that alternatives were being represented, but important that they are seen as temporary and transient, even where they are the only successful domestic situation on offer within a film's narrative. It would be easy to argue that this represents an ultimate conservatism within these films, or that the radical pretensions of the film-makers from the days of the Free Cinema movement were found wanting.

These film endings can, though, be read as a 'pragmatic acceptance' of what possibilities were realistically on offer to characters in these situations, before the liberation movements of the 1960s and 1970s and when the pressures of convention were still most keenly felt. In *Sapphire* there is in a sense an attempt to establish another kind of alternative family (alternative at least for early 1960s Britain) in the form of a mixed-race marriage. That this attempt doesn't get very far is the crux of the film. There is such a strong feeling against the idea of this marriage within David's family that one of them has murdered Sapphire to prevent the marriage. In terms of ideas about the family, what is particularly interesting is the level of threat that is felt to this particular family by the idea of miscegenation. Although Millie, who is David's sister and the murderer, could be dismissed as a typical film noir neurotic – she is sexually and emotionally unfulfilled after her husband has left her and their two daughters – her motives are quite clear. She sees her family under threat. There is a telling scene in which Millie reveals the extent of her feelings towards 'coloured people', just before she is accused of and admits to the murder. In this scene, Sapphire's brother, Dr Robbins, has been invited to the Harris family home by Inspector Hazzard, who is also present. Unlike Sapphire, Dr Robbins is clearly identifiable as black. As Inspector Hazzard is talking to and asking questions of the family, he has picked up a doll and is seemingly absent-mindedly carrying it around. It is a white doll and belongs to one or other of Mildred's daughters. After a while, the Inspector nonchalantly passes the doll to Dr Robbins, who in turn is seen to absent-mindedly play with it. The camera cuts between close up shots of the doll in Dr Robbins hands, and shots of Mildred looking increasingly anxious. Eventually there is an outburst from Millie in which she is seen to demonstrate her fear and hatred of coloured people. 'Get him out!' she shouts, 'I don't want his hands on my kids' toys!

Don't want him near my kids! Don't want his dirty hands on my children! Tearing up my family – they're mine!' She goes on to explain that she attacked Sapphire when Sapphire has told her that she was pregnant, and that Millie could go home and tell her daughters they were soon to have a new cousin.

The motive for this murder could be seen as merely fictional and exceptional. As one piece of evidence it cannot be used to form any definite opinion on ideas about the family. However, it does relate to other ideas already explored in previous chapters. In particular the fear of miscegenation, so articulately expressed in the Royal Commission on Population ten years earlier, coupled with the extreme importance attached to the family as the race in miniature, put this storyline into clearer perspective, as might the legacy of the eugenicist ideas about family from the same period. Furthermore, the writer, director and producer of the film have clearly taken racism as a 'social problem' to be the subject of the film and endeavour to explore the existence and rationale of racism in the film. That they chose to structure a social problem film around a murder, as opposed to any other dramatic device, that the site of the murder was the respectable white British family and that the motive for the murder was the fear of a black person 'tearing up' the family, are surely telling.

British New Wave in context

Before British New Wave

The films of the British New Wave engage with ideas about the family in ways which are particular to both their time and genre. We can see this more clearly by placing the genre in the context of other kinds of film which engage with ideas of family. Of these, two of the most important genres which were popular before the advent of British New Wave (and which continued to be popular during and after) were the melodrama and the social comedy.

In *Celluloid Sisters*, Janet Thumim tells us that melodrama was by far the most popular film genre of the 1940s. Within this genre, she argues, the most popular themes were the chronicling of domestic and emotional struggles within family groups. Thumim's research has shown that these struggles invariably deal with efforts to establish, maintain or defend the family, however that social unit is defined within the film. Furthermore, this 'preservation of the family' invariably transcends the importance of the individual, whether the film is a historical melodrama, like *The Wicked Lady*, a wartime melodrama such as *The Piccadilly Incident,* or a melodrama of middle-class nuclear family such as in *Brief Encounter.*[20]

Comedy becomes established as a specific genre in the 1950s which has its antecedents in the social comedies of the earlier period which are frequently concerned with familial and domestic matters. The social comedies often revolved around a recurring family group, for example the Rileys, the Aldrich family and, after the war, most popular of all, the Huggetts. Just as the melodramas were formulaic in their dealings with the family and the individual, these family social comedies – examples of which Len England called 'the family film' – were formulaic in their representation of the family group and gender.[21]

I want, then, to begin this section with a consideration of films from the melodrama and social comedy genres because they so frequently deal directly with families and because of their patterns of representing families which other researchers have noted. One way to examine these formulas of representation is to make a close reading of important films, and I have therefore chosen to discuss in detail examples which were amongst the most commercially successful and enduring films of the early postwar years: *Brief Encounter* (dir. David Lean, 1945) and *Here Come the Huggetts* (dir. Ken Annakin, 1948).

The Oscar-winning *Brief Encounter* is firmly established in the national psyche as a classic piece of cinema. *Here Come the Huggetts* may now have a less secure place in the national imagining, but in the late 1940s and 1950s it occupied a very central position. In *The Times* obituary for Kathleen Harrison, the film's female lead, it was suggested that as a result of their roles in the Huggetts series, 'in any popularity poll taken during the late 1940s, Kathleen Harrison and Jack Warner would have eclipsed an army of more glamorous actors'.[22] Furthermore, the Huggetts provided the inspiration for the first television soap. I would argue, then, that these films had a particularly clear cultural resonance which make them suitable for analysis in this context.

Brief Encounter is concerned with the telling of a story of a dilemma for 'an ordinary woman'[23] through her own recollections. Laura's dilemma centres around a relationship which springs up unexpectedly with another married person whom she meets by chance in a station café. Increasingly, she is aware of the contrast between the freedom, excitement and deep feelings associated with this relationship and the mundane nature of her life as a dutiful suburban wife and mother. The film is narrated in her own voice and its unfolding occurs as she sits in the library of her home, listening to Rachmaninov's Second Piano Concerto. Her husband, occupied with the *Times* crossword, sits opposite. We are never entirely sure if the events she describes have actually taken place or if they exist only in her imagination.

Three things are particularly interesting in relation to the film's representation of the family. The first is Laura's awakening to new dimensions of her sexuality and her ensuing doubts about her life as it had previously been constituted; the second, which is related to the first, is the way in which the narrative ends; and the third is the role of the minor working-class characters in unsettling the main narrative. I will look at these in turn.

Throughout the film we see the character of Laura (played by Celia Johnson) maintaining an extremely shaky control over feelings and situations which clearly frighten and panic her and yet to which she seems inextricably drawn. Her brief relationship with Alex is shown to develop almost against her will. As the narrative progresses, the dichotomy between her life with her husband and her life without him (either real or in her imagination) increases and she has to remind herself 'We're a happily married couple and must never forget that [. . .] I'm a happily married woman, this is my whole world and its enough; or rather it was until a few weeks ago . . .'. The phrases 'happily married couple' and 'happily married woman' seem to be uttered defensively, almost as if they could be understood as a mantra by which Laura is able to know and accept her life as it is.

Within the film there is indeed much evidence to suggest that Laura and Fred are 'happily married'. Fred appears gentle, caring and thoughtful. Laura knows him to be wise and understanding – the only person she knows who might be able to understand the predicament she is in and yet significantly she knows she will be unable to tell him, ever. They have a comfortable home with a servant and two healthy children whose biggest problems are shown to be deciding whether to go to the circus or the pantomime for a birthday treat. Laura is not shown to be unusually meek or compliant in her marriage. She is able to tell Fred to 'shut up' and 'stop fussing' when he tries to arrange for her to see a doctor. In many ways this family seems safe, comforting, healthy and balanced, and aside from her pain and dilemma over her relationship with Alex, there is much to support the idea that Laura was indeed happy and that this was 'enough'.

The ambiguity surrounding Laura's relationship with Alex (is it 'real'; is it imaginary?) is underlined by the closing of the narrative which finds Fred at Laura's side and commenting that she has been 'a long way away' and thanking her for coming back to him. It seems that there are three different ways in which we can understand this. We could assume that Fred's is a chance remark in which he is aware that Laura has been deep in thought for some time, perhaps as a result of listening to the music. In this understanding, it does not matter whether Laura has been daydreaming her relationship with Alex or whether she has been preoccupied with going over the events and feelings of the past few weeks which have revolved around an actual relationship with him. Fred is simply commenting that

Laura has been deep in thought and jokingly thanks her for returning to the 'real world'.

Alternatively, we could understand that Fred – the wise and caring husband whom Laura believes would be the only possible person to understand her predicament – is actually far more aware of what it is that has been preoccupying Laura and is attempting, gently, to let her know. Here, we could see that perhaps Laura has been involved in a dilemma over an extra-marital relationship and that Fred has been observing this and is aware that the dilemma appears to have been resolved. Yet another option would be that Laura has been fantasising her relationship with Alex, perhaps only for the duration of her evening in the library listening to the music, and that Fred is aware that she has been daydreaming/fantasising and is still able to let her know by thanking her for returning to him. Which are we to believe? And what does it matter?

If this incident occurred elsewhere in the film it would be easier to regard it as a coincidental remark on the part of Fred. It could be seen as an ironic joke between the film-makers and the audience in which the audience could enjoy the pleasure of knowing that which is unknown to an important character in the film. Occurring as it does at the very end of the film, this explanation seems weak. This scene and Fred's words are the last that we see and hear. They close the narrative, and given cinematic convention, are therefore vastly heightened in importance. We are indeed expected to read more into Fred's remarks than mere irony. The ambiguity of his remarks, coupled with their placing at the very end of the film, suggest that we are meant to see something here. But what is it?

Firstly, I would argue that the initial ambiguity – whether Laura is re-membering or fantasising her relationship with Alex – does not need to complicate our understanding of the film's ending. In either case, Fred is evidently welcoming Laura back from somewhere else and he clearly has an idea of where she has been, even if we are not aware of what it is that he understands. It is the welcoming back – from a real or fantasy relationship – which is most significant. There seems to be little question that Laura has indeed 'come back' even though the narrative has clearly demonstrated her discomfort with her domestic situation. Her coming back into the fold is acted out by Fred shepherding her into his embrace, enfolding himself around her as she remains seated in the chair from which she has remem-bered/fantasised her story. Our final image of Fred and Laura is of her return to the bosom of the family, while Alex, in good narrative tradition, is banished to the Empire to seek a new life. Thus both protagonists are returned to their 'proper' places.

Laura and Alex are seen to make the sensible choice, to reject the new-found pleasure and excitement of their brief encounter and to return dutifully to their families while putting a large distance between themselves. Their brief, tortured and ultimately sensible affair is thrown into sharp relief by the behaviour of the lower-class characters, snippets of whose lives pepper the narrative. These characters are the woman who runs the refreshment room at the station, the ticket inspector with whom she is having some kind of relationship, and Beryl, her assistant. It is worth pausing for a moment to consider why these characters appear and reappear throughout the film. Although minor characters, their role is not limited merely to enabling the progress of the narrative drive. In particular, their histories and current relationships are brought periodically into more central focus. The woman who runs the refreshment room tells the ticket inspector how she left her husband for another man with whom she went into business. This relationship was short-lived as the man in question died soon after they embarked upon their new life together. However, this relationship helped shape the woman's current position as proprietor of the refreshment room, as it provided the financial basis for this venture. Her current relationship with the ticket inspector is somewhat ambiguous, although it is indicated that they may be having a sexual relationship or that they have 'an understanding': when the woman is reticent with him in front of customers, the inspector remarks that she 'wasn't like that the other evening', implying a certain level of intimacy. The woman's assistant, Beryl, is also seen to be having a meeting with a man at the refreshment room. This meeting (he has evidently come to pick Beryl up from work for an evening out) again seems carefree and simple in contrast to that of Laura and Alex who are the only people remaining in the refreshment room at the end of the evening and whose presence is delaying the start of the younger couple's evening out.

What do these relationships add to our understanding of the central relationship between Laura and Alex? In the case of Beryl and the young man, it is possible to draw simple contrasts between an older couple married to other people and a younger, presumably unmarried couple; between the simplicity of the 'legitimate' relationship and the complexity and angst of the 'illegitimate' relationship – for Noel Coward, as screenwriter, the impossibility of illegitimate and clandestine relationships was a recurring theme. The role of the ticket inspector and the café proprietor is less clear though. An extra-marital relationship seems to have benefited the proprietor of the refreshment room, at least financially. There is no clear chastisement for her in the narrative for having left her husband, and this sits uneasily within the narrative, offering a counterpoint to the ending of the central plot.

Would it be too fanciful to make connections between this and ideas about class difference articulated by the Royal Commission on Population, which was established in the same year, or the similar ideas expressed by Beveridge in 1942? As discussed in Chapter Two, there was in both of these a concern that the middle classes (or 'the more successful' as Beveridge called them) needed to act with greater responsibility in relation to family and sexual matters, as the working classes could not be relied upon to behave in a responsible manner.

This is not to suggest that this was Coward's explicit intention – this seems hardly likely. Another reading of the film might suggest that Coward, following in the tradition of Forster and others, was using the idea of a potential extra-marital relationship to explore the wider idea of constraint and the control of desire in a respectable middle-class context. Yet even if Coward's primary concern was the impossibility of certain relationships, it is the impossibility of these relationships within a social context which is important. For Laura and Alex the social context is a middle-class world of duty, responsibility and constraint, the ethos of which was arguably to gain expression in the official discourse of the period which has already been discussed.

The idea that it is possible to make connections between a popular medium and the wider socio-political climate is certainly not new. Commentators on other media of the period have suggested similar connections there. Marjorie Fergusson, writing on women's magazines of the period, goes as far as to suggest that

> women's magazines played their part in . . . putting across postwar social policies such as those enshrined in the Beveridge Report of 1942 which firmly re-located women back in the home.[24]

I would not want to suggest that postwar policies are *enshrined* within popular films of the period – although a case could perhaps be made for this when considering the government's information films. I would argue though that there clearly is some resonance between social policy and popular film.

Here Come the Huggetts (dir. Ken Annakin, 1948) is a useful film for examining this argument. It is a film which is centrally concerned with a south London respectable working-class family who first appeared in Annakin's *Holiday Camp* of the previous year, a film which spawned many sequels on film and television. *Here Come the Huggetts* is the first to focus squarely on the Huggett family themselves. On one level the film is concerned with the everyday lives of a couple with adult or near-adult children, their work, their ways of entertaining themselves, and the ways in which they fit into their extended family and wider community.

The Huggett household comprises Joe Huggett (played by Jack Warner), his wife, Ethel (Kathleen Harrison) and their three daughters, Jayne, Susan and Pet. Although the Huggett family is clearly the central focus of the film, there are two overarching concerns which serve to frame the narrative. These are a debate about marriage and, connected to this, a focus on interlopers and threats to the family, and especially threats to marriages or potential marriages. Underpinning much of this are questions about the proper roles for men and women both within the family and outside.

The subject of marriage is brought up in the opening scene of the film. The discussion is inspired by the forthcoming marriage of Princess Elizabeth, a theme which is returned to throughout the narrative – half of the family go into central London to attempt to see the royal wedding procession – and which is again referred to in the closing scene of the film. This impending marriage is used initially to open discussion on the subject of marriage within the family. One Huggett daughter, Susan, makes a flippant remark about marriage, saying that she thought the main reason for marrying was to receive presents. This allows her mother to reprimand her and alert us to an early key point which the film has to make, which is the seriousness with which marriage needs to be viewed.

A perceived threat to the marriage of the Huggett parents, Joe and Ethel, is a major strand in the film's narrative. This threat is seen through the eyes of their youngest daughter, Pet, and involves the arrival of a cousin, Diana (played by Diana Dors). Pet starts to see her parents' marriage under threat through a series of misinterpretations of conversations and interactions between her father and cousin. She is also influenced by reading a newspaper article entitled 'Marriages on the Rocks – Post War Unrest Leads to Home Breakers Harvest'. Pet is reading this article as her father and cousin Diana are seen coming home from work together, with Diana asking Joe to come up to her bedroom to fix the window. This theme of a threat to this marriage is linked to the theme of external threats posed by interlopers into the family.

The theme of the interloper, which Annakin developed in *Holiday Camp*, can be seen again in *Here Come the Huggetts*. In *Holiday Camp* a crucial character is the sex murderer, who has been described by Marcia Landy as the 'embodiment of threats to the stability of the community' and 'the antithesis of the familial values that the film seeks to promote'.[25] In *Here Come the Huggetts* I would argue that the characters of Diana and Harold, the bookish young man who courts Jayne, embody different but related threats to the family, and can thus be usefully viewed as interlopers.

Although a distant relative, Diana is an immediately visible interloper into the family. With her peroxide hair, her sensuously laid back attitude, her irreverence for work and authority, she is immediately marked out as different from the Huggett daughters and the family in general. Her appearance, her values and her behaviour mark her as other. She is seen to pose two distinct threats to the family. The first is her perceived threat to the Huggett parents' marriage. This, largely a figment of Pet's imagination and unlikely as it may seem, must surely signify the danger associated with the sexually liberated, un-familiar woman. A second threat comes when, after Joe has reluctantly managed to secure Diana a secretarial post at his factory, he is held responsible for her oversights and is demoted. This threatens not only the financial stability of the family but also Joe's self-esteem which is seen to be tied up with the well-being of the family itself. (Intriguingly, Joe is only saved from an outright dismissal because his employer, Mr Campbell, is reluctant to dismiss 'a family man'.)

Although Diana is seen to take advantage of the services of the family – she accepted meals offered by Mrs Huggett, accepts the offer of one of the daughters' bedrooms, and accepted Joe's attempts to gain her a job – she finds the family stifling. She escapes to a pub in the evenings, complaining to a male character, 'I can't stand that Huggett place of an evening – it simply crawls with the family'.

The character of Harold also serves as interloper into the family. Harold is an earnest young man who forms a friendship with Jayne Huggett at the library in which she works. He is constantly reading and has a particular interest in psychology. Jayne has long been engaged to an airman, Jimmy, who has announced his imminent return and desire for an early wedding. Jayne is uncertain, having not seen Jimmy for some time, but is never able to communicate this to him. Harold, in his bookish way, goes about trying to dissuade Jayne from going through with the wedding. He has an obvious desire for Jayne himself which is not made clear to her until late in the narrative.

What is particularly interesting about this is that Harold is seen to attempt to influence Jayne against the idea of marriage *per se*. Even once he has made clear his feelings for her, he is seen to be mealy-mouthed about his intentions. When Jayne asks if he would want her to marry him instead of Jimmy, he is only able to mutter a feeble denial. He describes marriage as 'an archaic survival of a past age', although he seems uncertain in this, as if it is only something learned in a book. Indeed, his character and his reading habits combine to suggest this. Given his persistence in attempting to dissuade Jayne from marriage, it is interesting to see how unsuccessful he is and how he leaves the narrative.

In the closing scenes of the film, Harold's role as outside/interloper is re-emphasised when he appears at the back of the church as Jayne is marrying Jimmy. The sequence of shots does not allow him a benign presence. Rather, his late and furtive appearance, alone and as the couple are in the process of making their vows, is emphasised by the camera shots. Harold is seen sneaking along the pews, his movement emphasised by the static presence of the rest of the cast, as the camera zooms into Jayne and Jimmy making their vows. The film cuts to Harold looking even more furtive and perhaps panicked and then cuts to show two elderly Huggett relatives holding hands as Jayne and Jimmy are saying 'till death us do part'. In the next shot, Harold is seen to leave the church and the film cuts back to Jayne and Jimmy completing their vows. Harold is seen no more. Diana is similarly most obvious for her absence at the wedding, having been imprisoned for slapping a policeman and using bad language, and consequently disappearing from the narrative.

The film is clearly concerned with the state of marriage and the family in the postwar period. Its meditations on the seriousness and importance of marriage as well as its concerns for threats to both individual marriages and the institution of marriage echo the thoughts of the 1947 Denning Report into matrimonial causes, discussed previously, with its expression of the need to raise awareness of the importance of marriage. It also anticipates the thinking in the 1948 Development of Marriage Guidance report's concern for deteriorating standards in marriage.

It would be too simple though to see the film as simply reflecting such official discourse. The film has its own things to say about marriage and deviates from official policy in crucial ways. Most importantly, the idea that marriage should be encouraged for everyone – on which point these reports were in agreement – is not consistent with the logic of the narrative in *Here Come the Huggetts*. The threatening/interloping characters (chiefly Diana and Harold) are not reformed of their views and behaviour in relation to marriage and the family, as might be expected if there was to be a direct correlation between the film and the rhetoric of social policy. Instead, the characters are punished or banished, leaving the central characters to round off the story. Arguably what is happening here is the strengthening of the legitimate family and a marginalising of those who threaten it – a consolidation of the central characters and an abandonment of the peripheral; the apparent universality of social policy rejected in favour of an othering of familial outsiders.

The representation of the nuclear family, and particularly the marriage of the Huggett parents, would have been extremely familiar to the contemporary viewer. The homely domesticity, the sharply divided gender roles and the occasionally bad-tempered paternal authority were reproduced in countless films, not least by Jack Warner himself through his roles in the Huggetts and in the creation of Dixon, first in *The Blue Lamp* (1950) and later in *Dixon of Dock Green*. The Ealing comedies also portrayed this kind of marriage in films like *Passport to Pimlico* (1949) and *Hue and Cry* (1946). Moreover, the Huggett family films were produced alongside similar series featuring the Aldrich family, the Higgins family and the Jones family in a genre recognised at the time as 'family films'. Ken Plummer has described the representation of families of this kind as 'a major story of our times'.[26] In a later period these stories become concerned with 'a family of nostalgia, a family that existed in a "world we have lost"'.

Len England, writing for the Mass-Observation project in 1944, described the genre of the family film and the standardised characters who were to be found within it. He suggested that while the war had produced a number of serious family films, like the American *Mrs Miniver* and the British *Salute John Citizen*, the family genre tended to be lighthearted, ignoring 'the less pleasant aspects of life'.[27] He also identified a number of stereotypes within the family which resonate with the characters in the Huggett films. The father, he writes, 'is usually rather irate and apparently bad-tempered, always offering advice that is not accepted and which turns out to be right . . . always fond of his wife and kids and always doing his best for them.' The mother character, on the other hand, 'is less steadily characterised, but tends to be fluffy and talkative and seemingly frivolous. She is found to have a decided will of her own and usually gets her own way.' There is also usually an older daughter who brings strange men into the home. England also notes that marriage is particularly romanticised, and that marital crises, where they happen, are 'never really unpleasant' and are ultimately resolved.

There are echoes, too, of this depiction of family life in some of the Ministry of Information films which the government produced in the war years and beyond. While some of these films challenged conventional gender roles (for example through the support for young women's war work in the factory and in the field), others portrayed the apotheosis of divided gender roles through serious films like *They Also Serve*, dedicated to 'the housewives of Britain' and comic shorts such as the Food Flash series on 'Expectant Fathers'.[28]

It is tempting to see a direct contrast between this kind of sharply gender-divided marriage – which is represented in British New Wave films by the marriages of Arthur Seaton's parents in *Saturday Night and Sunday Morning* and by Joe Lampton's aunt and uncle in *Room at the Top* – and the gritty realism of the marriages of the younger generation of characters in British New Wave. Yet there are examples of a kind of realism in earlier films, for example in *It Always Rains on Sunday* (dir. Robert Hamer, 1947) in which the infidelity, the economic deals of marriage and the claustrophobia of the home are dealt with against a backdrop of a working-class London emerging from the war. The popular images of the marriages and families are, though, not best represented by Googie Withers and Edward Chapman in *It Always Rains on Sunday*, but by Jack Warner and Kathleen Harrison, the most popular of their contemporaries.

The messages about marriage in the films of the British New Wave and social problem films are not as immediately clear as they are in *Here Come the Huggetts* or *Brief Encounter*. Certainly, wider possibilities – extra-marital (including pre-marital) relationships, separations etc. – are represented. In drawing comparisons again with women's magazines of the period, we can see a number of contrasts. As Marjorie Fergusson has shown, pre-marital sex was 'strictly taboo' in popular women's magazines until the early 1970s with 'the rewards of repression and the punishment of promiscuity relentlessly reinforced . . . virginity and monogamy were two cultural ideals slow to vanish'.[29] Yet if we compare a contemporary novel, for example Colin McInnes's *Absolute Beginners*, yet another set of images about marriage and the family emerge. The family ('if you can call it that'[30]) in *Absolute Beginners*, according to the narrator, consists of himself, his parents, his half-brother 'plus numerous additions', by which we are meant to understand the lodgers who temporarily live with the rest of the family and who are presumed to be his mother's lovers. The miserable state of his parents' marriage is a constant and accepted fact for which no resolutions are offered.

Clearly both the extent and form of discussion about marriage, sexuality and the family in these various media are specific to each. The films of the British New Wave, like their French counterparts, do have a radical reputation and certainly many of those involved in their making had radical or liberal aspirations.[31] It is too simple though to see these films as wholly radical and undermining of convention. While individual marriages may be threatened within the narratives, with the possible exception of *A Taste of Honey*, the place of marriage as an institution seems barely contested. Furthermore, where marriages are threatened, the threats are resolved and/ or the characters punished.

In the few examples in which this is not so, a similar message nonetheless can be understood. In *The Leather Boys* there is no resolution to the threat to Dot and Reggie's marriage and neither character is punished. However, the film's main concern is early and hasty marriage and the need to take seriously the decision to marry. Dot and Reggie, who are 16 and 17, respectively, are shown to approach marriage with very little thought, ignoring the advice of the schoolteacher who warns them against such an early marriage in the opening scenes of the film. That their marriage should fail and be unresolved is therefore within the logic of the film, and is arguably compatible with the respect and concern for marriage which is in evidence in other films of this genre. The uncertain resolution to Vic and Ingrid's marriage in *A Kind of Loving* can similarly be related to their hasty decision to marry as a result of a pre-marital pregnancy.

Yet to accuse these film-makers of merely delivering up an ultimately conventional set of endings may be too harsh. The genre actively engages with notions of realism and the endings perhaps reflect a pragmatic acceptance of the constraints and culturally limited options available to the characters in the situations in which they find themselves. As Bert tells Arthur in *Saturday Night and Sunday Morning*, 'you've got to get married sometime . . . That's how things are, Arthur, there's no use going crackers over it'. This philosophy may well be as ingrained as the one which tells us that, in *A Taste of Honey*, Helen, the wayward mother, is still a more appropriate living companion for Jo as she prepares to give birth, than is the domesticated and reliable Geoff whose slinking away in the final scenes occurs without protest. David Morgan has theorised something similar when considering how and to what extent dominant ideas are disseminated from elites to non-elites. He has argued that,

> if, as would seem to be the case in matters to do with marriage and the family, non-elite members continue to give silent or vocal endorsement to the wider social order, this may not be a consequence of ideological indoctrination but through the 'dull compulsion' of everyday economic life. In the case of marriage and the family, this may be translated in terms of the relative lack of viable alternatives.[32]

On a more practical level, the film-makers had also to contend with the British Board of Film Classification. This set of films appeared at the same time as, and were instrumental in defining the limits of, the new X-rated certificate.[33]

Just as the interloper into the family fares badly in *Here Come the Huggetts* and *Brief Encounter*, so a similar fate tends to await them in British New Wave. Those who transgress the boundaries of marriage tend similarly to be severely dealt with. In particular, married women who have extra-marital affairs tend not to fare well in working-class realism. Alice Aisgill commits suicide in *Room at the Top*, while Brenda faces a back-street abortion in *Saturday Night and Sunday Morning* before returning submissively to her husband. Dot loses all chance of a reconciliation with Reggie after being found in bed with another man. Even the young single men around whom the narratives tend to revolve are shown to live out the consequences of pre-marital sexual relations which result in enforced responsibility, chastisement and/or punishment. Vic marries Ingrid in *A Kind of Loving*, Arthur is severely beaten in *Saturday Night and Sunday Morning*, and Joe's fate is sealed in *Room at the Top* by Susan's pregnancy. Homosexual characters appear from and return to the margins, thwarted, frustrated and alone, unless, like Melville Farr, they constrain themselves within a sterile marriage.

The Swinging Sixties

Although the films of the British New Wave precede the 'permissive moment' by a good few years, clearly the laws which are enacted in the mid to late

1960s period are themselves preceded by debate in the late 1950s and early 1960s of which those films are a part. The set of films known as Swinging London are perhaps more clearly identified with this permissive moment. (In his *Sixties British Cinema*, Robert Murphy has a subsection on the permissive society within his chapter on Swinging London.) As has been argued in previous chapters, the concept of the permissive society is one which is open to debate, and one which encompasses a number of contradictions. Arguably these contradictions manifest themselves in the films which attempt to deal with Swinging London.

Alfie, released in 1966, explores a certain kind of contemporary masculinity, but also explores the results of actions. This owes much to working-class realism and indeed the character of Alfie Elkins is arguably the apotheosis of the kind of masculinity suggested by British New Wave.[34] While it is masculinity and sexuality which are the film's most obvious concerns, ideas about the family are necessarily inscribed within the narrative. Alfie's lifestyle is the antithesis of familial and domestic life, and on the occasions where he is presented with the opportunity to settle down (especially with Gilda, with whom he has a child), Alfie actively refuses. Throughout most of the film, marriage and domestic life, where they are represented, are seen to be dull and safe, or practical and hollow: Gilda finally accepts a safe offer of marriage from the character of Humphrey, because the stability he offers is in direct contrast to the excitement and unpredictability of Alfie, to whom she is genuinely attracted. Lily and Harry's marriage is presented as dull and predictable until Lily begins her affair with Alfie, shattering the veneer of stability and comfort which marriage had been suggested to offer.

The film ends with two sombre themes, though, the first of which suggests that transgressing the conventional boundaries of relationships has its price to pay, while the second undermines the positive representations of Alfie's lifestyle and the negative representations of marriage, which have been dominant in the film up to that point. Firstly there are the abortion scenes, in which Alfie and Lily are punished for their affair. Not only do we see how harrowing the experience is for Lily, but direct contrasts are set up between this scene and the scenes of the baptism of Alfie's son by Gilda with which the abortion scenes are intercut. Alfie chances upon this happy family scene – Gilda is now shown to be happy and relaxed in her marriage to Humphrey – at precisely the same moment that Lily's pregnancy is being terminated. Secondly, just as Alfie, immediately after this experience, has resolved to settle down with Ruby (the older woman with whom he has been having an affair) he finds that the transient lifestyle backfires on him, as Ruby has found another, younger man. As the film ends, Alfie is left to profoundly question his way of life.

Georgy Girl, released in the same year, is 'an old-fashioned story of how a plain but good-hearted girl takes over her flatmate's husband (temporarily) and baby (permanently) and finds a kind of happiness with an ageing admirer'.[35] We are shown several different kinds of household and relationship in the film. The first of these is a representation which draws upon older notions of the family/household. The character James is head of a household in which he lives with his frail wife and the manservant who is Georgy's father. Georgy has been brought up in this house and, although she also has a flat of her own which she shares with her friend Meredith, she is a frequent visitor to the house and is still very much part of the family. Her father's employer has paid for Georgy's education and takes a keen interest in her life. We also see the flat which Georgy and Meredith share and from which they, and particularly Meredith, experience some of what Swinging London has to offer. Meredith, who has an initially flippant and later disdainful view of marriage and children, falls pregnant and marries Josh who moves in to share the flat too. Josh and Georgy make preparations for the birth of the child while Meredith becomes increasingly withdrawn and alienated from the experience of pregnancy and marriage. Once the baby girl is born, she is abandoned by her mother and left to the care of Josh and Georgy who begin a new relationship with each other. This relationship is short-lived and eventually James, who has been propositioning Georgy throughout the film, appears at the end to offer her marriage and a home for her and the child. The film ends with the scene of James and Georgy framed in a church doorway on their wedding day.

The film's ending can be read as conforming to convention and clearly has a lot in common with both the earlier British New Wave films and with *Alfie*, where a baptism rather than a wedding forms one of the ending scenes. The narrative does, however, include a number of unconventional elements which are suggestive of an altogether more liberating discourse. Robert Murphy has suggested that although Meredith is ultimately viewed with disapproval by the film, her defiance of the conventions of marriage 'is not quite snuffed out' by this disapproval.[36] Furthermore, it is only once she is married and expecting a child that the disapproval of her free and easy attitude to sex and relationships becomes evident. Georgy also transgresses the usual codes of behaviour in beginning an affair with her friend's husband, for which the narrative can hardly be seen to punish her. In this way, the film may ultimately be more in tune with a film like *Joanna* than *Alfie*. *Joanna*, which appeared two years later, in 1968, is set around one of Swinging London's main areas, Chelsea's King's Road. Sexual promiscuity is explored without the severe reprimands for characters and an interracial relationship between Joanna, the magistrate's daughter and a black nightclub owner is portrayed in what must have been neutral terms for the period.

Of course, most of London was not swinging, and a backlash to the Swinging London genre appeared which owed much to the working-class realism of the British New Wave. A most obvious connection between the two is made with *Life at the Top*, the sequel to *Room at the Top*. Here Lawrence Harvey's character, Joe Lampton, leaves his wife Susan to (unsuccessfully) pursue a new relationship with a swinging character represented by Honor Blackman, playing a BBC television reporter. The more powerful narratives centre on the plight of working-class Londoners in unfashionable parts of the city. The work of Ken Loach and Nell Dunn stands out here, as work with a particular cultural resonance.

The narrative in Loach's *Cathy Come Home* – which was described as 'the shocking story of our times which caused nationwide controversy when shown twice on BBC tv'[37] – is concerned with the falling apart of a particular family. The film explores the reasons for this breakdown, and focuses less on personal morality than on the material circumstances that bring about this state of affairs. The breakdown of this family is clearly seen to have economic, environmental and political causes. Responsibility is seen to lie with government and welfare authorities.

Poor Cow (1967), written by Dunn and directed and Loach, is concerned primarily with how human (and particularly female) sexuality is problematically contained within the ideal of monogamous marriage and the wider realities of material life. The central character, Joy, is played by Carol White, who also starred in *Cathy Come Home*. We see her giving birth to her first child in the opening scene and soon enter into her domestic world with husband, child and home. Her husband Tom earns a living through crime and is imprisoned early on in the narrative. We watch Joy as she begins her first and short-lived extra-marital relationship while Tom is in prison, and as she starts to discover her own sexuality she comes to realise she needs 'different men to satisfy different moods'.

Other aspects of female sexuality are explored in the film through the characters of Joy's Aunt Emm and Beryl, a woman Joy works with in a local pub. Aunt Emm educated Joy in the material need for women in their situation to have a man. She also shows how sex can be used to get her out of difficult situations, like paying the landlord 'in kind' when she is unable to find enough money for the rent. Beryl has a carefree attitude to prostitution and modelling, which she shares freely with Joy.

Both *Cathy Come Home* and *Poor Cow* show that an active socialist voice was to be heard within the mainstream of British film and television, commenting on marriage, relationships and the family, and, especially in the case of *Cathy Come Home*, intervening in the debates around the moral decline of the family to put forward an alternative case.

In conclusion

What, then, can we say about the representation of the family as a cultural construction in the examples shown? Certain differences are clearly evident over time and between genres. But equally, differences are discernible within genre, and certain continuities are also in evidence over time and between genres. The films of the British New Wave are pivotal in that they show representations, particularly of ordinary locations and working-class people, which had barely been seen on the screen before. Sometimes the representations of domestic life and relationships seems unduly hampered by convention in ways that later films do not. Yet in raising this criticism we need be aware of the exigencies of both the film industry and the broader culture through and into which the films were released. Furthermore the differences in representation between the British New Wave and Swinging London films are tempered by continuities which unite them with each other and at times with yet older films.

A fairly consistent theme within the examples discussed is, not withstanding exceptions, the primacy of one-to-one relationships, marriage and the nuclear family in the narrative and a repetition of stories about problems in and threats to these primary concerns. Equally consistent are resolutions to such threats and problems in which marriage and the nuclear family emerge perhaps battered but fundamentally unchallenged. Finally, the extended family tends to be represented here on the margins of the narrative, though it is possible to read the narratives of the British New Wave as showing the extended family in a more supportive and morally guiding role than is usually suggested.

Another safe conclusion to make is that, as there are differences and similarities between films on this subject, so there are differences and similarities between film and other media. This means that talking about, for example, a single 1950s image of the family in popular media makes no sense. There are different and competing images of the family, with particular forms of popular media offering their own realms of possibilities. The taboo of pre-marital sex for popular women's magazines may be bread-and-butter material for screenwriter and novelists. Similarly, the limits of what it is possible to discuss and publish in written form may be different from what is possible within the film industry. Many of the films discussed here were adapted from novels and stageplays in which tone and content were different.

There is also clearly some relationship between popular film and official discourse. Again, individual film-makers will make a difference here. In the examples discussed, the relationship between film and official discourse ranges from Ken Annakin's airing of official (and, it must be said, popular) concerns about the state of marriage as an institution in *Here Come the Huggetts*, to Ken Loach and Nell Dunn's exploration of sexuality and the impossible constraints of marriage in *Poor Cow*, or Loach's counterattack on the state and social services for their role in undermining certain families in *Cathy Come Home*. The relationship between popular film and official discourse in connection with ideas about the family will be returned to in Chapter Six.

CHAPTER FIVE

'Relatively speaking'

Family, experience, memory

Chapters Two and Three were concerned with national and local government policy and discourse relating to the family, while Chapter Four looked at the representation of family in British film of the period. In this chapter I want to develop a third and final research strand which will address the *experience* of 'family', that is, how family and domestic life was lived out and made sense of by people at that time. Now, analysing the experience of family is in many ways a simple idea. Having researched one aspect of the ideas about the family, through analysis of official discourse and the representation of family in a mass medium, there is a simple logic to seeing how such ideas are assimilated, (re)produced or resisted in everyday life. And for the period 1945 to 1970, and to obtain a representative sample, oral histories are an obvious primary source. However, working with oral sources necessitates engaging with a set of debates in oral history, particularly around the cultural construction of memory, the subjectivity of the interviewee and interviewer, and the form and content of the oral text. The simple idea of collecting examples of experience is complicated by the need to acknowledge that experience can only be related (in oral history or elsewhere) through present-day memory, and that memory as a source is itself highly contested.

This complication has produced one tension which has been at the heart of debate in oral history since at least the early 1980s. On the one hand there is the desire to uncover, reclaim and give voice to marginalised experience. On the other there are new theoretical debates about the cultural production of memory and subjectivity which focus largely on questions of language and form. Some oral historians – Elizabeth Roberts, for example, in her study of families in the 1940–70 period[1] – choose not to address these issues. I, though, believe we need to look in some detail at this tension and these debates in coming to some conclusions about how to proceed with this strand on experience and memory.

Oral history: democracy, recovery, empowerment

In a recent article in *Oral History*, Alistair Thompson referred to 'the democratic aspirations of oral history as a practice which recovers hidden histories and empowers people to make their own history'.[2] Few would argue that this has been a central tenet of oral history from the start. Oral history as a field of study (and as a way of thinking about the past) emerged alongside the new social history of the 1960s and 1970s. There was a consensus that its concerns were with the ordinary, the everyday, with a 'bottom-up history'. This meant not only that new subjects for historical concern were found – the working class and women in particular – but that new kinds of questions about the past were being asked which challenged existing paradigms in both professional and popular notions of history.

The new oral history had its detractors, especially in the professional field. Doubts were raised over the validity of oral accounts, over the reliability of memory. One now infamous review of Paul Thompson's *The Edwardians*, by Stephen Koss in the *Times Literary Supplement* from 1975, encapsulated many of these scepticisms:

> Over the years certain memories have faded or, at the very least may have been influenced by subsequent experience. How many of their childhood recollections were in fact recalled to them by their elders? What autobiographies or novels might they have since read that would reinforce certain impressions at the expense of others? What films or tv programmes have had an impact on their consciousness? . . . More generally, to what extent might the rise of the Labour Party in the post war decade have inspired retrospective perceptions of class status and conflict?[3]

Defences of oral history were made in the light of such criticism, notably by Paul Thompson, drawing upon other disciplines such as psychology and sociology. Methods of representative sampling were adopted alongside theories of the regularity in patterns of remembering and forgetting in order to make sources less vulnerable to attack. As important, questions were again raised about the reliability and objectivity of other, more conventional historical sources. Despite this, it is fair to say that some suspicion has lingered and the use and the objectivity of oral sources are still called into question.[4]

Oral history: memory, subjectivity, theory

For some theorists, this scepticism over the reliability of memory and the objectivity of oral history offered a fresh and exciting starting point for an all together more rigorous understanding of both memory and oral history. For the Popular Memory Group at the Centre for Contemporary Cultural Studies in Birmingham, Paul Thompson's early efforts at defending oral history were misguided. This group instead embraced the criticisms that had been levelled at oral history:

> From the point of view of the study of popular memory or of cultural pheno-mena generally, empiricist methods (whether the 'administered questionnaire' or the empiricist interrogation of the source) are of very little value. We might say, indeed, that *the study of popular memory can begin only where empiricist and positivist norms break down.* The alternative and stronger responses to Koss-like criticisms of oral history are, then, as follows: yes, indeed, memory and its narratives *are* cultural constructions in much the same way that your histories are. To illuminate both, and especially to help popular memory to a consciousness of itself, requires an understanding of specifically cultural processes and particularly of the making and remaking of memory, on both an individual and social level. In this way your 'problem' becomes our 'resource', your insuperable difficulty our agendum, your closure our starting-point.[5]

It must be said that there were concerns that this kind of theoretical positioning could, perhaps inadvertently, lead to elitist oral histories, with the theory becoming more important than the content of histories. Some oral history practitioners saw the language of radical theory reproducing the earlier attacks on oral history's reliability.[6] Others took up the challenges presented by such new theoretical discussion, acknowledging the relative naivety of some earlier oral history work. Reflecting on this, Raphael Samuel and Paul Thompson in their introduction to the edited collection of papers from the International Oral History Conference in 1987, write of early oral history

> practising a naive realism – at least until Luisa Passerini and Ron Grele began to challenge us – [which] was all but taken for granted. Inspired by the very abundance of the newly discovered sources in living memory which we had opened up, we made a fetish of everydayness, using 'thick' description, in the manner suggested by anthropologists, to reconstitute the small detail of domestic life: but we had little to say about dream-thoughts and the hidden sexuality of family relationships.[7]

More radically, oral historian Joan Sangster has recently called for an oral history enlightened by post-structuralist insights. Writing from a feminist perspective, she suggests that, 'asking why and how women explain, rationalise and make sense of their past offers insight into the social and material framework within which they operated, the perceived cultural patterns they faced and the complex relationship between individual consciousness and culture'.[8] We are urged by Sangster to consider how the influences of class, gender, culture or political worldview on memory can be seen in both the content and narrative form of the interview and furthermore to contextualise oral histories by surveying the dominant ideologies shaping interviewees' worlds.

None of this is to suggest that the embracing of a more rigorous theoretical basis need supplant the original democratic aspirations of oral history. Joan Sangster argues forcibly for a feminist oral history enlightened by post-structuralist insights but firmly grounded in a materialist–feminist context. Similarly, Samuel and Thompson in discussing the 'naive realism' of early oral history and the more recently theorised oral history, suggest that we do not have to choose one and jettison the other.

Methodological note

I need, then, to clarify my own position within these debates and to set out my principles of analysis. The work here owes more to the tradition of the Popular Memory Group than it does to the more rigorous empiricism of Paul Thompson's work in the period after the criticisms articulated by Stephen Koss. I have found it particularly useful to ask what sets of meanings are available from the oral texts I have collected. In essence, I see two distinct (though not exclusive) meanings from which my analysis will be drawn. Firstly, these memories contain ideas about and evidence of the 1945–70 period. They offer valuable information about families in that period which it would be difficult to gain from any other sources. Secondly, the tapes are my contemporary cultural products containing the memories of the past which existed for individuals on that day, produced in the particular circumstances of the interview. Information about the 1945–70 period can only be given here through the memory of individuals, and this memory is shaped by interviewees' subjectivity and culture, and is produced within contemporary culture. As primary sources, oral sources need to be understood in both of these ways. My analysis must be made within the dynamic set up by the two.

I believe that the oral evidence presented here gives voice to some of those people who were experiencing day-to-day domestic life at that time, and who had their own senses of 'family'. In this sense this oral history does seek to 'recover hidden histories', and in this way the oral accounts do contain evidence of life in the 1940s, 1950s and 1960s. However, this cannot be a simple exercise in showing the lived reality as opposed to the fictional accounts in contemporary film or the idealised and highly politicised versions of family life discussed by official bodies. Memory will be influenced by present-day subjectivity, by current debates and intervening experience, amongst other things. This means that the oral texts need to be thought about broadly and holistically and to be read in a number of ways. For example, as the subject of the family (and in particular its frailty and decline) has persisted as a crucial issue in many discourses, I need to be aware that what interviewees may have to say about their memories of family and domestic life is said within the context of these current and ongoing debates. This is not about treating the memories as unreliable; it is about appreciating their richness and complexity as sources.

The main sources used here are oral histories collected since 1991. Geographically, the focus is on what was the Metropolitan Borough of Woolwich and its immediate environs. Sources have been selected to be representative of gender, class and age. There is some ethnic diversity amongst interviewees – Scottish, Welsh, Jewish, as well as English – but ethnic difference is not directly addressed.[9] I have attempted to interview a sample of people who are broadly representative of the class diversity of the area in the period, though no sophisticated methods of representative sampling were used. Broadly, the interviewees fall into two age groups, though at the margins these begin to overlap. The oldest interviewee was born in 1912, the youngest in 1941 so two generations are represented. The first group includes those born before 1930 and who became adult and, for the majority, married before or during the Second World War. These are Betty (b. 1912), Gerald (b. 1915), Ted (b. 1916), Doug (b. 1916), Les (b. 1917), Irene (b. 1919) and Elsie (b. 1922). The second group, those born in or after 1930, include Yvonne (b. 1930), Anne (b. 1933), Sheila (b. 1936), Martin (b. 1937), Jim (b. 1938), Helen (b. 1939) and Christine (b. 1941).

The interviewees were found mostly through mainstream social organisations for older people – social groups, 'pop-in' centres and reminiscence groups, though some were university students and staff connected to the Popular Memory unit at the University of Greenwich. I have tried to be aware of how the selection of interviewees may have impacted upon the memories collected and consequently upon the analysis which is made.

A set of questions was produced to structure the interviews (see appendix). Aside from basic biographical detail, I focused on the following areas of enquiry: who was seen to be included in 'family' and the nature of extended family relationships; ideas about marriage and marital roles; gender and work inside and outside the home; and ideas about 'the decline of the family'. These areas were chosen not only to interact particularly with ideas in evidence in official discourse and policy (specifically the family wage, the gender division of labour, and the 'decline' of family life) but also to engage with ideas about the family which seemed to be absent in official discourse, such as the significance of extended families. Questions about the idea of the decline of the family were framed in a way to invite discussion of the legislation of consent and its impact upon family life in the period, although few interviewees mentioned this having much direct impact on their own lives.[10]

The question sheets produced were intended to act as a guide for a semi-structured interview rather than as a means to gaining statistically significant data. Although I have not adopted sophisticated methods of representative sampling, nor do I attempt to produce statistically significant data, I have not abandoned the empirical tools altogether and do seek to write about significant patterns which emerge from the oral material.

Clearly the evidence found and the patterns which emerged in the oral texts are reliant, at least in part, on the questions asked. Other incidental information, however, which I had not sought directly to uncover, emerged from the oral evidence (such as the gendered nature of responses), and this information has been included for analysis. In analysing this information, I noted the various responses and themes which emerged from individual tapes as they were transcribed. Once each tape and transcription had been analysed in this way, I began to note the patterns of responses formed, and these patterns shaped the presentation of the oral evidence. I have therefore organised the remembered experience of interviewees around four main themes: the ways in which people seem to have negotiated prevalent ideas about domesticity; gender difference in remembered experience; memories about the extended family; and ideas about the 'decline' of 'the family'.

It seemed initially that sources, especially the diaries, from the Mass Observation archive at the University of Sussex might make useful comparisons with the oral material I had collected. Of all the Mass Observation material, though evidently primary material from a different period, the diaries are most similar to oral histories, being personal accounts by a variety of individuals of their daily experiences. Furthermore, as with the oral accounts from the London Borough of Greenwich, diarists were encouraged to record their own responses to situations and to recount their own life experiences rather than recount the news stories of the day.[11] Much of the other work of Mass Observation was concerned with the pre-1945 period (the Worktown Project, the Day Surveys, Time Charts and Directive Replies), while the archive holds diary entries from 1939 to 1963. A wide range of people contributed to this archive which includes the writings of some 500 diarists. However, as Angus Calder and Dorothy Sheridan point out, after 1945 most of the contributors discontinued their diaries with only a few carrying on into the postwar years.[12] Further enquiries into these remaining few revealed that none had lived in the Metropolitan Boroughs of Woolwich or Greenwich, and indeed the archivist could find none from the pre-1945 period either. This information led me to question the usefulness of the Mass Observation sources for this study, and eventually to the elimination of the Mass Observation archive as a source for comparative analysis.

Remembered experience of family

Negotiating prevalent domestic ideas

The oral evidence suggests that there was diverse negotiation of prevalent domestic ideas amongst those interviewed. There is some evidence of people accepting prevalent ideas unquestioningly, though there is less evidence of people actively resisting them. More strikingly, there is much evidence that the particular circumstances of people's lives necessitated patterns of behaviour which ran against the grain of prevalent ideas. Here there is less a sense of active resistance to prevalent ideas than a sense of adapting one's own life to fit circumstances in spite of these. I will consider each of these responses to prevalent ideas, but it is the latter and most common response that will concern me most.

One area in which prevalent ideas were noticeably unquestioned by many interviewees was in considering marriage and marital roles. Anne was born in the early 1930s in South Africa of Anglo-Scottish parents. She emigrated to England in 1957, and as a child she had always expected to get married: 'No one ever thought of not getting married in those days.' She trained to be a nurse, though before finishing the training she had to take six months off with an injury. In this six months she met and married her husband. Returning to the training after marriage was not seen as an option for her: 'In South Africa, once you were married you weren't allowed to carry on with your training . . . so naturally I thought the same rules applied here.'

Gerald, born in Charlton in 1915, was also asked if he had always expected to get married:

Oh yes, yes. I wanted a good stable family life and as I say I met my wife when we were quite young – 17 and 14 – and that was when we were looking forward to being together all the time.

He also had clear ideas about their roles in the marriage:

> Then it was the man was the provider and I had that in my mind that my wife would not go to work when I married. I was going to provide for her and take care of her. It was a principle in those days. You married to take care of somebody.
>
> *Interviewer*: So would it have been against a principle or would it have seemed wrong for a wife to have worked?
>
> Oh yes, that would have been quite wrong then. I would never have approved – well you are being kept by a woman or being helped and that wouldn't suit me one little bit, still wouldn't.
>
> *Interviewer*: Would other people have felt it strange as well?
>
> That was the opinion of most people I should say in those days, most people.

Gerald's mother had had 12 children of which he was the youngest. She had not worked outside the home: 'not with all those kids she couldn't, no.' A generation later, in the 1930s, Martin's mother left her job on the birth of her first child: 'Of course she gave up work and never worked again, not externally anyway.' After this, Martin's mother had taken responsibility for the home. He could not remember his father doing housework while he lived at home.

Elsie, born in Woolwich in 1921, had also always expected to get married. In fact, when asked this question in the interview, she seemed puzzled that it should be asked at all. As a child she had also accepted that, as her mother was ill, it was her responsibility to look after her father and brothers:

> So you know I've not really had an easy life because before that I brought five brothers up. My mother was always ill so I just had to do everything for those . . . all [were] younger except one and my father didn't believe in, you know, having anybody in to help. I was the girl and I had to do it. I had a sister but she had heart trouble and she died at 18 so she couldn't do anything at all, so it was not only nursing her but it was looking after the five boys as well, see, so I didn't have an easy life but, as I say, I survived.
>
> *Interviewer*: But it was expected that you, as the girl, would be the one to look after them? Would it be all the cooking, all the cleaning?
>
> Everything. Washing, cooking, cleaning. And in them days they used to have a thing what they called bagwash. You used to put all the stuff in the bag and sent it out to be washed, and I said to my father 'Can I?' and he said, 'No, you are the girl you do the washing'. He wouldn't allow us to do anything

like that. I used to have to go to work, come home and do the washing, do the cooking, do the cleaning, so I never got much time to myself.

Interviewer: What age would this have been from?

From about the age of 7.

The evidence from remembered experience suggests little active or conscious rejection of prevalent domestic ideas amongst those interviewed. It is possible to speculate that this may have something to do with the mainstream social centres in which interviewees were found, or the fact that interviewees were self-selecting. It may be that in such settings, broadly conventional stories are easier to tell. Certainly, evidence of the active and conscious rejection of prevalent domestic ideas has been found elsewhere, for example in some of the interviews collected in the Hall–Carpenter Archive, which represents the memories of some people living outside of and sometimes consciously rejecting heterosexual norms.[13]

However, while the majority of interviewees did not actively resist or reject prevalent domestic ideas, circumstances often led them to adapt ideas to fit what was possible, necessary or desirable in their own lives. Elsie, quoted above, did not seem to question that she should have been expected to do all the housework in her parental home. (As such, her experience seems to run contrary to Janet Finch's demonstration that family responsibilities are essentially negotiated between individuals and are dependent on reciprocity.[14]) Neither did she express any determination for things to be different in her marital home. However, when she married, she and her husband shared domestic work. The reason she gives for this is not any conscious rejection of prevalent ideas, rather it is described as a product of circumstance and chance:

Oh, we used to share all the housework, yes, and I will tell you another incidence. My mother came down one day, and he was washing my baby's napkins and she said to me, 'You ought to be ashamed of yourself, letting that man do that washing.' She said, 'That is your job, you shouldn't be letting him do that,' and he came in and he said, 'Alright, Mum, I'm a motor mechanic and I want to get my hands clean,' so that passed off, but this is the way they were . . . Oh yes, my husband used to help out with all the chores. See my mother had never seen anything like that because my husband, his father died when he was only 14, and he had left four and he used to help his Mum do all the work and everything. See that's the difference in two families.

Helen tells how in her parental home in the 1940s and 1950s

things were a little different because my mother was ill quite a lot when we were children so therefore my father did a great deal of the shopping and the washing and the cleaning and that sort of thing . . . He even learned to plait hair, somewhat painfully, but he did a lot of the work, I must admit. He was a very good cook – my mother taught him, but as children we were expected to do quite a few chores indoors.

Christine also tells of her father doing substantial domestic work in the 1940s and 1950s. Her explanation for this is that her father had had to do domestic work in his parental home, as the family was so large:

My own father, because he came from a great big family – there used to be about ten or eleven of them – he didn't . . . when they married my Dad used to help my Mum. He did cooking, he helped do the cleaning, he helped bath us and do all the things men do today – a lot of men do today.

This contrasted sharply with Christine's husband's experience in his parental home and his early expectations of marriage. As Christine explains,

John, being an only child, was spoilt at home so his Mum did everything. She would get his clothes out. Well, when we got married I started doing that, and then I thought 'What the hell am I doing? It's like having a child' and I hadn't got a child, and I don't want one yet either, and I stopped doing it, and he used to say, 'Where's my pants?' and I would say, 'In that drawer' or 'In that cupboard', and he started to do more things.

Before the Second World War, Sheila's father had worked on the railways, and her mother had worked in the home. During the war, her mother went to work in a munitions factory, while her father was invalided out of the army. After the war, her mother continued to work and her father continued to stay at home, taking care of domestic duties. Sheila believes this suited both of her parents well, as her mother was much more keen on working outside of the home than her father was, and her father was content to stay at home.

Although these examples suggest a number of families were negotiating the prevalent domestic ideas to suit their own needs and preferences, I believe that evidence from the oral material points to these negotiations taking place very clearly within the framework of dominant ideas. Firstly, it might be noted that interviewees tended to refer to their fathers or husbands 'helping' in the home (Elsie, Christine, Gerald, Helen), the implication being that domestic work, while shared, was the woman's responsibility. Of the examples quoted above, one interviewee did not refer to her father as 'helping' in the home – Sheila refers to her father 'doing most of the work' in the home while her mother worked outside of the home. Her way of explaining this is interesting, though as she says 'in a way [her mother] became the male of the family', thereby explaining the deviation from gender roles as the adoption of different gender identities by her parents. At the same time, women's work outside of the home is referred to by a number of interviewees (Christine, Gerald, Doug) as 'having a little job', again suggesting that this work is not to be seen as significant.

It is also noticeable that where fathers in particular 'helped' with housework, this was seen by many interviewees (Sheila, Christine, Elsie, Helen) as unusual. Christine thought her father 'a rarity'. Helen thought her parents' domestic arrangement 'a little different', while Sheila thought her parents' arrangement 'quite unusual'. It might also be that in some cases there was a certain stigma attached to men working in the home. Helen remembers her uncles' reaction to her father's doing housework:

> His brothers used to have a go at him when we were quite small children. I can remember, sort of, uncles taking the mickey out of my father and sending him aprons for his birthday and things like that.

It has already been noted that Elsie's parents disapproved of her allowing her husband to participate in domestic duties. Helen similarly remembers an incident which occurred with her mother-in-law soon after she married her husband in 1965:

> When my husband and I got married, I can remember having a dreadful row with my mother-in-law. She came round for dinner one Sunday and we had only been married a few months and she said, 'Where's Terry?' and I said, 'Oh he's in the garden cleaning the shoes' and she nearly had a fit. 'My son's never cleaned shoes in his life!' She was horrified.

There is also a certain amount of disagreement between different interviewees on what might generally have been acceptable or expected at different times. Doug and Gerald, who were both married in the late 1930s, said it was usual and expected for wives not to do paid work. Betty and Elsie, both of whom worked for money in the 1940s, 1950s and 1960s, and Yvonne whose mother had worked outside of the home in the 1940s and 1950s disagree, saying there was nothing unusual in married women working outside the home at that time. Sheila, Christine and Martin all commented on how keen their mothers had been to take up paid employment in the same period. At this time, only Martin seems to have thought it was natural for his mother to have given up her job on the birth of her children.

How can we begin to comment on these differences? Perhaps class made a difference. Maybe for women of the middle and lower middle class it was less acceptable to work outside of the home for money – in the case of Martin, his father had a white-collar job in a local bank. It could also be that the type of work undertaken by women for money also helped determine the acceptability of that work. Betty ran a grocery shop, living with her husband and children in the same building, while her husband went out to work. Irene's mother had taught music from home, thereby earning money but not working outside the home.

However, simple explanations such as these will not explain all the differences. For each of the cases mentioned there are an equal number which defy such explanation. Yvonne's family may have been lower middle class, but her mother was determined to work outside of the home, even though her husband disapproved. Gerald and Doug who strongly disapproved of their wives working came from the same class background and lived in the same area as Elsie who remembers that it was acceptable and not unusual for married women to work outside the home.

It might be that the different memories suggest that people wish to remember their actions and thoughts as usual and reasonable. The man who remembers discouraging or not allowing his wife to work outside of the home might like to believe that this was normal and acceptable at the time. The woman who worked outside of the home in spite of the presence of such feeling may like to look back and see that she did not behave unusually. It is possible to relate this to the idea of subjects' attempting to achieve 'composure' – both in composing their own story and in attempting to find composure within themselves – which has been developed by Graham Dawson.[15] Dawson points out that composing stories about oneself is a deeply embedded cultural practice on many levels and that an important part of such storytelling is the development of an 'acceptable' version of the self among the many versions of the story that could be told. This acceptable version 'is a version of the self which can be lived with in relative psychic comfort, to enable, in other words, subjective composure to be achieved'.[16] And, perhaps, as Samuel and Thompson have commented, 'life, in short, is conceptualized teleologically'.[17]

Gendered memories

In *Family Fortunes*, the groundbreaking work on the world of the English middle classes in the nineteenth century, feminist historians Leonore Davidoff and Catherine Hall argue that gender is a crucial category of historical investigation. This idea is echoed and applied specifically to oral history by

Joan Sangster in her recent article in *Women's History Review* where she argues that 'the exploration of oral history must incorporate gender as a defining category of analysis, for women remember the past in different ways in comparison with men'.[18] Most recently, the idea of gender and the production of memory has been explored in some depth by Penny Summerfield in *Reconstructing Women's Wartime Lives*.[19]

Sangster, drawing on the work of Susan Geiger, G. Etter-Lewis and Isabel Bertaux-Wiame, suggests that in some studies women have been less likely than men to place themselves at the centre of public events, that women's narratives are more likely to be characterised by understatement and avoidance of the first person point of view, and that women's embeddedness in familial life may shape their view of the world and their consciousness of historical time. It is not my intention to engage with these specific claims here, rather they are cited as examples of an area of study with which I want to engage: the gendering of memory.

Some differences and patterns were noticed in responses to interviews, along gender and age lines. All the women were extremely forthcoming when interviewed on the subject of family and domestic life. All but one (Yvonne) had clear memories about the division of labour within the home in the period in question. This was not always true of male interviewees. It was noticed that in the older group, the majority of men (Ted, Doug, Les) seemed less interested in talking about family and domestic life and instead would change the subject of discussion frequently during the interview. Although asked similar questions to the women, their responses were often brief and used as a springboard for talking about other subjects, specifically work, recreation and wartime memories.

Doug, for example, was asked if other relatives lived nearby when he and his wife lived in Charlton:

> Oh yes, Mum and Dad was there and me sister was living in a block of flats across the road from there. I had a photo done of Charlton Lido when it first opened – me and a mate . . . [continues with a story about the opening of Charlton Lido].

A question about the experience of returning from the war to see his daughter, not seen since she was 6 months old, is answered in more detail before being located by a move from Charlton to Middle Park Estate, Eltham, where Doug 'got involved in football here and played three times a week'. Football is after this a recurring theme of the interview. In a similar vein, when asked where he was born, Doug answered 'Old Charlton. I was born at Old Charlton. I learned to swim in the Thames . . .'

It was as if questions on family and domestic life got in the way of the stories some men really wanted to tell. On occasion, I completely abandoned the prepared questions as the interviewee's responses were so limited. Ted agreed to an interview about family and domestic life but seemed oblivious to any attempt to bring him back to this subject. He spoke lucidly and at length about his experiences at work in the merchant navy, in the navy during the Second World War and about politics in the 1990s. Questions about the family were dealt with as if they were sidetracking him from his real story.

This was not noticed in the interviews with men from the younger age group, though with some their memories of who did what around the home in the 1940s and 1950s were noticeably more vague than those of the women. Jim was asked if he could remember if his father had done any housework, replying 'to be honest I don't remember who did it'. His only strong memory of housework was that as his mother worked outside of the home during the day, he and his brother came home from school and started preparing the dinner. Martin was asked if he had helped with housework as a child and he remembered doing errands. He was also asked if his sisters had helped in any particular way, but he had no clear memory of this – 'It's a long time ago, it's very difficult to remember.' This contrasts sharply with Anne who had very clear memories of who did what work in the home, memories which shaped her decision to give her own children the same domestic tasks, regardless of gender. Christine also remembered in detail her duties in helping out in the home and that her brothers 'didn't lift a finger'. This clarity of memory was typical of women interviewees.

It could just be that this group of women were especially clear and lucid, and that another group of women might not remember so clearly. Similarly, there could be personal and individual reasons why these particular men were less clear in their memories about the family. However, I think other explanations may be available to us, and, without wishing to generalise too rapidly from these observations, several things may help put them into context. Firstly, the men in the older age group clearly steered the interview from the familial and domestic to more public concerns. This could be understood as their moving from discussion of the private sphere to discussion of the public sphere. Given the history of gender relations in Britain, and their places within this, this may make some sense.

It would also be possible to argue that the younger men's lack of clarity of memory could be related to their not being 'embedded within familial life'[20] in the same way as the women. Furthermore, Barrie Thorne, editing a collection of feminist essays on the family, has argued that because families are structured around gender and age, women, men, girls and boys do not experience their families in the same way. She notes that there has been a call amongst feminists for the differentiating of family experience:

> Feminists have explored the differentiation of a family experience mystified by the glorification of motherhood, love and images of the family as a domestic haven. Feminists have voiced experience that this ideology denies: men's dominance and women's subordination within as well outside of the family, and the presence of conflict, violence and inequitably distributed work within the 'domestic haven.[21]

Again, it is too soon to say that this is what is happening in this particular group of interviews, but this argument may at least help put the gender differences that were noted into some context.

One further point which may help to put these differences into context is that studies of the family have themselves often been implicitly gendered. In the field of oral history, two examples illustrate this. *A Marsh and a Gasworks: One Hundred Years of Life in West Ham,* is a Newham History Workshop book which includes a chapter on family life, based largely on oral sources. In it the writer, Elsie Lewis, opens by explaining that in the chapter she 'wants to describe something of the experience of women who have lived in West Ham and Newham'.[22] The chapter is then concerned with women in the West Ham area in their domestic environments and the subject of family becomes almost synonymous with the subject of women. Not dissimilarly, Elizabeth Roberts introduces her recent oral history, *Women and Families,* by placing it in the context of her previous work, *A Woman's Place*:

> *A Woman's Place* was first published in 1984. It is an oral history of working class women in the period 1890–1940. This volume is, to some extent, a sequel to that book, but it also stands on its own account. Its chief focus remains the lives of women but, as the title indicates, there is consideration of families too.[23]

The link between women and the family as an area of study is thus made explicit.

Perhaps at this point it is useful to return to the questions raised earlier in the methodological note, about memory and the complex nature of oral testimony both as evidence of the past and as contemporary cultural product. We can see so far that the people interviewed offer us insight, through their memories, into how things may have been for them in the past. In this way the interviews have provided us with valuable evidence of the period. We can also see that differences in the quality of these memories may be noted along gender and perhaps age lines. We can start to put this into context by noting how some men steer the subject of the interview from the private to the public sphere; that, historically, women have tended to be more embedded in the family; and that studies of the family sometimes implicitly acknowledge this through their approaches. The gender differences in the oral evidence can therefore also be read as evidence of contemporary subjectivity and how that subjectivity has developed over the years since the events which triggered the memories actually took place.

The extended family

I want next to turn to look at the extended family and how it was experienced by the people in the sample. In looking at the oral evidence it became clear that, for many interviewees, extended families offered education, entertainment, practical support or community. Yvonne tells of an aunt who came to live with her family in Charlton during the war and stayed on after,

> and became a second mother. Different temperament to my mother, and she became very valuable. She was the one who told me that she had a bookcase with books in it, and she took me to the ballet, and I can remember when I got the School Matric . . . she took me to the ballet as a treat. My mother was not that way inclined.

Doug remembers large numbers of family gathering together at the weekend in Charlton:

> I had a good time in there, The Swan. All me family used to go there, and there used to be eighteen or twenty of us all get together, every Saturday night and have a sing-song. We used to like a sing-song.

However, he observes that 'once your Mum and Dad dies then all that dies all together'. Betty remembers her whole world as a child and young woman revolving around her family. Her family was large and close and she does not remember feeling the need to include many more people in her circle. There were family friends of long standing who formed part of this family circle, though, and it was one of these, a friend of her brother, that she married.

It is clear, too, that members of extended families offered practical support to one another. Elsie remembers her family operating as a supportive network. After being bombed out during the war she had gone to live with her husband's mother, where they came to an amicable financial and domestic arrangement – 'I said to her, "Mum, what if I go to work, you look after the children and we'll split the wage right down the middle", and this is what we did and it worked out very well.' After the war, Elsie's grandmother died and she inherited the tenancy of the house. Throughout this period, Elsie still went round to her parent's to do their housework, as her mother remained ill. Although that arrangement seems to involve little reciprocity of the kind Janet Finch has observed, the arrangements about work and child care with her mother-in-law clearly did.

A generation later, Christine also found accommodation through her extended family, an occurrence which involved the kind of favouritism which Finch also suggests is important in understanding how help between family members operates:

> Luckily for us, I suppose, Terry's aunt and uncle had a shop in Plumstead with like living quarters over the top and they had one son who had emigrated to New Zealand and so the top flat of those premises was empty. So, Terry being the favourite nephew got round his auntie and she let us have the top flat which is where we lived for about four years saving up to buy a house.

Meanwhile, Helen today lives in the house that her parents and grandparents had lived in, while Jim remembers living in one house with two other families (from his extended family) for a while in the late 1940s, recalling that this seemed to work out well for his parents' work and child care arrangements.

Gerald remembers both helping and being helped by members of his family. In 1945, when he and his wife and child were moving into a prefab, he remembers

> the family all got together and found little bits of furniture for me, because we lost ours during the war. We got a bed and table and things like that, and we slowly started to build our lives up . . . Families were so very, very important, very important to have a good close family, it was important. Without that you were lost, and as I say I had a very good supportive family, they were good to me and they helped us along.

He also remembers:

> One of my sisters she lost her husband and she was still quite young and she had four little children, but the rest of us – the family – we used to help her a couple of bob here and a couple of bob there and we used to be able to buy little things for her . . . the whole family used to muck in with a few shillings to help out.

Helping out in this way was not restricted to the family though. Gerald remembers neighbours helping each other out:

My old Dad, as I say, was an old engine driver, and if there was somebody in the street who was ill, he'd always had a load of old wood or bits of coal and things like that, and drop in their front garden – we all helped each other. Old people, we helped them particularly. They were vulnerable, they couldn't help themselves, they were vulnerable so there was always somebody taking something to Mrs so and so. My wife did, perhaps she'd cook a bit extra for an old lady who used to live next door but one to us. She was on her own, an old widow, she had nothing, so my wife used to take a meal into her when we had a meal, and all little things like that. Not big things, not important things, but they were important to those people who had nothing. Didn't have meals on wheels in those days, you depended on your neighbours, and we all helped each other.

This practical and financial support is part of the informal provision of social welfare discussed at the end of Chapter Three.

Decline of the family?

There is some disagreement between interviewees in their memories of the experience of family and whether the idea of 'the family' being in decline makes any sense in their own lives. Some clearly do believe that the sense of family has been in decline and that their own experience bears this out. For some this is about having once been a part of a large extended family living near one another and now finding that family has dissipated. For others it is about a sense of duty or commitment which they have felt for members of their family but which they feel has been lost in the present generation, echoing Michael Anderson's findings from 1983 that the possibilities of three-generational family reciprocity had all but disappeared from working-class communities.[24] In other cases, it may be fairer to describe these as *changes* in patterns of family obligation, in line with the findings of Janet Finch.[25]

No clear or simple patterns emerge though. Definitions of family feeling, of extended family and decline vary between interviewees. That there should be difference here should come as no surprise given the kinds of academic debate there have been on such senses of family. Carolyn Steadman's critique of Richard Hoggart and Jeremy Seabrook in her *Landscape for a Good Woman*, comes to mind in thinking about the different ways in which interviewees demonstrate their memories of family filtered through myths of decline.

Initially, when interviewing Irene, I thought she may have considered herself as living in an extended family network as she told me 'My mother-in-law lived near where I had been bombed out in Anne Street. I lived on the corner of Anne Street and Robert Street but she lived in Anne Street itself with my husband's brother and his two younger sisters, one of whom was still at school.' However, when I asked, 'So was there a lot of family living nearby?' she replied negatively, explaining that her husband had originally come from Waltham Abbey and that some of his family were still there. Her own parents had moved to the Sussex countryside and she did not consider herself as having much family nearby. Gerald, however, remembers his family being extremely close as a child, even though, as he was the youngest, several of his siblings had moved away from the area by the time he was born.

The experience of migration and emigration, and the impact of this on specific families, seems to influence how some interviewees remember the sense of family. Betty remembers her close-knit family circle being disrupted by emigration. Her siblings emigrated to New Zealand, and her daughter to the United States. Gerald also remembers how emigration impacted upon his extended family:

> There was no local work, so we used to go and find it elsewhere, and a lot of families had their children emigrated to Australia, New Zealand, Canada. They used to have schemes where you could go to Australia for ten pounds to emigrate, and people used to go. Families were broken up, they did scatter. My own family is quite scattered now. Well, I've got one brother, well he's dead now, but his family live in Australia, and two of my sisters married Americans and live in America. We were scattered and we went all over the place.

Gerald found this distressing, remarking that 'something had gone out of family life, the closeness had gone':

> People had lost their homes through the war and settled in other parts of the country, that's all they could do, and I think that when families broke up like that it was tragic, it was a loss – families ceased to be families. I've got nephews and nieces now that I wouldn't know if I saw them. They are strangers to me and that is terrible.

However Gerald's father had himself (e)migrated to London from Wales, leaving family behind and forsaking the kind of familial closeness which Gerald was himself to experience. He recalls: 'as I said, my father was a Welshman, so I've got people living in Wales – some I've seen, some I've not seen', and 'my grandparents died before I was born, so I never knew my grandparents, and I wouldn't have known those because they were Welsh people, they lived in Wales.' Ted and Anne also migrated to London, as had Jim and Betty's parents.

Sheila believes that 'family' has declined in importance and that this 'is partly a shame', although she believes that this has had benefits in the increased individualism and independence of children. She regrets, though, that people 'don't have the feeling of family that they used to have'. Yet she describes her relationship with her own children as very close and acknowledges that the 'family feeling' has persisted in their case. Anne, on the other hand, feels that for her the family is now stronger than it was back in the 1950s when she emigrated to London. She now has an extended family of husband, children and husband's family.

In conclusion

The small sample of oral sources dealt with here can only begin to address what family may have meant to different people in that area. This was a largely working-class area, dominated industrially by the docks and engineering works and noted, as many urban areas were, for its particular pattern of working-class family networks.[26] Research into other areas may produce widely differing accounts of family and domestic life. In focusing on agency and difference, this, though, is precisely the point.

This chapter has been concerned with remembered experience and has focused on three themes which emerged from analysis of the oral texts. There are clearly connections to be made between these themes, and between debates over remembered experience and with evidence from the previous three chapters. Some of the problems raised and the connections made within this chapter will be considered in greater detail and in further context in the next chapter. In particular, where and how interviewees get their ideas of the 'normal' will be addressed.

CHAPTER SIX

Conclusions

In this chapter, conclusions are organised into two sections which address the diverse nature of the material presented so far. The first section draws together the findings from the various research chapters, seeking to make connections between the different research strands, and clarifying ways in which the theoretical perspectives from the first chapter can be related to the evidence presented in the book. In the second section, I turn to the issue of the *relative* value of the evidence from the various research strands, and reflect upon what this kind of study may have to contribute to ways of thinking about families and historical method.

Relating theory to findings

In beginning to relate the findings of the previous chapters to the theoretical perspectives discussed in Chapter One, one question re-emerges: Why study these three different research strands – official discourse and policy, popular cultural representations, and remembered experience? In considering this issue, a second question emerges: How can we best evaluate the evidence from the various strands? A further issue, which follows on from this, is how we should assess the *relative* importance of official discourse and policy, popular cultural representations, and remembered experience for a study of ideas about the family.

An answer to the initial question can be begun through reference to the assumptions about culture and ideology with which the book began. It should first be noted that the use of official sources in the history of ideas has a long history of its own, and is an obvious starting point for an assessment of ideas about the family in the period after 1945. My own understanding of ideology is rooted in Gramsci's concept of hegemony as interpreted within cultural studies in the 1980s and 1990s. Added to this is a particular insistence on agency, which owes as much to culturalism as it does to more recent debates on difference and resistance, or on agency and structure.

Within Gramscian understandings of culture, there is a particular emphasis on ideology as a site of contestation and, within this, popular culture as a source of resistance to hegemony. Tony Bennett has argued for the importance of the contradictions within this:

> To the degree that it is implicated in the struggle for hegemony . . . the field of popular culture is structured by the attempt of the ruling class to win hegemony and by the forms of opposition to this behaviour. As such, it consists not simply of an imposed mass culture that is coincident with dominant ideology, nor simply of spontaneously oppositional cultures, but is rather an area of negotiation between the two within which – in different particular types of popular culture – dominant, subordinate and oppositional cultural and ideological values and elements are 'mixed' in different permutations.[1]

It is this contestation that suggests popular culture as a particularly useful strand of research in thinking about ideology.

To turn to the second assumption about culture and ideology with which the book started, and which I am arguing provides the beginnings of an answer to the question of studying these three disparate research strands, let us return to the issue of agency. Culturalism's emphasis on human agency – that, as E.P. Thompson insisted, human subjects are present at their own making – can be considered alongside the current move in cultural studies to focus on resistance to ideology (or where ideology fails to determine) and the recent contributions to the structure/agency debate made by Beck, Giddens and others. Together these suggest the significance of individual experience, especially in an area such as families and interpersonal relationships. From these various strands of debate, we can further extrapolate the need to consider individual accounts of family in an assessment of ideas about the family and, therefore, suggest that individual accounts for the period 1945 to 1970 can usefully be studied through oral history.

So, the understandings of ideology gained through consideration of hegemony and agency can suggest the inclusion of popular cultural sources (such as film) and individual accounts (such as oral histories) in a history of ideas about family. For these reasons, and in an attempt to further the development of methodological strategies, this book has considered three strands of research – official discourse/policy, popular cultural representations and remembered experience – which are not normally tackled together.

There are, however, problems associated with this approach. Firstly, spending one-third of the research time on each strand means that those strands remain only partially developed. A piece of work which focused solely on ideas about family in popular culture would necessarily expand research beyond the primary concern with film to consider more fully other popular cultural forms. A simple oral history of family might look beyond the one geographical area for comparative purposes, or might be able to expand the research in other ways, through a larger sample. Although these approaches would have the potential for producing research work which was more coherent and consolidated, it would not be able to address theories about ideology – in particular debates about hegemony and agency – in the way that a piece of research like this can. Neither would it add much to the development of methodological strategies.

There is also, still, the problem of weighing up the *relative* value of the different source material; but before addressing this issue, I will first attempt to make clear how the theoretical perspectives outlined in Chapter One can be related to the evidence from the various strands. Stuart Hall has argued that the problem of ideology concerns the ways in which ideas grip the minds of masses and become 'a material force'.[2] Following on from Gramsci's use of 'common sense' in understanding hegemony, Hall has also written about the process of 'naturalisation': the representation of an event or discourse such that it is legitimated by nature, rather than problematised by history. It is useful to consider these two theoretical perspectives in relation to the evidence from the various strands.

The evidence suggests that, within British culture in the period 1945 to 1970, there was a powerful normative force at work in official discourse, at both a national and local level. This has been shown in discourse ranging from national policies on the idea of the family wage and the creation of pseudo-normative families in local authority care of children, to the points system in local authority housing provision and support for the funding of family planning advice. Integral to this culture of the normative has been a set of gender-specific ideas, particularly connected to work and the care of the domestic sphere. Significantly, the evidence presented here has suggested that this normative discourse involved a naturalisation of such ideas, and that such ideas are frequently legitimated by reference to 'common knowledge', or 'what is obvious' and what is 'unnecessary to explain'.

It is possible to argue that this normative discourse is reflective of social realities of the period, that such ideas would have been usual or ordinary for people at that time. It would seem to make sense that this should be, at least in part, true – it would be absurd to argue that normative discourse could 'create' what it describes from nothing. Yet it is equally possible to see this normative discourse as hegemonic.

There are direct and indirect attempts to shape families – encouraging people to have more children; basing welfare provision on the assumption of the family wage; providing funding for mediation in divorce; promoting gender-specific domestic education and so on – which have an impact on people's experience of family and life in general. Noticeable here, too, are traces of eugenicist thought at a national and local level in both public and voluntary bodies, from the Beveridge Report, through the Royal Commission on Population, to local Medical Officer of Health reports and the case notes of Family Welfare Association workers.

As well as seeking to shape families, the normative discourse clearly also works to exclude those who do not exist within its frameworks of ideas. We can relate the narrow range of possibilities on offer within this normative discourse to the diversity of remembered experience. There is in this a further exclusion or alienation which can be associated with the sense of being unusual, which was an important finding to emerge from the remembered experience.

Both the key issues of the normative discourse and the interviewees' sense of atypicality rely upon a similar understanding of the normal, and clearly the interviewees' sense of atypicality comes from somewhere. One way of understanding this is to see interviewees' sense of the normal and the typical as an example of ideas becoming a 'material force' in Hall's sense. The taken-for-grantedness of certain family forms and certain ways of organising family life is clearly in evidence in the normative discourse of official publications, and specifically in the language of local bodies; yet the idea that it was possible to organise things differently is clearly embedded in the consciousness of interviewees, especially as they describe the ways in which they negotiated dominant ideas. It is possible to see this as part of the hegemonic process: the normative discourse of official sources articulates the common sense, taken-for-granted ideas about the family which are further articulated in the interviewees' sense of the normal and the usual. That many interviewees negotiated these common-sense ideas in ways that suited their own circumstances can attest to hegemony as a site of contestation.

The three patterns of negotiating prevalent ideas which I observed in analysing the oral sources, and which were discussed in Chapter Five – broadly unquestioned acceptance; 'running against the grain'; and active resistance – are reminiscent of the 'three hypothetical positions from which decodings of a televisual discourse may be constructed', which Stuart Hall described in the influential article 'Encoding, decoding', referred to in Chapter Four.[3] In this article, Hall nominated these positions as, firstly, the 'dominant–hegemonic position', where the viewer is operating within the

123

dominant code and which is the ideal case of 'perfectly transparent communication'; secondly, the 'negotiated position', in which audiences understand quite adequately what has been dominantly defined and professionally signified, and accord this a privileged position, while reserving the right to make a more negotiated application to 'local conditions'; and thirdly, the 'oppositional position', in which viewers understand the literal and connotive inflection of televisual discourse, but decode the message in a globally contrary way. That Hall's model seems roughly translatable to understandings of remembered experience is significant. It suggests a more general application of the dominant–negotiated–oppositional model is possible, while rescuing Hall's model from the criticism that, in focusing on media relations, it has little to say about relations between the individual subject and ideological structures.[4]

To return to the popular cultural representations, we can relate these to Gramsci's notion that popular culture is a site of particular resistance to hegemony, and one in which emergent forms of consciousness become articulated. The limited comparative analysis of popular culture in this book also attests to the idea of the relative autonomy of different elements of the culture, as, for example, the discourse on family in films of this period was more varied and offered more possibilities than were to be found in women's magazines. The films of the British New Wave can be related to Gramsci's sense of the process of new forms of consciousness emerging through popular culture, as they prefigure, and contribute to, that adaptation of hegemony which became known as 'the permissive society'.

However, it must be stressed that although oppositional forms may relate to new forms of consciousness emerging, the research on popular culture here saw particular limits to those oppositional forms. These limits may have been partly the result of the constraints of the industrial and institutional structures from which they emerged, but also, arguably, are to do with the taken-for-grantedness of certain ideas about the family which are ingrained within the texts. Clearly, not all popular culture is oppositional or obviously resistant to hegemony, and in other examples we have seen coherent articulations of the hegemonic order.

There is another example of emergent consciousness within popular cultural representations, and this relates to the new social identity of the consumer. While this emergent social identity is being represented within film, consumerism is also being contested in other parts of the culture, particularly for its potential impact upon families. In the material I considered from the Family Welfare Association, there is a concern that new ideas about consumption and spending may have a detrimental effect on the stability of family life and on the ability of families to stay together in the face of debt and recrimination. This concern was also articulated in the films of the

British New Wave, and was specifically gendered, with women being shown to have a problem by being caught up in consumerism. Domestic life is also sometimes seen to be influenced by the arrival of new consumer goods – particularly the television – which impact upon communication within families. It is possible to relate these concerns to the kind of cultural criticism of consumerism (and especially Americanisation) which appeared in Britain in the postwar period, perhaps best represented by Richard Hoggart's concern about the impact of such popular culture on working-class families, communities and identities. There is an irony, though, in the representation of women and consumerism in the films of the British New Wave, as going to the cinema was an intrinsic part of consumption. Those (especially female characters) who are seen flicking through magazines or engrossed in television game shows, could just as easily be placed in the cinema, watching the very kind of films of which they were a part.

Some of these concerns about family, community and consumption are echoed in remembered experience in the idea of loss of community interaction and informal care networks which many interviewees commented upon. Connected to this perceived decline in community interaction is a set of ideas about the individual and the extended family. The films of the period offer apparently conflicting ideas about the generational crisis in, and simultaneous support offered by, extended families. The Family Welfare Association clearly thought the extended family had a duty to support its troubled members, and that it was right and proper that the widest number of family members should be called upon to contribute practically and financially in resolving clients' problems. Contrasted to this, the normative discourse of official publications up to the 1970s seems much more concerned with the nuclear family than the extended family, although at the same time the local authorities were increasingly aware of the number of older single people who were not sufficiently cared for by family, friends and neighbours. The oral histories record regret that extended families seemed to become more geographically dispersed. Within the evidence from the various strands, the dominant definition of family as nuclear or extended seems to be especially contested. The discourse of official publications and policy seems to favour a predominantly nuclear definition of family, as little or no evidence could be found in which attention was directed at broader understandings of family. The evidence from the strands, taken together, would seem to question whether hegemony had been won in this area.

It can also be noted that official concern often takes an anxious form which sees 'the family' under attack or in decline. Within this there is also more of a concern with preserving individual nuclear family units than with identifying what is good and useful about family life, and seeking to nurture this. It has already been noted that a common-sense approach to the preservation of individual family units is identifiable. The wider concern with preservation needs also to be addressed. In *All that is Solid Melts into Air*, Marshall Berman draws upon Marx's words to explore the idea that the essential condition of modernity is one of perpetual change.[5] This perpetual change, Berman argues, results in both individual and cultural anxiety and a desire to hold on to the solid while all the time it melts into air. He takes the example of 'the nation' as an idea people hold on to in the face of uncertainty and perpetual change.

Although Berman does not address the idea of family, it is a connection that is useful to make here. While it is easy to see concern about the family as a 'moral panic', it is also possible to understand it as a response to the change and panic of modernity. Anthony Giddens's argument that modernity is a post-traditional order, in which the question 'how shall I live?' needs to be answered on a daily basis, is relevant here, as it emphasises the choices that are increasingly evident in the domestic and the personal spheres.[6] Much of what threatens 'the traditional family' can be seen as aspects of the modern condition – economic, technological and scientific change interacting with cultural change and producing new tensions in existing social relations. Attempts to shore up the traditional family can be seen as trying to turn back the clock, to negate the influence of change, to contain 'progress'. Furthermore, as has been argued here, crises in 'the family' have been a focal point for the expression of many different anxieties around aspects of modernity (for example immigration and emigration, Empire and the development of international capital). At a personal level, traditions within families – Christmases, anniversaries, holidays (the occasions which provide the settings for family snaps) – may also provide ways of creating fixed points in an ever-changing world. The chronicling of these in family photograph albums can be a way of making these 'solid'.[7] It is difficult to say how the official or intellectual anxieties relate to the everyday concerns of people, though there may be some commonality in the experience of change which has characterised modernity.

History, theory, methodology

The drawing together of evidence from the various chapters, and the relating of theoretical perspectives to the findings of the different strands, is clearly useful in coming to conclusions regarding ideas about the family in this period. There remains, however, the problem of weighing up the relative value of the different source material, a problem which has methodological implications. The theoretical perspectives influencing the choice of research strands are useful for making some general points here. Firstly, in accepting the relative autonomy of culture and ideology from economic conditions, as Stuart Hall has done,[8] we can further assume the relative independence of different areas of ideological discourse, an idea initially developed by Althusser, and reworked through readings of Gramsci in the 1980s. As such, it is possible to argue for the need to look at different elements within ideological discourse for a rounded picture, and specifically to look beyond just official discourse *or* popular culture *or* remembered experience for the articulation of ideology. Similarly, the understandings of hegemony and agency outlined here *necessitate* the use of disparate sources. The value of the research strands, then, is greater than the sum of their parts because an understanding of ideology within these theoretical frameworks would be incomplete without each component part. While we are able to concern ourselves with the relative value of each, we should not lose sight of this.

The evidence from the various research strands clearly needs to be read in relation to each other. Furthermore, an understanding of ideological discourse from one strand can resolve problems which may be inherent in another. This suggestion needs to be considered in some detail. If we were simply to look to official discourse for an understanding of 'the family' in these years, we would find a set of fairly fixed and clear-cut ideas. We could come away with the image – popular in much of the current debate about the family – that families were, on the whole, uniform, conventional and, above all, knowable. While families *may* have been less diverse then than they are now, nevertheless the evidence from the oral sources suggests this is too tidy an image. We can see from the majority, who neither entirely conformed to nor actively rejected prevalent ideas, that assumptions about, for instance, the family wage or specific gender roles did not always make sense, as much diversity occurred within this model. Furthermore, while official discourse is concerned almost exclusively with the nuclear family, interviewees were often as or more concerned with extended family networks. Indeed, when interviewees spoke of the 'decline of the family', it was the decline of *extended* family links which was most often and most sadly lamented. By using popular cultural sources, we can see that this hegemony was contested, and by utilising the evidence from oral sources we can argue that human agency meant that the dominant discourse did not directly determine lived experience.

However, the oral history strand, read in isolation, could potentially fall into the trap of excessive relativism. One crucial issue raised by the discussion of remembered experience in Chapter Five was the sense of difference in interviewees' accounts, and the privileged place given to notions of agency within my argument confirms the importance of such difference. In the opening chapter it was observed that recent studies which have foregrounded difference and resistance have been criticised for abandoning material analysis in favour of relativism.[9] Consideration of agency may rescue discussions of ideology from the tendency towards determinism; there is a need, though, to rescue discussion of agency from a tendency towards relativism.

One way to rescue agency from relativism is offered by making reference to the *patterns* which can be seen to overlay difference, and the material framework within which social agents exist. Within the oral evidence presented here, such patterns may be available through reference to the suggestion that, although the majority of interviewees negotiated prevalent ideas about the family in order to suit their own needs and circumstances, the evidence pointed to these negotiations taking place within the framework of prevalent ideas. In Hall's terms, the interviewees understand dominant codes and accord these a privileged position, but adapt those codes to 'local conditions'. Those prevalent ideas or dominant codes can be seen to have a material basis, one which in this instance is articulated clearly, if not exclusively, in official discourse and policy. While we can value the sense of difference and the importance of the role of human agency in understanding the remembered experience, we need to see such difference and agency as operating within the boundaries of hegemonic codes, however contested they may be.

Popular culture has been taken here to be an area of contestation between official discourse and remembered experience. In popular cultural forms it is possible to find a wider sense of debate about the family than is usually in evidence in official discourse. As well as debate about the family we can also find challenges to, and assimilation of, official discourse. However, popular culture does not exist outside of hegemony, and as well as being shaped by hegemonic ideas, popular culture will at times feed into official discourse (*Cathy Come Home* is one of the most striking examples of the period) and impact upon its formation. Popular culture can also be a source of normative ideas, as has been suggested by Chapter Four, and which is echoed in this passage of autobiographical writing about a 1950s childhood:

> And, of course, it was from books that I really acquired my conviction that we were strange. Not in *The Famous Five*, not in *The Secret Seven*, not in Jennings, not in E. Nesbit, not even in *Eagle* or *Girl*, did any family behave itself like mine. We *children* might try to model ourselves on such stories – but where were our jolly grandparents; our even jollier cousins; our benevolent, pipe-smoking, dog-walking dad; our smiling, sweetly sewing mum? Where was our warm, secure and immutable world of grown-up certainties?[10]

Finally, the relationships between centre and locale, between official and voluntary bodies, between national and local concerns, between individual case histories and the formation of policy, and between the visible and invisible, which were traced in Chapter Three, add to the sense of connectedness between the different areas of ideological discourse.

In conclusion

The study of history is still over-reliant on documentary sources, as can be witnessed through analysis of any new publishers' catalogue. In this book I have tried to affirm the importance of studies of popular, non-literary culture and oral histories in understanding the past. It is suggested here that when such sources are taken to be as important as documentary sources, different kinds of insight into the past are made possible. Furthermore, the evidence from these various research strands suggests that historical method can benefit from exposure to the widest possible range of ways of analysing ideas. Historians can benefit from the kind of engagement with theoretical perspectives which is often shied away from in professional, as well as public, circles. Engagement with new methodological tools, too, from literature, film studies and other disciplines can add to the ways in which historians are able to understand areas of the past.

'The family' is such a contested notion in Britain at the start of the twenty-first century. Historians, whose job it is to make sense of the present through understandings of the past, need to find ways of making sense of these debates. Through the sources, findings and methodology developed here, it is hoped that this book may in some way better equip us to face that challenge.

CHAPTER SEVEN

Postscript: New families?

From the permissive moment to the present

This chapter brings elements of the history up to date. It aims to do this in three ways. Firstly, it will survey the major trends and developments in the practice of family life in Britain from the late 1960s to the beginning of the twenty-first century; secondly, it will begin to put these trends and developments into wider socio-economic and cultural context; and finally it will survey the major developments in government policy and the law surrounding family in this period.

Demographic changes

The chapter begins by looking at demographic changes over the period. Here, the first thing to note is a set of trends connected to personal relationships and domestic life which are revealed in the statistics produced by official sources. To begin with trends related to marriage, the statistics show that the period after the 1960s saw a number of new patterns emerge (see Figure 7.1). In brief, these were a decrease in the number of marriages; a sharp rise in the number of marriages ending in divorce; and a rise in non-marital cohabitation, including the emergence in demographic surveys of cohabitation as a category of analysis in its own right.[1]

The crude figures show that in Britain there were some 459,400 marriages in 1971 and only 304,800 in 1998. The marriage rate (the number of people marrying in any given year per thousand of the population aged 16 and over) fell in England and Wales from 69 per 1,000 in 1971 to just 27.7 per 1,000 in 1998, with a similar scale of fall in evidence in Scotland. At the same time, the divorce rate (the number of people divorcing per thousand

Thousands

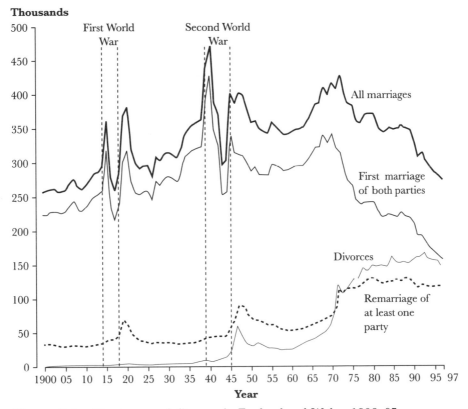

Figure 7.1 Marriages and divorces in England and Wales, 1900–97.
Source: Population Trends 100, National Statistics © Crown Copyright 2001.

of the married population) rose in England and Wales from 5.9 per 1,000 in 1971, the year that the Divorce Reform Act 1969 came into effect, to 12.9 per 1,000 in 1998.[2]

As cohabitation, unlike both marriage and divorce, is not required by law to be recorded, it is more difficult to gain accurate figures about numerical developments in this area. However, it is possible to gain some insight from social surveys, such as the annual General Household Survey, and these suggest that by the late 1990s, around 12 or 13 per cent of respondents to surveys were men and women cohabiting.[3] Although historical studies have suggested there has been a long tradition of non-marital cohabitation in Britain,[4] in the period in question levels rose substantially and there is evidence of cohabitation becoming a significant demographic trend.

Another notable development has been the increase in households which contain children and only one parent – 'one-parent families' as they are currently known in official publications. Figures are also uncertain here

131

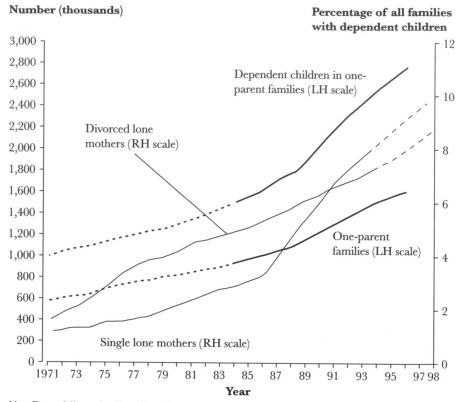

Number (thousands)

**Percentage of all families
with dependent children**

Note: Dotted lines signify either absence of estimates in intervening years, or omission of estimates which showed minor variation from the trend line

Figure 7.2 'Best estimates' of trends in one-parent families in Britain, 1971–98.
Source: Population Trends 100, using *General Household Survey.* National Statistics © Crown Copyright 2001.

because outside of census years, accurate figures are not officially collected. However 'best estimates' have been complied in the *General Household Survey* which suggest that, while in 1971 (the census year) there were around 600,000 one-parent families with around 1 million children living in such households, by 1996, there were some 2 million one-parent families containing around 2,750,000 children. Within this growth in numbers, and since the mid-1980s, there has been a move towards more single (never married) women than divorced women heading one-parent families, with women who had never married forming the majority after 1990[5] (see Figure 7.2).

There have also been several developments in reproductive trends which are worthy of comment (see Figure 7.3). Over this period, the birth rate (the number of live births per thousand of the population of all ages) fell from 16.1 in 1971 to just 11.8 in 1999, noticeably lower than the birth rate had

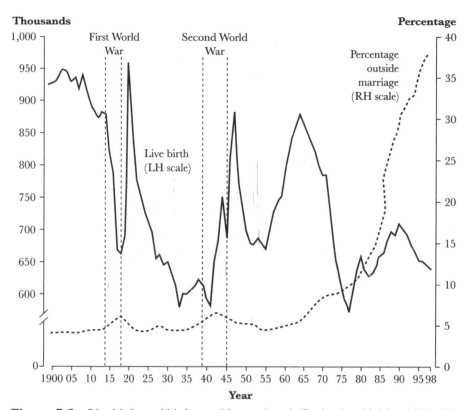

Figure 7.3 Live births and births outside marriage in England and Wales, 1900–98.
Source: Population Trends 100, National Statistics © Crown Copyright 2001.

been when the Royal Commission on Population had sat in the second half of the 1940s.[6] This decline can be related to several other trends. Firstly, there has been a general move towards smaller families and a decline from an average of 2.4 children per woman in 1971 to an average of 1.8 children per woman in the late 1990s. This figure includes childless women, who have grown in number over these years, a period in which demographers suggest has seen childlessness become a growing trend in Britain.[7] It can be noted that there is, however, some ethnic diversity concealed within these figures with, for example, women from south Asian and (to a lesser extent) African/Caribbean ethnic minorities having more children on average and showing no decline in birth rate.[8]

There has also been a trend towards those women who are having children having them later in life and, in particular, delaying the birth of their first child. In England and Wales, the average age of married first-time mothers rose from 23.9 years to 29.4 years between 1971 and 1999. And, despite the significant incidence of teenage and under-age pregnancies in Britain during this period, the average age of women giving birth has risen steadily. In 1976, 69 per cent of all live births were to women in their twenties, and 20 per cent to women in their thirties. By 1998 these percentages had become much more equal, at 48 per cent and 42 per cent, respectively.[9] While the overall number of live births declined, the percentage of these births which were occurring outside of marriage rose sharply and steadily throughout the period, as Figure 7.3 shows. In 1971 there were 901,600 live births, of which 73,900 (or 8.2 per cent) were outside of marriage. By 1999, although the number of all live births had fallen to 700,200, the number of these babies born outside of marriage had risen to 271,600, or 38.8 per cent of all live births.[10]

Not only were the number and rate of births outside of marriage changing, but the patterns of registering these births was changing too. The Office of National Statistics, in its regular series *Birth Statistics*, began to note how births outside of marriage were registered by parents, distinguishing between joint registration (i.e. by both parents) and sole registration (by the mother alone). It showed that there was a trend towards the joint registration of such births and a move away from sole registration. In 1971, 54.5 per cent of all births outside marriage were registered by the mother alone, with 45.5 per cent being jointly registered. By 1999 the position was reversed, with 80 per cent being jointly registered and only 19.9 per cent registered by mothers alone.[11]

Furthermore, from 1986, the Office of National Statistics began to differentiate joint registration of births outside of marriage between those registered by parents giving the *same* address and those giving *different* addresses. The statistics showed that while joint registrations at different addresses remained almost static (and sole registrations fell), joint registrations with both parents giving the same address rose steadily from 46.6 per cent in 1986 to over 61 per cent in 1999. The implication of this is clearly that although more children were being born outside of marriage, most of these were being born to cohabiting couples.

We have been able, then, to see a number of trends emerging from demographic statistics which seem to suggest that family and domestic life has been in a state of flux in recent decades and which might support the idea that 'the traditional family' has been in decline in this period. However, caution is required here as these statistics offer only a partial view of what has been happening over these years. It could be argued, for example, that marriage as an institution was in many ways resilient over these years. Significantly, the large majority of people still married at some point in their lives. Figures for England and Wales show that, in 1971, 78.9 per cent of the population over the age of 16 had ever married, and in 1998 this figure had only dropped to 70.8 per cent,[12] and part of this decrease may possibly be explained by the trend for first marriages to be delayed by both men and women. Even when the divorce rate had settled into the low teens in the early 1980s, when it was famously predicted that one-third of all marriages would end in divorce,[13] this still meant that 66 per cent of marriages could be expected to endure. Furthermore, the rise in divorce rates coincided with a rise in remarriage rates (see Figure 7.1), suggesting again a resilience in the idea of marriage, even where individual marriages had failed.

Another way in which such statistical surveys give only a partial view of the practice of family life is that they tend only to compile information on family members who are living in the same household, thereby excluding non-resident family members. For example, some 'one-parent families' may well consist of two parents in practice, though only one is permanently resident with the child or children. Partly as a response to this, there has been a recent broadening of interests within official publications and new concern shown for the demography of the elderly, kin and wider relationships.[14]

Finally, caution needs to be taken with seeing non-marital cohabitation as *replacing* marriage. Soon after the *General Household Survey* began to give figures for cohabitation it was suggested that the popularity of this kind of domestic arrangement may be largely due to the emergence of temporary, pre-marital cohabitation as a cultural phenomenon.[15] This suggestion is confirmed in recent reports such as *Population Trends* from the Office of National Statistics, where it is argued that 'amongst couples about to marry, living together before marriage has become the norm rather than the exception, and all but a few couples cohabit premaritally'.[16] If this is so, it would suggest that instead of *replacing* marriage, cohabitation is for many heterosexual couples a stage before marriage and that, therefore, rather than providing evidence for the decline of marriage, pre-marital cohabitation is part of the changing route *to* marriage.

The cause of changes in demographic patterns is always hard to determine, for there can be as many reasons for individual life changes as there are people to live out those lives. What is helpful, though, is to attempt to understand these changes by placing them in a wider social and cultural context, to see how demographic change fits in with broader developments both within a culture and on an international scale. This is what the following sections begin to do.

Transformations in domestic and personal relations

The demographic statistics and patterns discussed above show us the broad quantitative changes in family and domestic life in Britain in the last three decades of the twentieth century. Moving away from the national demographics, sociological studies which address targeted quantitative change are able to show some of the detail within these broad changes. Such developments in the organisation of domestic and personal relationships are further revealed in the *qualitative* work which has been done by a number of researchers in this period.

A number of these studies suggest that new forms of domestic, social and emotional relationships (and non-relationships) have been developing which open up new possibilities for living and which, wittingly or otherwise, challenge the hegemony of the conventional nuclear family. The research shows that people in Britain and elsewhere in Europe are living together – and apart – in more diverse ways, not merely through the rise in non-marital cohabitation which has been charted by demographers, but also through patterns of serial monogamy, separation and divorce and remarriage/re-cohabitation[17] and the growth of cross-household familial relationships (what Proctor and Padfield have referred to as 'transhabitation' and what Murphy calls 'couples living together apart'[18]). Research also suggests an increase in the significance of adult friendship networks,[19] a phenomenon which may be related to the growth of national and international cultures and economies, and the emergence of 'families of choice' – which may include friends, lovers and ex-lovers – who are incorporated into, and which sometimes supplant, families of origin.[20]

Household formation is one area of research of particular interest here. Patterns of household and family formation amongst young people have become increasingly interesting to sociologists concerned with young people's transitions into adult life. Studies have shown that across much of northern Europe, young people are remaining in the parental home for longer periods of time.[21] New patterns of growth in non-familial households have been identified in both British and European contexts, with studies by de Jong Gierveld and Beekink in 1989 and Jones and Wallace in 1992 and 1995.[22] Particularly in urban areas, sharing accommodation with friends, lovers, acquaintances and strangers may be becoming normative, especially amongst the young.[23] It has been suggested that such households might constitute a form of family. A forthcoming piece of research by Sue Heath is concerned with the establishing and the dynamics of non-familial households amongst young people and the extent to which these households replicate and therefore redefine familial-type relationships.[24] While new family/household forms might be emerging, a withdrawal from the family household is also apparent, with an increase in solitary living having been identified as a cultural trend: between 1971 and 1991, one-person households rose from 18 per cent to 27 per cent of all households in Britain.[25]

The work on family and household formation overlaps with work on divorce, remarriage and step-families where contributions have been made by Jacqueline Burgoyne, David Clark, Christopher Cullow and others.[26] The rise in divorce and remarriage since the end of the 1960s, and the resultant growth in step-familial relationships, has led some observers to describe step-families as the new extended family,[27] an idea which supports the suggestion that family forms may have been subject to change rather than simply to decline. A reaffirmation of the commitment to family is in evidence in the lived reality of daily life revealed in the work on family obligation and responsibility which has been extensively researched by Janet Finch. In her *Family Obligation and Social Change*, she focuses on the qualitative aspects of family life, and she argues that family responsibilities are in essence negotiated between individuals, are dependent on reciprocity and factors such as ethnicity, gender and locality, and cannot be simply predicted by the biological relationship between family members. In collaboration with Jennifer Mason, Finch has further argued that family and kin relationships should be seen more in terms of *responsibility* than of obligation.[28]

These pieces of research have emerged in the context of new critiques of the interpersonal domain and the organisation of everyday life. The essence of this critique is captured in Anthony Giddens's *The Transformation of Intimacy* in which he argues that, although filtered through existing inequalities and traditions, modern cultures have witnessed a radical democratisation of the interpersonal domain in which equal partners have emerged with the freedom to choose lifestyles and forms of partnership.[29] In relationships between men and women, this can be connected to developments in gender relations and in the separation of sexuality from reproduction enabled by developments in contraceptive technology (which are discussed more fully in the following section). Thus, it is argued, though still existing within the network of obligations and responsibilities which Janet Finch and Jennifer Mason have identified, late modernity has seen the emergence of 'pure relationships', entered into solely for what they can bring to each partner and existing only as long as those (usually emotional) benefits remain. We can further relate this to the wider theory of reflexive modernity, referred to in Chapter One, which has been developed by Giddens and Ulrich Beck, though it should be noted that both Giddens and Beck have been criticised for the limitations of their approaches, specifically Giddens's tendency to ignore the implications of parenting to the idea of the pure relationship and Beck's exclusive focus on heterosexuality.[30] Connected to this, others have commented on the convergence of patterns in both heterosexual and homosexual ways of life centred around the search for and maintenance of a satisfactory primary emotional relationship as a key part of personal identity.[31]

Wider cultural transformations

Aside from developments in personal relationships and family and household formation, the period since the end of the 1960s has seen a number of social, cultural, economic and technological transformations which can be seen to have impacted in some way upon the practice of family life in Britain. These transformations include developments in gender relations; changing patterns of employment; technological advances in communications; developments in reproductive technologies; increased ethnic diversity in Britain; and the changing patterns of religious beliefs.

The first thing to note about developments in gender relations is the advent and impact of the new wave of feminism which grew strongly in Britain from the late 1960s onwards. Aside from changes in the law surrounding gender relations (which are discussed in the following section), this period saw gender become a central issue in many areas of society, opening up the possibilities for most women to make choices about their lives which had not been open to previous generations. Not only did the rights of women move sharply up the agenda, but also there developed a new focus on masculinity, its cultural limitations and possibilities.

The successes of feminism in changing the gender culture in Britain clearly had implications for the ideas about women and families contained within the postwar settlement of Beveridge. Part of this change is in evidence in developments in women's paid employment which has sharply increased over the period. Other economic transformations have interacted with this, particularly the decline in traditional industry after the 1970s and the rise of new light industry and service industries which have attracted women workers, often on a part-time basis. Changing employment patterns which have occurred as a result of these wider economic and industrial transformations have unsettled the family wage model of male breadwinner and female homemaker.

As well as changes in the workplace, technological advances in communications and transport have impacted upon how, where and when people can and may want to work. These mean that people can often work from home on a part-time or full-time basis, but also that greater distances for commuting to work are possible. Both possibilities have had the potential to impact upon how people live together (and apart) and how family and domestic life is lived out.

In another area of transformation, changes in reproductive technology and practice are coming from many different directions, both from within and outside the conventional family. Conception has been made possible outside of the body, first with the 'test-tube babies' of the late 1970s and later through the more sophisticated techniques of assisted conception.

Women (sometimes family members) are able to act as surrogate mothers for infertile women. Some women are actively choosing planned single parenthood through artificial insemination; some men and women are actively choosing to remain childless[32] (and even organising pressure groups to promote the rights of non-parents[33]); while others are choosing to parent in same-sex relationships.[34] Much public debate has taken place over the question of women bearing children conceived through *in vitro* fertilisation after the menopause.[35] Recently, a case came before the European Court of Human Rights in which a transsexual man applied for the right to be named as the father of his eldest daughter, conceived through artificial insemination by donor.[36] In contraceptive technology, the development of the contraceptive pill has been seen as a point at which female sexuality could become detached from reproduction, enabling amongst other things, more equal relationships between men and women to emerge.

These transformations, and the debates which surround them, feed into, and are part of, wider cultural debates about the sanctity of the individual and the development of individualised, customised lifestyles associated with postmodernity; the personal rights agenda; and ideas about the natural and unnatural, and the elasticity of boundaries between the two. They are also clearly related to developments in science and technology, health care, longevity and economics, which make many of these lifestyle choices possible.

Cultural transformations of another kind have seen ethnic diversity increase in Britain over the whole of this period. Whereas in the earlier part of the post-Second World War period men had often come alone from parts of the former Empire, increasingly, as the period went on, whole families came to settle in Britain. The particular relevance of this growing diversity to this study is that different patterns of organising family life are evident amongst the various ethnic groups and that these different patterns add to the growing sense of diversity within family forms and the organisation of personal and emotional life as a whole. Research from the late 1980s suggested the following trends amongst some of the larger ethnic minority groups:

> Compared with either white or Afro-Caribbean ethnic groups, Indian, Pakistani and Bangladeshi groups tend to have larger households and larger families, with more dependent children per family and more families per household . . . These Asian groups also have a much smaller proportion of lone parent families . . . Compared with either white or Asian ethnic groups, Afro-Caribbean groups have a higher preponderance of lone parent families . . . They also have more families with a female head.[37]

This diversity has become more pronounced in recent years with the newer groups of immigrants from eastern and south-eastern Europe and elsewhere.

The decline of formal religion – or more specifically of Christianity – during the second half of the twentieth century can be connected to many of the developments outlined in this section in that the specific moral codes of the Church – with their clear guidelines for the organisation of family and personal life – have ceased to hold sway for many people. The growing secularisation of many sectors of society may have opened up the possibility of new ways of living and organising the personal. However, the growing popularity on non-Christian religions, with their various teachings on family and sexual behaviour (related in part to the growth in ethnic diversity) complicates this trend while providing a counterbalance to the decline of formal Christianity.

Clearly there are points of connection between these various transformations and it would be wrong to see these developments as discrete and unconnected, for many of them are very much bound up with each other. Equally, 'the family' has been a crucial point of reference for a multitude of contemporary debates, both for those concerned primarily with social relations and also for a much broader set of debates about contemporary culture.

Developments in policy and the law

These trends in demographics and transformations in the wider culture have been the subject of enquiry, policy and legislative change and new legal interpretation over the period. This section surveys these developments in policy and law, taking a thematic rather than a chronological approach. The main sources to be used here are John Dewar, *Law and the Family* and Lorraine Fox Harding, *Family, State and Social Policy.*[38]

As has been noted in previous chapters, 'family policy' in Britain, in contrast to that in some other countries, has tended to be implicit and at times contradictory. Similarly, 'family law' is an ill-defined area of law, comprising many disparate legal rules and concepts, each with its own particular history and pattern of development. Moreover, 'family' is not clearly defined in law, but relies upon the precedent of past legal judgment and judicial review.

Shifting definitions and understandings of family

Two areas in which definitions of family have been expanded and adapted in law over this period are, firstly, cohabitation and, secondly, births outside marriage (what used to be called illegitimacy). Although there is no direct legislation in which the rights of non-marital heterosexual partnership is enshrined, and the legal regulation associated with marriage has not been extended to cohabitation, under certain parts of the law, such cohabitation is recognised, especially where it can be shown to be of a long-term and stable nature. These areas of recognition include succession to tenancies, liability to maintain each other under social security law, liability to maintain children (under the Children Act 1989 and the Child Support Act 1991), the right to restraining orders in respect of violence, and, in certain circumstances, rights to inheritance.[39]

In consideration of illegitimacy, there has been a shift in both the status of and language surrounding children born outside of marriage. This has coincided with the rise in births outside marriage and the predominance of the joint registration of these births by both parents (as noted above). Although a succession of Acts from the 1950s onwards had sought to reduce the disadvantages of illegitimacy, until the mid-1980s there was a sharp legal distinction between legitimate and illegitimate children, i.e. those born within or outside marriage, with many legal (as well as social) benefits falling to the legitimate child.

The Family Law Reform Act 1987 removed the legal distinction between legitimate and illegitimate children in all but a few cases, stating, as a general principle, that 'all references (however expressed) to any relationship between two persons shall . . . be construed without regard to whether or not the father and mother of either of them, or the father and mother of any person through whom the relationship is deduced, have or had been married to each other at any time'. When the law came into force in 1989, there was also a change in language to accompany the change in status, with the terms 'legitimate' and 'illegitimate' being replaced in legal use by the terms 'within marriage' and 'outside marriage', respectively. In effect, the law had begun to recognise some forms of non-marital relationship, and any children which may be produced outside of marriage, as constituting 'family'.

In 1988, though, in contradiction to this broadening of the parameters of family, the Thatcher government introduced a new concept in law to *restrict* the definition of family with the adoption of section 28 of the Local Government Act 1988 and its idea of the 'pretended family'. This rather confused measure, which at the end of the century was still on the statute books, was an attack upon what was seen as the 'intentional promotion' of homosexuality in (predominantly Labour-controlled) local authorities. It specifically forbade the promotion of the acceptability in state schools of homosexuality (but not other unconventional family forms) as a 'pretended family relationship'. Although clearly a homophobic measure, it was also an attempt to ring-fence the idea of what in law constituted a family, perhaps in part because the parameters of family had been expanding in other areas of the law.

In stark contrast, in 1999, there was a significant widening of the legal definition of family coming not from a change in government policy but from judicial review with the law lords ruling in the Martin Fitzpatrick case, which was discussed early on in Chapter One. This was the case of a man's attempt to succeed to the tenancy of his deceased male partner's housing association flat. The case ended up in the House of Lords with a major review of the meaning of family. We have already noted that the law had begun to recognise the right to succeed to a tenancy in cases of non-marital heterosexual cohabitation. The law lords ruled that if a man and a woman who were not married but who lived together in a stable and permanent relationship could be considered to be a family, then there were no reasonable grounds not to extend the same recognition to two men or two women living together in such a relationship. That this ruling could appear at a time when section 28 remained law is an example of the contradictory nature of law relating to the family.

One final area of change within understandings of family has been in the various relations between parents, children and the state. This change has involved a reappraisal of children's rights and the rights and responsibilities of parents. Children have become recognised as more autonomous individuals, especially since the Children Act 1989, and are able to initiate legal action relating to aspects of their care. The 'non-intervention principle' was outlined in the same Act. Within relations between parents, children and the state, this stated that courts should not make any order in family cases unless it was clearly in the child's interests. As such, as well as promoting the position of the child, the non-intervention principle can be seen to promote the idea of family autonomy in the resolution of domestic and family matters.

These changes in the definition and understanding of family, at times contradictory, bring us on to discussion of developments in specific policy areas.

Shifting attitudes to policy on families

John Dewar has noted that in recent years in family law there has been increasingly less emphasis placed on the exclusivity of the legal status of marriage and more emphasis put on constructing 'status-like relationships' around new organising concepts.[40] As well as being important to the shifting definitions of family, this is part of a sea-change in political thinking about family and responsibility. As part of the project of welfarism, the long-term trend until the 1980s had been for a gradual reduction in the range of family members who would be legally responsible for each other financially, with a corresponding rise in responsibility for the state. The period since the 1970s has seen conscious attempts at reversing this trend. The reason for this may be to do with the ever-expanding budget for social security, but may also be to do with a desire to shift responsibility away from the state and back on to family members for other reasons, including suspicions about the efficiency of a system of welfare organised in such a way and the effects upon the wider society of the reduction in family responsibility. This is perhaps best seen in the Child Support Act's attempts to enforce child maintenance from absent parents (usually fathers), but can also be seen in the removal of the general availability of social security payments to young people under the age of 18, the introduction of the lower level of social security payments for those under 25 and the introduction of partial payments for private residential care for the elderly, all of which put pressure, if not a legal requirement, on immediate family members to provide some level of financial or practical support.[41]

The Conservatives' review of welfare and morality after their 1979 general election victory was the first major review of the permissive moment. This was clearly signalled in the 1983 electoral campaign through the idea of a return to 'Victorian values', which Jeffrey Weeks has characterised as 'a reassertion of what were conceived as traditional familial and sexual standards'.[42] It is in this context that we need to place the idea of the 'pretended family' which appeared in section 28. Indeed, Weeks has argued that although there may have been a considerable amount of homophobic feeling and prejudice behind this measure, its real purpose was something different:

> Their underlying concern was more strategic; quite clearly to make unlawful any activities that undermined the family. Individual, privatised homosexuality, as legalised by the 1967 Act, could be accepted. Public displays which affirmed the equal merits of lesbian and gay lifestyle ('pretended family relationship') could not be. In effect the new provision insisted on a return to the narrow interpretation of the 1967 Act. Anything that went beyond that threatened the hegemony of the family.[43]

It should be noted that political concern about the family at that time was not only a British phenomenon, but as Weeks has argued elsewhere, was a feature throughout the developed world.[44]

Moving on into the 1990s, family was signalled as an important theme of the 'New' Labour project in both rhetoric and the formation of policy. In a key extract from his conference speech a few months after the 1997 general election victory, Prime Minister Tony Blair explained the Labour thinking on family.

> We cannot say we want a strong and secure society when we ignore its very foundations: family life. This is not about preaching to individuals about their private lives. It is addressing a huge social problem . . . Every area of this government's policy will be scrutinized to see how it affects family life. Every policy examined, every initiative tested, every avenue explored to see how we strengthen our families.[45]

In this speech we can trace ideas that stretch back to the beginning of the period with which this book is concerned. Blair's commitment to scrutinise every policy to see how it affects family life and to seek to strengthen families across policy areas recalls the Royal Commission on Population's observation that family had tended to be overlooked or only given a minor place in social policy and the proposal that, in future, family should be given a central place in policy across the board.[46] The speech also reaffirms the idea of family as the key foundation for society.

As well as encouraging an awareness of family across policy areas, the Labour government was keen to develop the first ever explicit family policy in Britain. In 1998 the Home Office, headed by Jack Straw, produced a Green Paper entitled *Supporting Families* in which proposals for the new family policy were laid out. Again parallels can be drawn between the ideas about the importance of family in this document and in the earlier public enquiries. In the summary leaflet for *Supporting Families*, the opening statement reads: 'Families are at the heart of our society and the basis of our future as a country',[47] while the 1946 *Report of the Committee on Homeless Children* had proposed that 'it is upon the family that our position as a nation is built'.[48] Further continuities can be seen in the *Supporting Families* Green Paper's call for the development of parenthood education in schools and for better guidance for couples preparing to marry (both of which were in evidence in most of the enquiries into marriage, family and population in the early postwar years) and in the proposals to enhance the reconciliation process amongst couples planning to divorce (which had been one of the main proposal to come out of the series of enquiries into marriage and divorce in the 1940s and 1950s).

The resemblances in ideas about the family from the two periods is striking, but one important difference is in the dropping of the term 'the family' in Blair and Straw's rhetoric and its replacement with 'families' and 'family life'. This could be taken to indicate a move away from the monolithic idea of 'the family' which was almost universal in earlier policy and rhetoric.

However, some researchers have criticised Labour's thinking on family as reductionist and backward-looking. Elizabeth Silva and Carol Smart suggest that, especially in the conference speech, the Labour position acknowledges social change while attempting to hold on to the early postwar ideal of the family. In particular, they take issue with the idea of strengthening families, arguing that

> Strong families are, of course, seen as conjugal, heterosexual parents with an employed male breadwinner. Lone mothers and gay couples do not by definition constitute strong families in this rhetoric. On the contrary, they are part of the problem and part of the process of destabilizing the necessary fortitude of the proper family.[49]

What is certainly clear from the Green Paper is that family policy for Labour is mostly about child-raising, and might easily be called 'parenting policy' instead. In the summary leaflet, the 'three simple principles' of family policy are described as: 'Children must come first'; 'children need stability'; and 'families raise children'. This may be part of a wider shift towards a more child-centred culture in Britain, but it certainly retains the idea that, as far as public policy is concerned, family is about parents and dependent children. This is reiterated in the section of the Green Paper where, after discussing the general family policy, a small section is devoted to 'the wider family'.

Developments in marriage, divorce and the law

The changes in the law concerning births outside of marriage, as well as the limited recognition of cohabitation in various sections of the law discussed above, have contributed to changes in the status of marriage over this period. There are several changes within marriage which should also be noted. One area of change, with significance for understandings of the nature of marriage, was over the question of rape within marriage.

In the law connected to rape, the key issue is that of consent. Until the early 1990s, through agreeing to marry, a woman was deemed to have given *general* consent to sexual relations with her husband, thereby exempting the husband from charges of rape, other than in exceptional circumstances (legal decisions in the 1980s had done away with this exemption in cases where there was a judicial separation, or where a non-molestation order or *decree nisi* had been awarded). In 1990, the Law Commission recommended that the idea of general consent be abandoned and the exemption of husbands to charges of rape within the marriage be removed. Although no statutory change to the law was to occur, in the following year the House of Lords decided that the marital rape exemption was no longer to be considered part of the common law, noting that such a concept was out of keeping with contemporary notions of marriage as a partnership of equals.[50] We might also connect this to the development of the concept of domestic violence within the law. During the twentieth century, and increasingly since 1970, there has been a growing intolerance of physical violence between family members. In our period, the first piece of significant legislation is the Domestic Violence and Matrimonial Proceedings Act 1976. This allowed county courts to provide non-molestation orders for applicants or for a child living with an applicant as well as providing for exclusion orders restricting those named from the conjugal home, with a judge being allowed to attach the power of arrest to such an order. Men and women who were either party to a marriage or who were living in the same household 'as husband and wife' were eligible to apply for such orders on the grounds of their partner's violence or the threat of violence. Two years later, these powers were extended in the magistrates courts in the Domestic Proceedings and Magistrates' Courts Act 1978.

The Family Law Act 1996 provided for a significant extension to those who could apply for such orders under the law on domestic violence. After the enactment of this legislation, a set of 'associated persons' – which includes those who have been married to one another, cohabitees and former cohabitees, certain relatives (including parents, siblings, grandparents and relatives-in-law), and even flat-mates – can apply for non-molestation or occupation orders (provided, in the case of the latter, that they already have a right to occupancy through, for example, a tenancy agreement). The Act also, arguably, extended the idea of what constitutes family, by expanding the range of those given access to such rulings under family law.

This idea of marriage as a partnership of equals, which had been evoked in the removal of the marital rape exemption, can also be seen in the changes in taxation for married couples which have occurred over this period, most significantly in income tax. For income tax purposes, married couples were treated as a single unit since the beginnings of the tax in the Napoleonic Wars, with the husband receiving an automatic tax allowance in respect of supporting a wife (with no account taken of the wife's actual financial circumstances). Despite many and varied changes to the income tax system over the years, it was not until the early 1970s that the possibility of separate taxation was introduced, and then only for earned income. Further change came in the 1990s with the introduction in 1990 of fully independent taxation for both parties to a marriage, with married women becoming responsible for completing their own tax returns, and changes to the married couples allowance in 1993 which allowed for married couples to divide the allowance equally between them or choose which partner should claim it solely.[51]

Turning to policy on divorce, a number of trends become apparent. The 1969 divorce reform, implemented in 1971, had introduced the idea of the 'no fault' divorce which began to turn divorce law away from the idea of crimes against marriage. This trend away from assigning blame in divorce cases continued throughout the period and culminated in the removal of the fault clauses from the law in section II of the Family Law Act 1996. This section of the Act consolidated another trend which was towards placing greater emphasis on attempting to reconcile the parties in a divorce application through new provisions for mediation and the introduction of the idea of a 'period for reflection and consideration' after the application for a divorce had been made. Thus, in the period since 1970, the concerns of the law in divorce cases has moved away from deciding whether a divorce should be granted and moved towards either providing the means for reconciliation or, where this is not possible, managing the divorce (distributing money, property, and responsibility for and contact with any children etc.) in the best interests of all parties.[52]

Changing ideas about gender

Some of these changes in marriage – particularly over the question of rape within marriage and the taxation of parties to a marriage – can be connected to broader developments within gender law since the 1960s. There have been a number of moves towards gender equality in official thinking since that time, and two major pieces of legislation occurred early in the period: the Equal Pay Act 1970 and the Sex Discrimination Act 1976. The Equal Pay Act, which was not implemented until 1975, made it illegal to pay different amounts to people who were doing the same work, or who could be deemed to be workers of equal worth. The Act therefore outlawed the practice of paying men and women different rates for essentially the same work, although it can be noted that it did little or nothing to address the issues of low-paid work tending to be done by women, or gender differentials in work experience, training etc.[53] The Equal Pay Act was amended in 1983 to enable a woman to claim equal pay with a male colleague in the same establishment if it could be proved that her work was of equal value although she was doing a different job. The Sex Discrimination Act had a wider remit and made it illegal, with a few exceptions, to discriminate on the grounds of gender in the significant areas of employment and education, including both direct and indirect discrimination. The Equal Opportunities Commission was established to promote the law in this area.

However, in terms of policy on gender-related issues, there has been less of a move towards equality in some areas. Successive governments' policies on child care have, for example, been criticised by feminists in particular for failing to provide adequate state-run nurseries to enable mothers to more easily enter the workforce or otherwise develop their own lives. Government policy has fluctuated on this matter over these years. In the early 1970s, Heath's Conservative government did propose an expansion of the state nursery system, although this was later abandoned. In the 1980s and 1990s, the general trend within government thinking has been towards supporting the development of employer or private child care, with state provision being reserved primarily for a minority of families with special problems, for example where children are at risk of abuse.[54]

Regulating reproductive technology and practice

Early on in this period there was significant deregulation of family planning when the 1970–74 Conservative government allowed contraceptives to be universally available (and free of charge) on the NHS to those over the heterosexual age of consent. However, other developments in reproductive technologies and practice have come under close official scrutiny and have been the object of much deliberation and increased regulation in this period. In particular, concern was expressed over egg, embryo and sperm donation, as well as surrogacy (where a woman agrees to carry a child through pregnancy with the intention of handing over the child to the father and his partner), and the resultant confusion and ambiguity over who should be deemed the parents of any child born after such interventions. In 1984, the Department of Health and Social Security *Report of the Committee of Inquiry into Human Fertilisation and Embryology* (the Warnock Report) appeared,[55] leading to the Surrogacy Arrangements Act 1985 and the Human Fertilisation and Embryology Act 1990.

The Surrogacy Arrangements Act was designed to outlaw commercial surrogacy, but allowed for women to act as surrogate mothers if they were not to profit financially from the experience (although they were to be allowed to claim reasonable expenses). This was a swift response to a high level of public debate about surrogacy, but did little to clarify the broader issues. The Human Fertilisation and Embryology Act, on the other hand, was rather more far-reaching and dealt with a number of key concerns in the field. Chief amongst these was the resolving of ambiguities over whom the law would recognise as being the legal parents of a child born through the donation of eggs, embryos or sperm or carried by a surrogate mother. In particular, and of interest to the subject of this book, the Act gave quite specific definitions of the meaning of mother and father. A mother, it said, is 'the woman who is carrying or has carried a child as a result of the placing in her of an embryo or of sperm or eggs, and no other woman is to be treated as the mother of the child'[56] (except for in the case of adoption). This definition of a mother was clearly stated to include a woman who, though carrying a child, had *not* produced the egg which had resulted in the formation of an embryo, but for whom an egg had been donated. A father, the Act said, is either the husband of a woman receiving such fertility treatment, regardless of whether his own sperm was involved in the conception, or if there is no husband, a man (for example a woman's partner) for whom treatment was being offered together with the mother. In either case, no other man (except in the case of adoption) was to be regarded as the father, and if the sperm of a man or any embryo created using his sperm was used after his death, he was not to be treated as the father. The Act also provided for a child conceived using the genetic material of one or both parties to a marriage but carried by a surrogate mother to be treated (through a parental order) as the child of that married couple. This provision was not extended to unmarried couples, even where there existed a stable and long-standing cohabiting partnership.

This Act did manage to clarify some of the issues surrounding new reproductive technology. However, the manner in which this clarification was made did in many ways uphold a conventional view of what a family is and what a father and a mother are. It rejected, rightly or wrongly, the opportunity to expand the general understanding of these categories which the ambiguities of the new reproductive technologies had thrown up. There was also to be more state regulation and control of reproductive technologies, with the prohibition of anyone providing or experimenting in human fertility treatment except in pursuance of a licence, and the creation of the Human Fertilisation and Embryology Authority to license, regulate and monitor clinics which provide infertility treatment and centres which carry out human embryo research.

The Act also provided for the first (and, so far, only successful) legislative limitation to the Abortion Act 1967. The upper limit for abortion had been set at 28 weeks gestation by the 1967 Act. Numerous private member's bills had sought to undermine this limit but had been unsuccessful. The Human Fertility and Embryology Act reduced the limit to 24 weeks, largely, it was argued, in recognition of medical advances which had increased the viability of foetuses after this stage in a pregnancy.

What is interesting about the set of definitions developed in the Human Fertility and Embryology Act is not that men and women who were not genetically linked to their children could be considered in law to be their parents, nor that men and women who were genetically the mother and father of such children could be deemed not to be their parents (because this has been the basis of adoption law for many years[57]) but rather that the law showed that definitions of parenthood were not fixed and indeed could change alongside both technological developments and developments in social practice. Also, as Jeffrey Weeks has argued, these issues which the Warnock Committee and later both the government and Parliament had to grapple with, had also exposed the limitations of the Wolfenden strategy, which had underpinned the legislation of consent of the 1960s, of distinguishing between private rights and public policy in moral matters.[58]

In conclusion

Some tentative conclusions from the information presented in this chapter may be possible. Clearly there has been some change within the patterns and trends in the organisation and practice of family life in Britain since the end of the 1960s, and some of these patterns and trends contrast quite sharply with those of the 1950s in particular. This could therefore be characterised as a period of diversification. However, whether this represents a change in the quality of family life is open to question. Furthermore, I would suggest that we should not underestimate the continuities and contradictions within these developments. I would add that such change within families must be understood in the context of wider cultural change on a national, and especially a global, level. A final conclusion would be that it may be more accurate to see such developments as limited *changes to* rather than a decline in family life and that, in some ways, family forms and the processes of family formation are changing rather than declining. This is perhaps best seen in the examples of cohabitation and births outside marriage. Although cohabitation has become a common domestic arrangement, research suggests this is usually pre-marital rather than non-marital (at least amongst most heterosexuals) and that cohabitation is now a standard part of the route to marriage. Similarly, the large rise in births outside marriage does not suggest a similarly large rise in births to single mothers, as it might have done in the 1950s. Rather, it is part of a new pattern of cohabiting (though as yet unmarried) couples becoming parents together.

Policy and the law surrounding families has struggled to recognise such change at the same time as generally favouring marriage (and the preservation of individual marriages in particular) over other family forms. Policy and the law have sometimes appeared contradictory, even within the same administration. This can perhaps be best explained firstly by the separation of legislature and judiciary, and the resultant autonomy of various parts of the apparatus of law-making; and secondly by policy on families being pulled in two or more different directions by the competing demands of different aspects of the ruling political philosophy. Clearly the full complexity of developments within the formation and organisation of family and domestic life is not yet represented in policy and the law, and is almost certainly not yet fully recognised by researchers. As such, I would suggest, argument and discussion about familly is likely to remain central to contemporary culture and debate.

APPENDIX

Questions for semi-structured oral history interview

General questions

Where and when were you born? What were your parents' occupations? Where did you live?

Can you tell me about your family?

Who lived in your home?

Did other family members live nearby? How much contact would you have had with them? Did family members help each other out? In what ways? Did this change over time?

How important was family to you? In what ways?

Marriage

Did you ever marry? Did you always expect to marry? Did this seem the 'natural' thing to do? Do you remember people who didn't marry?

What were your expectations of marriage?

Would you say it was an equal relationship? Did each partner have their own roles?

[if appropriate] What changes in circumstance did the war bring? What impact did these have on your marriage? Were these lasting impacts? Was it easy to readjust after the war?

Work

Tell me about the work you did. Did you work outside the home?

What attitudes towards women working outside the home do you remember? What was your own attitude? And that of other family members? Were your attitudes typical?

Turning to domestic work – who did what around the home? Did this change over time? Was this the usual pattern for people you knew?

Decline of the family?

Do you remember any talk of the family being in decline? Does this make any sense in your own life?

Chapter One Introduction: The idea of the family

1. 'Oxo halts "dated" TV family's gravy train', *The Guardian*, 31 August 1999, p.3.

2. There is a painful irony in the other newspaper stories featuring Linda Bellingham that year which chronicled her attempts at legal intervention relating to domestic violence.

3. 'Lords' gay ruling redefines the family', *The Guardian*, 29 October 1999, p.1.

4. Ibid.

5. Departmental Committee on Procedure in Matrimonial Causes, *Final Report*, Cmd 7024, 1947, para. 10.

6. Cmd 7566, 1949, para. 4.

7. Quoted in Ronald Fletcher, *The Abolitionists* (Routledge, London, 1988), p.5.

8. Ibid., p.6.

9. Jacqueline Rose, 'Margaret Thatcher and Ruth Ellis', *New Formations* 6 (1988), p.20, quoted in Jeffrey Weeks, 'Pretended family relationships', David Clark (ed.), *Marriage, Domestic Life and Social Change* (Routledge, London, 1991), p.215.

10. P. Glick, 'The family life cycle', *American Sociological Review*, 12 (1947), pp.164–74, quoted in B. Jane Elliott, 'Demographic trends in domestic life, 1945–87', in Clark (ed.), *Marriage, Domestic Life and Social Change*, p.105.

11. Raymond Williams, *Keywords* (Fontana, London, 1976), pp.133–4.

12. Diana Gittins, *The Family in Question* (Macmillan, London, 1985), p.2.

13. Michele Barrett and Mary McIntosh, *The Anti-social Family* (Verso, London, 1982), p.33.

14. Michele Barrett, *Women's Oppression Today* (Verso, London, 1980), p.187.

15. B. Jane Elliott provides a very useful account of the demographic trends of the period in her article 'Demographic trends in domestic life', in Clark (ed.), *Marriage, Domestic Life and Social Change*.

16. See particularly Slavoj Zizek, *Mapping Ideology* (Verso, London, 1994) for the parameters of this debate.

17. Terry Eagleton, *Ideology* (Verso, London, 1991).

18. Ibid., p.1.

19. Stuart Hall, 'The problem of ideology: Marxism without guarantees', in David Morley and Kuan-Hsing Chen (eds), *Stuart Hall – Critical Dialogues in Cultural Studies* (Routledge, London, 1996).

20. This latter way of thinking about ideology is evident in Karl Mannheim's *Ideology and Utopia*, trans. Edward Shils (Routledge & Kegan Paul, London, 1960; first published 1936).

21. See, for example, Gianni Vattimo, *The End of Modernity* (Polity Press, London, 1988).

22. Raymond Williams, *Culture and Society* (Penguin, London, 1958) and *The Long Revolution* (Penguin, London, 1961); E.P. Thompson, *The Making of the English Working Class* (Penguin, London, 1963).

23. Louis Althusser, *For Marx* (Allen Lane, London, 1969) and 'Ideology and ideological state apparatus (notes towards an investigation)', *Essays on Ideology* (Verso, London, 1984; first published 1970).

24. Graeme Turner, *British Cultural Studies*, 2nd edition (Routledge, London, 1996), pp.65–6, 194–7.

25. Ibid., p.199.

26. John B. Thompson, *Studies in the Theory of Ideology* (Polity Press, London, 1984), p.5.

27. Perry Anderson, 'The antinomies of Antonio Gramsci', *New Left Review* 100 (November 1976/January 1977).

28. Michel de Certeau, *The Practice of Everyday Life* (University of California Press, Berkeley, 1984).

29. Michael Anderson, *Approaches to the History of the Western Family 1500–1914* (Macmillan, London, 1980), p.14.

30. See particularly Peter Laslett (ed.), *Household and Family in Past Times* (Cambridge University Press, London, 1972).

31. See particularly Edward Shorter, *The Making of the Modern Family* (Collins, London, 1976) and Phillipe Aries, *Centuries of Childhood* (Penguin, Harmondsworth, 1962; first published Paris, 1960).

32. Leonore Davidoff and Catherine Hall, *Family Fortunes* (Routledge, London, 1992) and Leonore Davidoff, Megan Doolittle, Janet Fink and Katherine Holden, *The Family Story* (Longman, London, 1998).

33. Elizabeth Roberts, *Women and Families: An Oral History 1940–1970* (Blackwell, Oxford, 1995).

34. A fuller account of these is given in Chapter Six.

35. Anthony Giddens, *The Transformation of Intimacy: Sexuality, Love and Eroticism in Modern Societies* (Polity Press, Cambridge, 1992).

36. See Henning Bech, 'Report from a rotten state: "marriage" and "homosexuality" in Denmark', in Ken Plummer (ed.), *Modern Homosexualities* (Routledge, London, 1992) and Jeffrey Weeks, *Invented Moralities* (Polity Press, Cambridge, 1995).

37. See Eve Sedgwick, *Epistemology of the Closet* (Berkeley, New York, 1990); J. Katz, *The Invention of Heterosexuality* (Dutton, New York, 1995); and Jeffrey Weeks, Catherine Donovan and Brian Heaphy, *Families of Choice: Patterns of Non-heterosexual Relationships – A Literature Review* (South Bank University, London, 1996).

38. Richard Dyer, *The Matter of Images* (Routledge, London, 1993), p.3.

39. John Hill, *Sex, Class and Realism* (British Film Institute, London, 1986), p.2.

Chapter Two 'Family planning':
Families, policy and the law

1. Stuart Hall, 'Reformism and the legislation of consent', National Deviancy Conference (eds), *Permissiveness and Control* (Macmillan, London, 1980).

2. Royal Commission on Population (hereafter RCP), *Report*, Cmd 7695, 1949, p.iii.

3. Ibid., para. 617.

4. Ibid., para. 362.

5. Ibid., para. 651.

6. Ibid., para. 329.

7. Ibid., para. 330.

8. Ibid., para. 412.

9. Ibid., para. 418.

10. See Nicholas Timmins, *The Five Giants* (HarperCollins, London, 1995), pp.55–6.

11. Committee on Procedure in Matrimonial Causes (hereafter CPMC), *Final Report*, Cmd 7024, 1947, para. 10.

12. Royal Commission on Marriage and Divorce (hereafter RCMD), *Report*, Cmd 9678, 1955, pp.iii–iv.

13. CPMC, *Final Report*, para. 4.

14. Departmental Committee on Grants for the Development of Marriage Guidance (hereafter DCGDMG), *Report*, Cmd 7566, 1949, para. 6.

15. RCMD, *Report*, paras 35–7.

16. Ibid., para. 327.

17. DCGDMG, *Report*, para. 4.

18. RCMD, *Report*, para. 1162.

19. DCGDMG, *Report*, para. 5.

20. Denise Riley, *War in the Nursery: Theories of the Child and Mother* (Virago, London, 1983), p.196.

21. RCP, *Report*, para. 99.

22. Scottish Home Department Committee on Homeless Children, *Report*, Cmd 6911, 1946, paras 43 and 47.

23. Home Office, *Interim Report of the Care of Children Committee*, Cmd 6760, 1946, p.4.

24. Ibid., p.6.

25. Liz Heron (ed.), *Truth, Dare or Promise* (Virago, London, 1985), p.5.

26. Roy Parker, 'Family and social policy: an overview', in R.N. Rapoport, M.P. Fogarty and R. Rapoport (eds), *Families in Britain* (Routledge & Kegan Paul, London, 1982), pp.358–9.

27. From the Preface to Susan Pedersen, *Family, Dependence and the Origins of the Welfare State* (Cambridge University Press, Cambridge, 1993).

28. Timmins, *The Five Giants*, p.49.

29. No payment was to be made for the first child at this point.

30. See Eva M. Hubback, 'The family allowances movement, 1924–1948', in Eleanor Rathbone (ed.), *Family Allowances* (Allen & Unwin, London, 1948).

31. RCP, chapter 14.

32. Timmins, *The Five Giants*, p.263.

33. Quoted in Timmins, *The Five Giants*, p.55.

34. *Social Insurance and Allied Services Report*, Cmnd 6404, 1942, p.53.

35. RCP, *Report*, paras 518 and 493.

36. Ibid., para. 512. It is interesting to note in advocating the provision of day nurseries the RCP does not consider the benefits or implications that this may have for children but concentrates solely on benefits for the mother.

37. CPMC, *Final Report*, paras 28 and 4.

38. RCMD, *Report*, para. 327.

39. Timmins, *The Five Giants*, p.322.

40. Jeffrey Weeks, *Sex, Politics and Society* (Longman, Harlow, 1981), p.256.

41. Lorraine Fox Harding, *Family, State and Social Policy* (Macmillan, Basingstoke, 1996), p.174.

42. See Alan Sked and Chris Cook, *Post-war Britain* (Penguin, Harmondsworth, 1979) for fuller details.

43. See Timmins, *The Five Giants*, pp.144–5.

44. RCP, *Report*, para. 673.

45. Graham Crow, 'The postwar development of the domestic ideal', in Graham Allan and Graham Crow (eds), *Home and Family* (Macmillan, London, 1989), p.20.

46. Riley, *War in the Nursery*, pp.167–8.

47. Jennifer Craik, 'The making of mother: the role of the kitchen in the home', in Allan and Crow (eds), *Home and Family*, p.147.

48. Timmins, *The Five Giants*, p.145.

49. See for example G.C. Peden, *British Economic and Social Policy* (Phillip Allan, London, 1985 and 1991).

50. Jane Lewis, *Women in Britain* (Blackwell, Oxford, 1992), p.25.

51. Janet Walker, 'Interventions in families', in David Clark (ed.), *Marriage, Domestic Life and Social Change* (Routledge, London, 1991), p.191.

52. See Janet Finch and Penny Summerfield, 'Social reconstruction and the emergence of companionate marriage, 1945–59', in Clark (ed.), *Marriage, Domestic Life and Social Change*.

53. Heron (ed.), *Truth, Dare or Promise*, p.4.

54. RCMD, *Report*, para. 51.

55. This view seems to have been particularly popular in the Women's Co-operative movement. For a fuller account see Elizabeth Wilson, *Only Halfway to Paradise* (Tavistock, London, 1980), pp.69–74.

56. RCMD, *Report*, para. 54. My emphasis.

57. Stuart Hall, 'Reformism and the legislation of consent', in National Deviancy Conference (eds), *Permissiveness and Control*, (Macmillan, London, 1980), p.13.

58. There was nothing unusual in these two subjects being the subject of a common investigation. Both were integrally connected in the history of the law where they were seen to be aspects of the same moral problem.

59. Committee on Homosexual Offences and Prostitution, *Report* (Wolfenden Report), Cmnd 247, 1957, paras 12 and 14. This may well reflect the trend mentioned above for people to withdraw increasingly into a more private lifestyle.

60. See Harriet Jones and Michael Kandiali (eds), *The Myths of Consensus* (Macmillan, London, 1996) which developed from an Institute of Contemporary British History Conference in 1995.

61. Wolfenden Report, para. 45.

62. Stuart Hall, 'Reformism and the legislation of consent', p.16.

63. Hansard, 6 December 1968, p.2034.

64. Ibid.

65. Hansard 741 (1966–67), p.946.

66. Ibid., p.1004.

67. Timmins, *The Five Giants*, p.267.

68. Hansard 732 (1966–67), p.1075.

Chapter Three   Families, charities and local authorities

1. Martin Loney (ed.), *The State or the Market: Politics and Welfare in Contemporary Britain*, 2nd edition (Sage, London, 1991), p.137.

2. Andrew Land, *The Development of the Welfare State 1939–1951*, Public Record Office Handbook No. 25 (HMSO, 1992).

3. Roy Parker, 'Family and social policy: an overview', in R.N. Rapoport, M.P. Fogarty and R. Rapoport (eds), *Families in Britain* (Routledge & Kegan Paul, 1982).

4. London Borough of Greenwich (hereafter LBG), *Report of the Medical Officer of Health* (hereafter *MOH Report*), 1965, p.45.

5. These figures are taken from the Metropolitan Borough of Greenwich (hereafter MBG), *Report of the Medical Officer of Health*, 1945–49, and the Metropolitan Borough of Woolwich (hereafter MBW), *Annual Report on the Health of the Metropolitan Borough of Woolwich*, 1945 to 1955.

6. LBG, *MOH Report*, 1968, p.94.

7. LBG, *MOH Report*, 1970, pp.94–5.

8. MBW, *Minutes of Proceedings* (Maternity and Child Welfare Committee), 11 October 1944, minute 17. My emphasis.

9. MBG, *Minutes of Proceedings* (Public Health, Maternity and Child Welfare Committee), 22 November 1944.

10. LBG, *MOH Report*, 1965, p.48.

11. LBG, *MOH Report*, 1966, p.12.

12. LBG, *MOH Report*, 1965, p.107.

13. Ibid., pp.105–6.

14. Ibid., p.102.

15. Ibid.

16. See, for example, J. Donzelot, *The Policing of Families: Welfare versus the State* (Hutchinson, London, 1979); S. Cohen, *Visions of Social Control* (Polity Press, Cambridge, 1985); and D. Howe, *The Consumers's View of Family Therapy* (Gower, Aldershot, 1989).

17. Janet Walker, 'Interventions in families', in David Clark (ed.), *Marriage, Domestic Life and Social Change* (Routledge, London, 1991), p.207.

18. Oral interview with Mr A.H. Wilcox (1993). Mr Wilcox worked in the Medical Officer of Health's department and was responsible for producing the MOH's annual report in the 1950s and 1960s. Tape and transcript held in University of Greenwich Oral History Archive.

19. Interview with Mr A.H. Wilcox, transcript p.6 and p.19.

20. Walker, 'Interventions in families', p.191.

21. LBG, *MOH Report*, 1966, pp.99–100.

22. LBG, *MOH Report*, 1967, p.97.

23. LBG, *MOH Report*, 1969, p.99.

24. MBG, *Municipal Tenant's Handbook*, 2nd edition (1953), p.11.

25. Parker, 'Family and social policy', p.361.

26. LBG, *Minutes of Proceedings*, April 1965, p.33.

27. LBG, *MOH Report*, 1966, p.70.

28. MBG, *Minutes of Proceedings*, 21 March 1945, and MBW, *Annual Report on the Health of the Metropolitan Borough of Woolwich for the Year 1946*, p.10.

29. MBG, *Minutes*, 20 December 1944.

30. LBG, *MOH Report*, 1965, p.97

31. Denise Riley, 'War in the nursery', *Feminist Review* 2 (1979), and *War in the Nursery: Theories of the Child and Mother* (Virago, London, 1983).

32. MBW, *Minutes of Proceedings* (Maternity and Child Welfare Committee), 16 April 1947.

33. LBG, *MOH Report*, 1965, pp.105–6.

34. Ibid., 1965, p.106.

35. MBW, *Annual Report on Health*, 1956, pp.21–2.

36. See especially MOH reports for the MBW, MBG and LBG.

37. MBW, *Annual Report on Health*, 1957, p.27.

38. Information from MOH reports.

39. See Jane Lewis, *The Voluntary Sector, the State and Social Work in Britain* (Edward Elgar, Aldershot, 1995).

40. Madeline Rooff, *A Hundred Years of Family Welfare* (Michael Joseph, London, 1972).

41. Family Welfare Association pamphlet (n.d.), p.3. The pamphlet must date from between 1952 and 1957 as it indicates that its patron is Queen Elizabeth II and a foreword is written by Sir Colin Jardine, the FWA chairman who died in 1957.

42. Family Welfare Association, 79th Annual Report of the Council, 1946/47, p.3.

43. FWA, *Annual Report*, 1947/48, p.3.

44. FWA, *Annual Report*, 1959/60, p.5.

45. See discussion further on.

46. FWA, *Annual Report*, 1954/55, p.4.

47. Ibid., p.3.

48. FWA pamphlet (n.d.), pp.3–4.

49. Deptford and Greenwich COS and CAB, *Annual Report*, 1944–45, p.5.

50. FWA, *Annual Report*, 1959/60, pp.8–9.

51. FWA, *94th Annual Report of the Council*, 1960/61, p.6.

52. FWA pamphlet (n.d.), p.15.

53. It was a condition of use that these case notes should remain anonymous. The references given are to the document's classification number in the London Metropolitan Archive. This example is from case notes A/FWA/GL/B6/6.

54. A/FWA/GL/B6/3.

55. A/FWA/GL/B6/12.

56. A/FWA/GL/B6/129.

57. A/FWA/GL/B6/3.

58. A/FWA/GL/B6/129.

59. See, for example, A/FWA/GL/B6/3.

60. See (1) Adrian Webb and Gerald Wistow, 'Social services', in Stewert Ranson, George Jones and Kieron Walsh (eds), *Between Centre and Locality: The Politics of Public Policy* (Allen & Unwin, London, 1985), and (2) Adrian Webb and Gerald Wistow, *Planning, Scarcity and Need* (Allen & Unwin, London, 1986).

Chapter Four   'Family viewing': Family, popular culture, representation

1. The Monopolies Commission, *Films: A Report on the Supply of Films for Exhibition in Cinemas* (HMSO, London, 1966), PP HC206, p.92.

2. Peter Lewis, *The Fifties* (Heinemann, London, 1978), p.208.

3. Eric Hobsbawm, *The Age of Extremes* (Penguin, Harmondsworth, 1994), pp.500–2.

4. I am indebted to David Lusted for this information.

5. For example, Janet Thumin's unpublished work on female audiences and their negotiation of the televisual discourses of the 1950s (seminar paper given at the University of East London's Cultural Studies Department 'Visiting Speaker' programme, 6 June 1996).

6. Stuart Hall, 'Encoding, decoding', in Simon During (ed.), *The Cultural Studies Reader* (Routledge, London, 1993).

7. Richard Dyer, *The Matter of Images* (Routledge, 1993), p.1.

8. John Hill, *Sex, Class and Realism* (British Film Institute, London, 1986), p.1.

9. Raymond Williams, *Culture and Society* (Pelican, London, 1958).

10. Anecdotal evidence from colleagues who were living in the United States at the time.

11. Janet Thumim, *Celluloid Sisters: Women and Popular Cinema* (Macmillan, London, 1992).

12. *The Guardian*, 13 August 1963, quoted in John Hill, *Sex, Class and Realism*.

13. *Daily Express*, 3 April 1959.

14. *Sunday Express*, 25 January 1959.

15. *Saturday Review*, 11 April 1959.

16. I am using this term to avoid using any anachronisms.

17. See Marcia Landy, *British Genres: Cinema and Society 1930–60* (Princeton University Press, Oxford, 1991).

18. Richard Dyer, '*Victim*: hegemonic project', in *The Matter of Images* (first published 1977).

19. See Richard Dyer's essay 'Sad young men' in *The Matter of Images*.

20. Thumim, *Celluloid Sisters*, pp.36–7 and 60–1.

21. Len England, 'The film and family life', in Jeffrey Richards and Dorothy Sheridan, *Mass-Observation at the Movies* (Routledge & Kegan Paul, London, 1987; first published 1944).

22. *The Times*, 8 December 1995.

23. Laura Jesson describes herself in this way.

24. Marjorie Fergusson, *Forever Feminine – Women's Magazines and the Cult of Femininity* (Heinemann, London, 1983), p.22.

25. Landy, *British Genres*, p.317.

26. Ken Plummer, *Telling Sexual Stories* (Routledge, London, 1995), p.152.

27. England, 'The film and family life', p.292.

28. These films can be seen at the Imperial War Museum film and video archive in London.

29. Fergusson, *Forever Feminine*, p.48.

30. Colin McInnes, *Absolute Beginners* (Allison & Busby, London, p.29; first published 1959).

31. See John Hill, *Sex, Class and Realism*.

32. David Morgan, 'Ideologies of marriage and family life', in David Clark (ed.) *Marriage, Domestic Life and Social Change* (Routledge, London, 1991), p.120.

33. Sir John Woolfe, co-producer of *Room at the Top*, at a screening of the film at the National Film Theatre, London, March 1995.

34. Robert Murphy makes this argument in *Sixties British Cinema* (British Film Institute, London, 1992).

35. Ibid., p.143.

36. Ibid.

37. Quoted from the cover of the book which accompanied the television play.

Chapter Five 'Relatively speaking': Family, experience, memory

1. Elizabeth Roberts, *Women and Families: An Oral History 1940–1970* (Blackwell, Oxford, 1995). Roberts points out in her opening chapter that it is not intended to discuss here [oral history's] potential or its limitations'. She also asserts that the research adopted 'no particular theoretical standpoint' (p.3).

2. Alistair Thompson, Michael Frisch and Paula Hamilton, 'The memory and history debates: some international perspectives', *Oral History* (Autumn 1994).

3. Stephen Koss, Review of Paul Thompson's *The Edwardians*, *Times Literary Supplement*, 5 December 1975.

4. See Henry Hodysk and Gordon McIntosh, 'Problems of objectivity in oral history', *Historical Studies in Education* 1, 1 (1991), and Wayne Roberts 'Using oral history to study working class history', Canadian Oral History Association Conference, Toronto, 1991, both quoted in Joan Sangster, 'Telling our stories: feminist debates and the use of oral history', *Women's History Review* 3, 1 (1994).

5. Popular Memory Group, 'Popular memory: theory, politics, method', in Richard Johnson, Gregor McLennan, Bill Schwarz and David Sutton (eds), *Making Histories* (Hutchinson, London, 1982), p.226.

6. See Thompson *et al.*, 'The memory and history debates', p.34.

7. Raphael Samuel and Paul Thompson, *The Myths We Live By* (Routledge, London, 1990), p.2.

8. Joan Sangster, 'Telling our stories: feminist debates and the use of oral history', *Women's History Review* 3, 1 (1994), p.6. Penny Summerfield has a very useful account of the history of debates within feminism about oral history and theory in *Reconstructing Women's Wartime Lives* (Manchester University Press, Manchester, 1998), pp.9–16.

9. Today the London Borough of Greenwich is an ethnicly diverse area with around 13 per cent of people from various ethnic minorities. The large Asian population in some areas of the borough did not settle substantially until the 1970s. (Source: Commission for Racial Equality, Greenwich.)

10. This would seem to resonate with Elizabeth Roberts's findings in the north-west of England where she reported 'little evidence that these measures had a direct impact on our respondants during this period'. Roberts, *Women and Families*, p.13.

11. See the note on the Mass Observation archive in Angus Calder and Dorothy Sheridan (eds), *Speak for Yourself* (Oxford University Press, Oxford 1985), pp.246–53.

12. Ibid., p.250.

13. Hall–Carpenter Archives, *Inventing Ourselves* and *Walking After Midnight* (Routledge, London, 1989). See also Kevin Porter and Jeffrey Weeks (eds), *Between the Acts* (Routledge, London, 1991).

14. Janet Finch, *Family Obligation and Social Change* (Polity Press, London, 1989).

15. Graham Dawson, *Soldier Heroes, British Adventure, Empire and the Imaginings of Masculinites* (Routledge, London, 1994).

16. Ibid., p.23.

17. Samuel and Thompson, *The Myths We Live By*, p.8.

18. Leonore Davidoff and Catherine Hall, *Family Fortunes* (Routledge, London, 1987), and Sangster, 'Telling our stories', p.7.

19. Summerfield, *Reconstructing Women's Wartime Lives*.

20. See Sangster, 'Telling our stories'.

21. Barrie Thorne, 'Feminist rethinking of the family: an overview', in Barrie Thorne and Marilyn Yalom (eds), *Rethinking the Family* (Longman, New York, 1982).

22. Newham History Workshop, *A Marsh and a Gasworks: One Hundred Years of Life in West Ham* (Parents' Centre Publications, London, 1986).

23. Roberts, *Women and Families*, p.1.

24. Michael Anderson, 'Some salient features of the modern family', in British Society for Population Studies, Occasional Paper 31, *The Family* (London, 1983).

25. Finch, *Family Obligation and Social Change*.

26. See, for example, Michael Wilmott and Peter Young, *Family and Kinship in East London* (Routledge & Kegan Paul, London, 1957).

Chapter Six   Conclusions

1. Tony Bennett, Colin Mercer and Janet Woollacott (eds), *Popular Culture and Social Relations* (Open University Press, Milton Keynes, 1986), pp.xv–xvi.

2. Stuart Hall, 'The problem of ideology: Marxism without guarantees', in David Morely and Kuan-Hsing Chen (eds), *Stuart Hall – Critical Dialogues in Cultural Studies* (Routledge, London, 1996), p.27.

3. Stuart Hall, 'Encoding, decoding', in Simon During (ed.), *The Cultural Studies Reader* (Routledge, London, 1993), p.100.

4. Graeme Turner, *British Cultural Studies*, 2nd edition (Routledge, London, 1996).

5. Marshall Berman, *All that is Solid Melts into Air* (Verso, London, 1983).

6. Anthony Giddens, *The Transformation of Intimacy* (Polity Press, Cambridge, 1992).

7. See Patricia Holland, 'Introduction: history, memory and the family album', in Jo Spence and Patricia Holland (eds), *Family Snaps – The Meanings of Domestic Photography* (Virago, London, 1991).

8. Stuart Hall, 'The rediscovery of "ideology": the return of the "repressed" in media studies', in Michael Gurevitch, Tony Bennett, James Curran and Janet Woollacott (eds), *Culture, Society and the Media* (Methuen, London, 1982).

9. See Turner, *British Cultural Studies*, pp.204, 211–12.

10. Harriett Gilbert, 'Growing pains', in Liz Heron (ed.), *Truth, Dare or Promise: Girls Growing Up in the Fifties* (Virago, London, 1985), p.52.

Chapter Seven   Postscript: New families?
From the permissive moment to the present

1. For example, in 1979, the family information section of the Central Statistical Office's, *General Household Survey* was expanded to include information on past and present experience of cohabitation.

2. All figures taken from *Population Trends* 100 (Office of National Statistics, 2000).

3. *General Household Survey*, quoted in *Population Trends* 100, p.28. Figures for same-sex couples are not included in this survey.

4. For example John Gillis, *For Better, For Worse: British Marriages 1600 to the Present* (Oxford University Press, Oxford, 1985).

5. *General Household Survey*, quoted in John Haskey, 'Demographic issues in 1975 and 2000', *Population Trends* 100, p.29.

6. See Chapter Two.

7. *Population Trends* no. 100, pp.5, 7, and C. Shaw, 'Recent trends in family size and family building', *Population Trends* 58 (1989).

8. A. Coote, H. Harman and H. Hewitt, 'Changing family structure and family behaviour', in John Eekelaar and Mavis Maclean (eds), *A Reader on Family Law* (Oxford University Press, Oxford, 1994).

9. Bev Botting and Karen Dunnell, 'Trends in fertility and contraception in the last quarter of the 20th century', *Population Trends* 100, pp.32–38.

10. *Population Trends*, no. 100, p.63.

11. 'Live births outside marriage: age of mother and type of registration', *Population Trends* 100, p.63, table 3.2.

12. 'Population: age, sex and legal marital status', *Population Trends* 100, p.56, table 1.6.

13. John Haskey, 'The proportion of marriages ending in divorce', *Population Trends* 27 (1982).

14. John Haskey, 'Demographic issues in 1975 and 2000', p.27.

15. A. Brown and K. Kiernan, 'Cohabitation in Great Britain', *Population Trends* 25 (1981).

16. John Haskey, 'Demographic issues in 1975 and 2000', p.27.

17. Demos, quoted in 'Truce in the war of the sexes', *The Guardian* 2, 6 March 1995, p.3.

18. Michael Murphy, 'Family and household issues', in A. Dale (ed.), *Looking Towards the 2001 Census*, OPCS Occasional Paper 46 (OPCS, London, 1996).

19. L. Rubin, *Just Friends: The Role of Friendship in our Lives* (Harper & Row, New York, 1985), and C. Becker, *Living and Relating* (Sage, London, 1992).

20. See Jeffrey Weeks, Catherine Donovan and Brian Heaphy, *Families of Choice: A Literature Review*, South Bank University Social Science Research Papers, March 1996.

21. Ann Berrington and Mike Murphy, 'Changes in the living arrangements of young adults in Britain during the 1980s', *European Sociological Review* 10 (1994), no. 3.

22. Jenny de Jong Gierveld, Aart Liefbroer and Erik Beekink, 'The effect of parental resources on patterns of leaving home among young adults in the Netherlands', *European Sociological Review* 7 (1991), no. 1; G. Jones and Claire Wallace, *Youth, Family and Citizenship* (Open University Press, Buckingham, 1992); G. Jones, *Leaving Home* (Open University Press, Buckingham, 1995).

23. Berrington and Murphy, 'Changes in the living arrangements of young adults'; Jones and Wallace, *Youth, Family and Citizenship*; and G. Jones, *Leaving Home*.

24. Sue Heath, *Young Adults and Shared Household Living* (ESRC Project, University of Southampton, forthcoming).

25. Figures produced in *Social Trends* 27 (1997), quoted in 'Home alone', *The Guardian*, 20 January 1998, p.13.

26. See Jacqueline Burgoyne and David Clark, *Making a Go of it* (Routledge & Kegan Paul, London, 1984); Jacqueline Burgoyne, R. Ormrod and M. Richards, *Divorce Matters* (Penguin, Harmondsworth, 1987); Christopher Cullow, 'Making, breaking and remaking marriage', in David Clark (ed.), *Marriage, Domestic Life and Social Change* (Routledge, London, 1991).

27. For example, Lorraine Fox Harding, *Family, State and Social Policy* (Macmillan, Basingstoke, 1996), p.74, and Cheryl Williams, 'National Step-families Association', *The Guardian 2*, 15 October 1997, p.3.

28. Janet Finch, *Family Obligation and Social Change* (Polity Press, Cambridge, 1989), and Janet Finch and Jennifer Mason, *Negotiating Family Responsibilities* (Routledge, London, 1993).

29. Anthony Giddens, *The Transformation of Intimacy: Sexuality, Love and Eroticism in Modern Societies* (Polity Press, Cambridge, 1992).

30. See Carol Smart and Brendan Neale, *Family Fragments?* (Polity Press, Cambridge, 1999).

31. See Henning Bech, 'Report from a rotten state: "Marriage" and "Homosexuality" in Denmark', in Ken Plummer (ed.), *Modern Homosexualities* (Routledge, London, 1992), and Jeffrey Weeks, *Invented Moralities* (Polity Press, Cambridge, 1995).

32. Fiona McAllister with Lynda Clarke, *Choosing Childlessness* (Family Policy Studies Centre, London, 1998).

33. For example, the British Organisation of Non-Parents and No Kidding!

34. See 'One dad good, two dads better?', *The Times*, 9 November 1999, pp.10–11.

35. See, for example, 'Mother, 54, plans her second baby by test-tube', *The Guardian*, 2 August 1997, p.2, and 'Test-tube mum expects again at 55', *The Guardian*, 12 September 1998, p.7.

36. The case was brought, and lost, by Stephen Whittle. See 'In the name of the father', *The Guardian*, 22 April 1997, p.17.

37. A. Coote, H. Harman and H. Hewitt, 'Changing family structure and family behaviour', p.39, using J. Haskey, 'Families and households of the ethnic minority and White populations of Great Britain', *Population Trends* 57 (1989).

38. Fox Harding, *Family, State and Social Policy*.

39. Ibid. pp.116–17.

40. John Dewar, *Law and the Family* (Butterworths, London, 1992), p.71.

41. Fox Harding, *Family, State and Social Policy*, p.126.

42. Jeffrey Weeks, *Sex, Politics and Society*, 2nd edition (Longman, Harlow, 1989), p.294. See also James Walvin, *Victorian Values* (Cardinal, London, 1988).

43. Weeks, *Sex, Politics and Society*, p.295.

44. Jeffrey Weeks, 'Pretended family relationships', in David Clark (ed.), *Marriage, Domestic Life and Social Change* (Routledge, London, 1991).

45. Quoted in 'Blair calls for age of giving', *The Guardian*, 1 October 1997, p.8.

46. See Chapter Two.

47. Home Office, *Supporting Families – Summary Leaflet* (HMSO, London, 1998), p.1.

48. Scottish Home Department Committee on Homeless Children, *Report*, Cmd 69, 1946, para. 43. See Chapter Two of this book.

49. Elizabeth Silva and Carol Smart, 'The "new" practices and politics of family life', in Silva and Smart (eds), *The New Family?* (Sage, London, 1999), p.3.

50. See Fox Harding, *Family, State and Social Policy*, pp.112–14.

51. Ibid., pp.128–31.

52. In January 2001 the Lord Chancellor's Department announced the government's intention to ask Parliament to repeal Part II of the Family Law Act 1996 because the various new models for reflection and reconciliation had proved to be less successful or workable than anticipated. However, the sentiments of this section of the Act are still worth noting.

53. Jane Lewis, *Women in Britain Since 1945* (Blackwell, Oxford, 1992).

54. See Fox Harding, *Family, State and Social Policy*, pp.166–71. Local conditions do vary, though, according to the specific policy of local authorities.

55. Department of Health and Social Security, *Report of the Committee of Inquiry into Human Fertilisation and Embryology*, Cmnd 9314, 1987.

56. Human Fertilisation and Embryology Act 1990, paragraph 27, subsection 1.

57. The Adoption Act 1926, an earlier example of changing thinking about definitions of family, created the legal process of adoption, allowing for the removal of parental status from biological parents and the transferring of this status to adoptive parents by means of a court order.

58. Weeks, *Sex, Politics and Society*, p.297.

Primary sources

Official publications

Abortion Act 1967

Committee on Grants for the Development of Marriage Guidance, *Report*, CMD 7566, 1949

Committee on Homosexual Offenses and Prostitution, *Report*, Cmnd 247, 1957

Committee on Procedure in Matrimonial Causes, *Final Report*, Cmd 7024, 1947

Committee on Social Insurance and Allied Services, *Report*, Cmd 6404, 1942

Divorce (Reform) Act 1969

Hansard, 1945–70

Home Office, *Training in Childcare: Interim Report of the Care of Children Committee*, CMD 6760, 1946

Home Office, Ministry of Health and Ministry of Education Care of Children Committee, *Report*, Cmd 6922, 1946

Home Office, *Supporting Families – Summary Leaflet* (HMSO, London, 1998)

Home Office, *Supporting Families: A Consultation Document* (HMSO, London, 1998)

NHS (Family Planning) Act 1967

Royal Commission on Marriage and Divorce, *Report*, Cmd 9678, 1955

Royal Commission on Population, *Report*, Cmd 7695, 1949

Scottish Home Department Committee on Homeless Children, *Report*, Cmd 6911, 1946

Sexual Offences Act 1967

Local authority and voluntary sector papers

Deptford and Greenwich Family Welfare Association, *Annual Report*, 1944/45 to 1948/49

Family Welfare Association (formerly the Charity Organisation Society), *Annual Reports of the Council*, 1944/45 to 1964/65

Family Welfare Association Area 6 (Lewisham, Greenwich and Deptford), *Annual Report*, 1949/50 to 1964/65

Family Welfare Association, *The Family Welfare Association*, pamphlet (n.d.)

Greenwich Council of Social Service, *4th Annual Report*, 1969

London Borough of Greenwich, *Forward to Modernity: A Systematic Approach to Local Authority Management*, 1968

London Borough of Greenwich, *Minutes*, 1965 to 1970

London Borough of Greenwich, *Report of the Medical Officer of Health*, 1965 to 1970

Metropolitan Borough of Greenwich, *Minutes of Proceedings*, 1943 to 1965

Metropolitan Borough of Greenwich, *Municipal Tenants' Handbook*, 1949 to 1953

Metropolitan Borough of Greenwich, *Report of the Medical Officer of Health*, 1945 to 1956

Metropolitan Borough of Woolwich, *Annual Report on the Health of the Metropolitan Borough of Woolwich*, 1945 to 1962

Metropolitan Borough of Woolwich, *Minutes of Proceedings*, 1943 to 1962

Filmography

A Kind of Loving (1962), cert. X, dir. John Schlesinger, sc. Willis Hall and Keith Waterhouse from the novel by Stan Barstow

Alfie (1966), cert. X, dir. Lewis Gilbert, sc. Bill Naughtton from his own play

A Taste of Honey (1960), cert. X, dir. Tony Richardson, sc. Shelagh Delaney and Tony Richardson from Delaney's stageplay

Billy Liar (1963), cert. A, dir. John Schlesinger, sc. Keith Waterhouse and Willis Hall based on the novel by Keith Waterhouse

Brief Encounter (1945), dir. David Lean, sc. Noel Coward

Georgy Girl (1966), dir. Silvio Narizzano, from the novel by Margaret Forster

Here Come the Huggetts (1948), dir. Ken Annakin

Holiday Camp (1947), dir. Ken Annakin

It Always Rains On Sundays (1947), dir. Robert Hamer, sc. Angus Macphail, Robert Hamer and Henry Cornelius, from the novel by Arthur la Bern

Joanna (1968), dir. Mike Sarne

Life at the Top (1965), dir. Ted Kotchoff

Look Back in Anger (1959), cert. X, dir. Tony Richardson, sc. Nigel Keane from the stageplay by John Osbourne

Poor Cow (1967), dir. Ken Loach, sc. Nell Dunn

Room at the Top (1959), cert. X, dir. Jack Clayton, sc. Neil Paterson from the novel by John Braine

Sapphire (1959), cert. A, dir. Basil Dearden, sc. Janet Green

Saturday Night and Sunday Morning (1959), cert. X, dir. Karel Reisz, sc. Alan Sillitoe from his own novel

The Blue Lamp (1950), cert. A, dir. Basil Dearden, sc. T.E.B. Clarke from the novel by Ted Willis

The Leather Boys (1963), cert. X, dir. Sidney J. Furie, sc. Gillian Freeman, based on the novel by Eliot George

Victim (1961), cert. X, dir. Basil Dearden, sc. Janet Green

Oral sources

It was agreed to let interviewees remain anonymous, so pseudonyms have been used. All tapes and transcripts are held at the University of Greenwich Oral History Archive.

Anne, born 1933, interviewed in 1992
Betty, born 1912, interviewed in Woolwich, 1992
Christine, born 1941, interviewed 1992
Doug, born 1916, interviewed 1991
Elsie, born 1922, interviewed 1991
Gerald, born 1915, interviewed 1993
Helen, born 1939, interviewed 1992
Irene, born 1919, interviewed 1991
Jim, born 1938, interviewed 1993
Les, born 1917, interviewed 1993
Martin, born 1937, interviewed 1993
Sheila, born 1936, interviewed 1992
Ted, born 1919, interviewed 1992
Yvonne, born 1930, interviewed 1993

Secondary sources

All places of publication are London unless otherwise stated.

Louis Althusser, 'Ideology and ideological state apparatus (Notes towards an investigation)', *Essays on Ideology* (Verso, 1984; first published 1970)

Michael Anderson, *Approaches to the History of the Western Family 1500–1914* (Macmillan, 1980)

Perry Anderson, 'The antinomies of Antonio Gramsci', *New Left Review* 100 (November 1976)

Phillipe Aries, *Centuries of Childhood* (Penguin, 1962; first published Paris, 1960)

Michele Barrett, *Women's Oppression Today* (Verso, 1980)

Michele Barrett and Mary McIntosh, *The Anti-social Family* (Verso, 1982)

Ulrich Beck, *Risk Society: Towards a New Modernity* (Sage, 1992)

Marshall Berman, *All that is Solid Melts into Air* (Verso, 1983)

Ann Berrington and Mike Murphy, 'Changes in the living arrangements of young adults in Britain during the 1980s', *European Sociological Review* 10 (1994), no.3

Muriel Brown, *Introduction to Social Administration in Britain*, 6th edition (Hutchinson, 1985)

Jacqueline Burgoyne and David Clark, *Making a Go of it* (Routledge and Kegan Paul, 1984)

Jacqueline Burgoyne, R. Ormrod and M. Richards, *Divorce Matters* (Penguin, Harmondsworth, 1987)

David Clark (ed.) *Marriage, Domestic Life and Social Change* (Routledge, 1991)

A. Coote, H. Harman and H. Hewitt, 'Changing patterns of family life', in John Eekelaar and Mavis Maclean (eds) *A Reader on Family Law* (Oxford University Press, Oxford, 1994)

Timothy Corrigan, *A Short Guide to Writing about Film* (HarperCollins, New York, 1994)

Jennifer Craik, 'The making of mother: the role of the kitchen in the home', in Graham Allan and Graham Crow (eds), *Home and Family* (Macmillan, 1989)

Graham Crow, 'The postwar development of the domestic ideal', in Graham Alan and Graham Crow (eds), *Home and Family* (Macmillan, 1989)

Ann Dally, *Inventing Motherhood* (Burnett Books, 1982)

Graham Dawson, letter to *Oral History* (Spring 1996)

Graham Dawson, *Soldier Heroes, British Adventure, Empire and the Imaginings of Masculinites* (Routledge, 1994)

John Dewar with Stephen Parker, *Law and the Family* (Butterworths, 1992)

Michael Drake (ed.), *Time, Family and Community* (Blackwell, Oxford, 1994)

Michael Drake and Ruth Finnegan, *Sources and Methods for Family and Community History: A Handbook* (Cambridge University Press, 1994)

Richard Dyer, *The Matter of Images* (Routledge, 1993)

Terry Eagleton, *Ideology* (Verso, 1991)

Felicity Edholm, 'The unnatural family', in Martin Loney *et al.* (eds), *The State or the Market* (Sage, 1991)

John Eekelaar and Mavis Maclean (eds), *A Reader on Family Law* (Oxford University Press, Oxford, 1994)

B. Jane Elliot, 'Demographic trends in domestic life, 1945–1987', in David Clark (ed.), *Marriage, Domestic Life and Social Change* (Routledge, 1991)

Friedrich Engels, *The Origins of the Family, Private Property and the State* (Penguin, 1986; first published 1884)

James Fentress and Chris Wickham, *Social Memory* (Blackwell, Oxford, 1992)

Marjorie Fergusson, *Forever Feminine* (Heinemann, 1983)

Janet Finch, *Family Obligation and Social Change* (Polity Press, 1989)

Janet Finch and Jennifer Mason, *Negotiating Family Responsibilities* (Routledge, 1993)

Janet Finch and Penny Summerfield, 'Social reconstruction and the emergence of companionate marriage, 1945–59', in David Clark (ed.), *Marriage, Domestic Life and Social Change* (Routledge, 1991)

Ronald Fletcher, *The Abolitionists* (Routledge, 1988)

John Fox and David Pearce, '25 years of population trends', *Population Trends*, 100 (HMSO, 2000)

Lorraine Fox Harding, *Perspectives in Childcare Policy* (Longman, Harlow, 1991)

Lorraine Fox Harding, *Family, State and Social Policy* (Macmillan, 1996)

Anthony Giddens, *The Transformation of Intimacy* (Polity Press, Cambridge, 1992)

Diana Gittins, *Fair Sex* (Hutchinson, 1982)

Diana Gittins, *The Family in Question* (Macmillan, 1985)

Jack Goody, *The European Family* (Blackwell, Oxford, 2000)

Antonio Gramsci, *Selections from the Prison Notebooks* (Lawrence & Wishart, 1976)

Stuart Hall, 'Reformism and the legislation of consent', in National Deviancy Conference (eds), *Permissiveness and Control* (Macmillan, 1980)

Stuart Hall, 'The rediscovery of "ideology": the return of the "repressed" in media studies', in Michael Gurevitch, Tony Bennett, James Curran and Janet Woollacott (eds), *Culture, Society and the Media* (Methuen, 1982)

Stuart Hall, 'Encoding, decoding', in Simon During (ed.), *The Cultural Studies Reader* (Routledge, 1993)

Stuart Hall, 'The problem of ideology – Marxism without guarantees', in David Morley and Kuan-Hsing Chen (eds), *Stuart Hall – Critical Dialogues in Cultural Studies* (Routledge, 1996)

Tamara Hareven, 'The history of the family and the complexity of social change', *American History Review* 96 (1991), no.1

Jose Harris, 'Some aspects of social policy in Britain during World War Two', in W.J. Mommsen (ed.), *The Emergence of the Welfare State in Britain and Germany, 1850– 1950* (Croom Helm, 1981)

John Haskey, 'Demographic issues in 1975 and 2000', *Population Trends* 100 (HMSO, 2000)

David Henige, *Oral Historiography* (Longman, 1982)

Liz Heron (ed.), *Truth, Dare or Promise* (Virago, 1985)

Jurgen Hess, 'The social policy of the Atlee government', in W.J. Mommsen (ed.), *The Emergence of the Welfare State in Britain and Germany, 1850–1950* (Croom Helm, 1981)

John Hill, *Sex, Class and Realism* (British Film Institute, 1986)

Eric Hobsbawm, *The Age of Extremes* (Penguin, Harmondsworth, 1994)

Richard Hoggart, *The Uses of Literacy* (Chatto & Windus, 1957)

Eva M. Hubback, 'The Family Allowances movement, 1927–1948', in Elennor Rathbone (ed.), *Family Allowances* (Allen & Unwin, 1948; a new edition of *The Disinherited Family*, 1924)

Keith Jenkins, *Re-thinking History* (Routledge, 1991)

Annette Kuhn, *The Power of the Image* (Routledge, 1992)

Marcia Landy, *British Genres: Cinema and Society 1930–60* (Princeton University Press, Oxford, 1991)

Jorge Larrain, 'Stuart Hall and the Marxist concept of ideology', in David Morley and Kuan-Hsing Chen (eds), *Stuart Hall – Critical Dialogues in Cultural Studies* (Routledge, 1996)

Jane Lewis, *Women in Britain Since 1945* (Blackwell, Oxford, 1992)

Jane Lewis, *The Voluntary Sector, the State and Social Work in Britain* (Edward Elgar, Aldershot, 1995)

Jane Lewis, David Clarke and David Morgan, *Whom God Hath Joined Together: The Work of Marriage Guidance* (Routledge, 1992)

Trevor Lummis, *Listening to History* (Hutchinson, 1985)

Fiona McAllister with Lynda Clarke, *Choosing Childlessness* (Family Policy Studies Centre, 1998)

Karl Mannheim, *Ideology and Utopia*, trans. Edward Shils, (Routledge & Kegan Paul, 1960; first published 1936)

David Morgan, 'Ideologies of marriage and family life', in David Clark (ed.), *Marriage, Domestic Life and Social Change* (Routledge, 1991)

David H.J. Morgan, 'Risk and family practices: accounting for change and fluidity in family life', in Elizabeth B. Silva and Carol Smart (eds), *The New Family?* (Sage, 1999)

Ferdinand Mount, *The Subversive Family* (Jonathan Cape, 1982)

Mike Murphy, 'Family and household issues', in A. Dale (ed.), *Looking Towards the 2001 Census*, OPCS Occasional Paper 46 (OPCS, 1996)

Robert Murphy, *Sixties British Cinema* (British Film Institute, 1992)

Roy Parker, 'Family and social policy: an overview', in R.N. Rapoport, M.P. Fogarty and R. Rapoport (eds), *Families in Britain* (Routledge & Kegan Paul, 1982)

Luisa Passerini, 'Work, ideology and consensus under Italian fascism', *History Workshop Journal* 8 (1979)

G.C. Peden, *British Economic and Social Policy* (Phillip Allan, 1991; first published 1985)

Melanie Phillips, *Who Killed the Family?* BBC 2, 31 October 1995

Popular Memory Group, 'Popular memory: theory, politics, method', in Richard Johnson, Gregor McLennan, Bill Schwarz and David Sutton (eds), *Making Histories* (Hutchinson, 1982)

Kevin Porter and Jeffrey Weeks, *Between the Acts* (Routledge, 1991)

Stewert Ranson, George Jones and Kieron Walsh (eds), *Between Centre and Locality: The Politics of Public Policy* (Allen & Unwin, 1985)

Jeffrey Richards and Dorothy Sheridan, *Mass-Observation at the Movies* (Routledge & Kegan Paul, 1987)

Denise Riley, *War in the Nursery: Theories of the Child and Mother* (Virago, 1983)

Elizabeth Roberts, *Women and Families: An Oral History, 1940–70* (Blackwell, Oxford, 1995)

Madeline Rooff, *A Hundred Years of Family Welfare* (Michael Joseph, 1972)

Michael Roper, 'Historians and the politics of masculinity', in Michael Roper and John Tosh (eds), *Manful Assertions* (Routledge, 1991)

Raphael Samuel, *Theatres of Memory* (Verso, 1995)

Raphael Samuel and Paul Thompson (eds), *The Myths We Live By* (Routledge, 1990)

Joan Sangster, 'Telling our stories: feminist debates and the use of oral history', *Women's History Review* 3 (1994), no.1

Edward Shorter, *The Making of the Modern Family* (Collins, 1976)

Elizabeth Silva (ed.), *Good Enough Mothering* (Routledge, 1996)

Elizabeth Silva and Carol Smart (eds), *The New Family?* (Sage, 1999)

Alan Sked and Chris Cook, *Post-war Britain* (Penguin, Harmondsworth, 1979)

Carol Smart, 'Regulating families or legitimating patriarchy?', in John Eekelaar and Mavis Maclean (eds), *A Reader on Family Law* (Oxford University Press, Oxford, 1994)

Jo Spence and Patricia Holland, *Family Snaps: The Meanings of Domestic Photography* (Virago, 1991)

Carolyn Steedman, *Landscape for a Good Woman* (Virago, 1986)

Penny Summerfield, *Reconstructing Women's Wartime Lives* (Manchester University Press, Manchester, 1997)

Pat Thane, *The Foundations of the Welfare State* (Longman, 1982)

Pat Thane (ed.), *The Origins of British Social Policy* (Croom Helm, 1978)

Alistair Thompson, Michael Frisch and Paula Hamilton, 'The memory and history debates: some international perspectives', *Oral History* (Autumn 1994)

Alistair Thompson, letter to *Oral History* (Spring 1996)

John B. Thompson, *Studies in the Theory of Ideology* (Polity Press, Cambridge, 1984)

Paul Thompson, *The Voice of the Past: Oral History* (Oxford University Press, Oxford, 1988)

Paul Thompson, 'I piccoli e il grande', letter to *Oral History* (Autumn 1995)

Frances Thorpe and Nicholas Pronay, *British Official Films in the Second World War* (Clio Press, Oxford, 1980)

Janet Thumim, *Celluloid Sisters: Women and Popular Cinema* (Macmillan, Basingstoke, 1992)

Nicholas Timmins, *The Five Giants* (HarperCollins, 1995)

Graeme Turner, *British Cultural Studies*, 2nd edition (Routledge, 1996)

Janet Walker, 'Interventions in families', in David Clark (ed.), *Marriage, Domestic Life and Social Change* (Routledge, 1992)

James Walvin, *Victorian Values* (Cardinal, 1988)

Adrian Webb and Gerald Wistow, 'Social services', in Stewert Ranson, George Jones and Kieron Walsh (eds), *Between Centre and Locality* (Allen & Unwin 1985)

Adrian Webb and Gerald Wistow, *Planning, Scarcity and Need* (Allen & Unwin, 1986)

Jeffrey Weeks, *Sex, Politics and Society*, 2nd edition (Longman, Harlow, 1989)

Jeffrey Weeks, 'Pretended family relationships', in David Clark (ed.), *Marriage, Domestic Life and Social Change* (Routledge, 1991)

Jeffrey Weeks, Catherine Donovan and Brian Heaphy, *Families of Choice: Patterns of Non-heterosexual Relationships*, South Bank University Social Science Research Papers, 1996

Jeffrey Weeks, Catherine Donovan and Brian Heaphy, 'Everyday experiments: narratives of non-heterosexual relationships', in Elizabeth B. Silva and Carol Smart (eds), *The New Family?* (Sage, 1999)

Raymond Williams, *Culture and Society* (Penguin, 1958)

Raymond Williams, *Marxism and Literature* (Oxford University Press, 1977)

Peter Wilmott and Michael Young, *Family and Kinship in East London* (Routledge & Kegan Paul, 1957)

David Wilson and Chris Game, *Local Government in the UK* (Macmillan, 1994)

Elizabeth Wilson, *Only Halfway to Paradise* (Tavistock, 1980)

Janice Winship, *Inside Women's Magazines* (Pandora, 1987)

Slavoj Zizek (ed.), *Mapping Ideology* (Verso, 1994)

INDEX